THREE
PLAYS
by
MAE
WEST

Page from Playbill of *Sex*, 1926.

Shubert Archive

THREE
PLAYS
by
MAE
WEST

Sex
The Drag
The Pleasure Man

Edited by
Lillian Schlissel

Routledge
New York

Published in 1997 by
Routledge
29 West 35th Street
New York, NY 10001

Library of Congress Cataloging-in-Publication Data
West, Mae.
    [Plays. Selections.]
    Three plays by Mae West : Sex, The drag, The pleasure man / edited
by Lillian Schlissel.
        p.   cm.
    Previously unpublished plays.
    Includes bibliographical references.
    ISBN 0-415-90932-5 (hb).--ISBN 0-415-90933-3 (pb)
    1. Women--Social conditions--Drama. 2. Sex customs--Drama.
I. Schlissel, Lillian. II. Title.
PS3545.E8332A6   19976
812'.52--dc21   97-24425

CONTENTS

INTRODUCTION
BY LILLIAN SCHLISSEL

Mae West's plays, *Sex*, *The Drag*, and *The Pleasure Man* are published here for the first time. *Sex*, which opened at Daly's 63rd Street Theatre just north of Broadway in 1926, gave West her first starring role in the theatre and marked the beginning of one of the most extraordinary American careers.

Mae West began writing as a teenager on the vaudeville circuit. She wrote encores to her songs because she was so sure audiences would call her back. She wrote night club acts, two novels, scripts for her Hollywood films, and, of course, her stage plays. She was a writer as much as a performer, and the likelihood is that if she had not written her own material, there would have been no stellar career.

The Mae West scripts are part of the Manuscript Collection of the Library of Congress—*The Ruby Ring* (1921), *The Hussy* (1922), *The Chick* (1924), *Sex* (1926), *The Drag* (1927), *The Pleasure Man* (1928), *Diamond Lil* (first and second versions, 1928, 1964), *Frisco Kate* (1930) and *The Constant Sinner* (stage version of the novel *Babe Gordon*, 1931), *Catherine Was Great* (1944), *Come On Over* (also called *Embassy Row*), 1946), and *Sextette* (first and second versions, 1952 and 1961). *Sex* and *The Drag* were copyrighted under the pseudonym Jane Mast, but it was an open secret that the plays were Mae West's.

She was never an original writer. Critics accused her, as they had accused Brecht, of "pirating, plagiarizing, shamelessly appropriating."[1] Writers who claimed she had stolen their work often pursued her in the courts, but she defended her claim. Once she had "bor-

1

rowed" a script, she was convinced that even the original idea had always been hers.

On the stage, Mae West played the "tough girl." In *Sex*, her self-congratulatory bravado and cocky invitation to sexual adventure carried the play, but unlike other "fallen women" of the day, the sexuality she displayed was closer to comedy than to passion.

Critics who applauded her smart-mouthed quips sometimes suggested that the flamboyant sexuality that became her trademark was a disguise. No real woman could be so brazen, so self-contained, or so funny. That a woman who played the bawd for half a century should have stirred debate about her sexual identity is part of the intrigue that has surrounded Mae West's style and career.

The "gay plays," *The Drag* and *The Pleasure Man*, are at the heart of the question. Readers have searched the yellowing pages of the scripts in the Library of Congress as if the leaves were written in some ancient hieroglyphic that would reveal a secret if rightly deciphered. The trouble is that *The Drag* and *The Pleasure Man* heighten questions of sexual transformations; they do not resolve them. For one thing, the scripts refute West's statement that she wrote because she needed material for the stage. She never appeared in *The Drag*, and she never appeared in *The Pleasure Man*. Each play was meant to be performed by a company of gay actors while she starred in the heterosexual playgrounds of *Sex* and then *Diamond Lil*. Yet she was obsessed with the gay plays, revising and rewriting them through the 1970s, hoping to turn them into films.

The publication of *Sex*, *The Drag*, and *The Pleasure Man* places Mae West's work beside contemporary plays like Eugene O'Neill's *Anna Christie* (1922), Oscar Hammerstein's *Showboat* (1927). and Ben Hecht and Charles MacArthur's *Front Page* (1929). Sometimes similarities are striking—Brecht's *Threepenny Opera* opened in Berlin in 1928, only a few weeks before *Diamond Lil* opened in New York. Lotte Lenya's role as the Whore Jenny bears close resemblance to Mae West's Margy LaMont in *Sex* and to her role in *Diamond Lil*. After all, it was Brecht who wrote "in our day sex undeniably belongs to the realm of comedy."[2]

The vulgarity of Mae West plays was meant to disrupt standards of propriety. The speech was intended to sow the seeds of revolution. No victory is so triumphant as a dirty word spoken in public; no guerrilla warfare so subversive as the moment when an audience, in spite of its best intentions, laughs at a really low joke. West's assault on the standards of decency would be played out in the arena of sexual license, but her enduring significance is her comedy where words are weapons and wit is the arsenal of attack.

The current interest in Mae West—the new essays in cinema journals, the new critical studies—attests to the fact that we are catching up with ideas that interested her, with her belief that virtue is unconnected to sex, and that sexual identity ranges over human experience from heterosexuality, to bisexuality, to homosexuality. In the plays, ethical choices are constructed out of sexual identity, but sexual identity is unstable.

For me, this book goes back twenty years, to 1974 when I first read the plays in the Library of Congress and pursued the possibility of getting them into print. My thanks to the Roger Richman Agency for its permission to publish these uncut scripts, and to Routledge, which over the past five years has patiently waited until legal matters were cleared. For readers who have long believed Mae West is an underrated figure, these plays provide the basis for new assessments of her impact on American theatre and letters.

Born in 1893, Mae West was the daughter of Matilda and Jack West. Her mother was a "refined" Austrian corset model and her father a small-time boxer known in Brooklyn as Battlin' Jack. She was a streetwise kid who grew up in Bushwick, a neighborhood where the dialect, like Cockney, was a life-long affliction. Her mother put her on the stage when she was six. West played Little Eva in *Uncle Tom's Cabin,* and Sis Hopkins in *Huck Finn,* and always managed to make her lace-trimmed bloomers more important than her lines.

Although she rarely acknowledged his influence, Jack West was important in her life. He took her to the fights and taught her the boxer's regimen of weightlifting; by the time she was a teenager, she was all strut and swagger, moving around the stage like a bantamweight fighter.

She went out on the road when she was sixteen and teamed up with a hoofer billed as Frank Wallace, born Frank Szatkus, son of a

Lithuanian tailor. They were married in Milwaukee on April 11, 1911. But like Fanny Brice, whose marriage to a Springfield barber ended abruptly, Mae ditched Wallace when she got back to New York in June.

She spent the summer in Coney Island saloons, with Jimmy Durante, who worked at Diamond Tony's on the boardwalk, and with songwriter Ray Walker, who played piano all night while Dutch Schultz held a gun to his head. Walker wrote a song for her called "Goodnight Nurse" (words by Thomas Gray). It was the first piece of sheet music with her photograph on the cover. She was an ordinary girl, a pretty brunette.

In 1911, she was getting small parts in musical revues, mostly through young men she dated on their way to becoming writers and producers. She was in *A la Broadway* and in *Vera Violetta*. A *New York Times* reviewer noticed an unknown "with a snappy way of singing and dancing," but Sime Silverman of *Variety* wondered if this "tough soubret" out of Brooklyn, who danced the Turkey (also the Fox Trot, the Monkey Rag, the Grizzly Bear, and the Shimmy) was not "just a bit too coarse for this $2.00 audience."[3]

She studied "big time" performers like Eva Tanguay, who sang "I Don't Care." She imitated the black vaudevillian Bert Williams, and listened to the fast-paced jokes of Jay Brennan and Bert Savoy. "In an era that did not allow recognition of the homosexual, let alone admission of being one, Bert was an outspoken example, yet so funny about it that nobody seemed to mind." Savoy played cheeky dames named Margie and Maude, gossipy secretaries and beauticians, party girls, and flirts. He wore a red wig and enormous picture hats. His camp humor played to audiences from New York to the Klondike. By 1920 he was the darling of the critics and *Vanity Fair* called him "The reigning Ziegfeld beauty." Savoy's one-liners were razor sharp. The minister asks at choir practice, "Don't you know the Ten Commandments?" and Margie snaps, "No, but if you'll hum a bit for me, I think I can play the tune." Offstage, Savoy was just as outrageous. Stopping in front of Saks Fifth Avenue, he told friends, "It's just too much. I don't care if he is building it for me. . . . I'll never live in it!"[4] Mae West onstage probably owed more to Bert Savoy than to any woman in the theatre before 1920.[5]

After 1919 West was playing in a string of revues. She was Mayme

Dean of Hoboken in *Sometime*, and Shifty Liz in *The Mimic World* (1921). She was flashy and pretty, but her streetsmart manner offended some audiences, and *Variety* kept warning her to "tame down" her stage presence or she would "hop out of vaudeville into burlesque."[6] She was always writing her own material, impatient for the break that would make her a star. She wrote a night club act where Harry Richman did a kind of male striptease while she sang "Frankie and Johnnie"—in a version she had learned from JoJo the Dog-Faced Boy at Diamond Tony's in Coney Island. The act took Richman and West to the Palace Theatre, but Richman quit and went to work with Nora Bayes, while West settled into a period with little work.

The big break did not come, and though she denied it all her life, film historian Jon Tuska believes that she went to work in burlesque. The Billboard Index between 1922 and 1925 includes notice of a performer spelling her name "May West" who appeared in *Playmates, Girls from the Follies, Round the Town, French Models, Lena Daly and Her Tobasco Company,* and *Snap It Up.*"[7]

Those years might have shaken the confidence of any actor, but West was indomitable. She apprenticed herself to a new craft and turned herself into a playwright. Her first script was called *The Ruby Ring* (1921), which set her at the center of the play as a "jazz baby." Jim Timony, a lawyer and friend of the family, hired a young screen writer, Adeline Leitzbach, to work with her, and together West and Leitzbach wrote *The Hussy* (1922). The plays were practice pieces in which Mae West wrote of herself as the dazzling heroine so beautiful no man could resist her, so virtuous that her dancing and wisecracks could be forgiven, and so wise she'd find a rich husband at the end of the story

Leitzbach and other young women were moving into the business of the theatre, writing for vaudeville and for film. Anita Loos honed her skills on *Gentlemen Prefer Blondes,* which opened in 1926. Blues singers Ma Rainey and Bessie Smith wrote almost a third of their own lyrics. Blanche Merrill, still in high school, began writing skits for Fanny Brice and soon became her principal writer. Dorothy Parker worked for *Vogue* and *Vanity Fair*.

Elinor Glyn wrote pulp fiction romance, a new genre that led some wags to snicker, "Would you like to sin/ With Elinor Glyn/ On a tiger skin/ Or would you prefer/ To err with her/ On some other fur?"[8]

Hollywood paid Glyn $50,000 in 1925 to endorse Clara Bow, a twenty-one-year-old redhead, as the "IT" girl. Dorothy Parker sneered, "'IT,' hell, she had Those." With "those" and no experience at all, Clara Bow earned $1000 a week, starring in movies as fast as the studios could turn them out.[9]

Clara Bow arrived in New York in 1925 to make *Dancing Mothers* at Paramount's Astoria studio. Mae West was thirty-one. She had been in vaudeville and burlesque for twenty-five years, and she could see no reason she should not generate the same excitement on the stage as Clara Bow on the screen. But there was one difference. In her early films, Clara Bow did not speak. Mae West, on the other hand, was about to launch a frontal assault on verbal taboos and turn the Broadway stage into a battlefield.

Timony bought a script called *Following the Fleet* for $300 from Jack Byrne of East Orange, New Jersey (throwing in another $10 for a hat for the playwright's wife). *Following the Fleet* was a third-rate sex play set in a Montreal brothel. Business is interrupted by the arrival of a "society lady" drugged and dumped by a blackmailing pimp. A prostitute named Margy LaMont tries to help Clara escape, but Clara accuses Margy of stealing her jewelry. The scene shifts to Trinidad, where— as befits melodrama—Clara's son falls in love with Margy. Since he cannot marry a fallen woman, he returns to his mother and Margy goes back to the brothel.

Clara Bow had just finished a movie called *The Fleet's In,* in which she played a taxi dancer, and Mae West was certain she could do better. She began by changing the ending of her play. In her version, the prostitute dumps Clara's son, chooses her sailor sweetheart, and they dance off together to start a new life in Australia. As the final curtain comes down, the hooker is heroine. Then Mae West retitled the play with a single word—*Sex.* She said later that Edward Elsner, the director, kept talking about how the play exuded "Sex, low sex. The way he said it, it sounded like the best kind."[10]

Considering that her credentials were modest, that she produced the play with money she borrowed from her mother, the success of *Sex* was astonishing. In writing of a hooker and a happy ending, Mae West challenged Broadway rules. Charles MacArthur and Clarence Randolph adapted Somerset Maugham's *Rain* in 1922. The production starred Jeanne Eagels as the tough-talking Sadie Thompson, and the scene was the distant landscape of a Pacific island, but nothing in the stage version altered the bleak ending Maugham had written for the original story. Jack McClellan's play *The Half Caste* was another tale of "Love and Sacrifice on the islands of Forgotten Men in Samoa," and *White Cargo* (1924), which featured Annette Margulies as Tondalayo, the part that would make Hedy Lamarr a star in film, was similarly catastrophic at the final curtain.

Broadway indulged itself in scores of "sex plays," all of them obedient to the unwritten rule that prescribed ruin for fallen women. John Colton's *Shanghai Gesture* opened at the Martin Beck Theatre in 1926, with Florence Reed as Mother Goddam, an oriental madam who ruled over an elaborate bordello with rooms called the Gallery of Laughing Dolls, the Little Room of the Great Cat, and the Green Stairway of the Angry Dragon. Mother Goddam sacrifices her own child, a hopeless drug addict, for revenge. *Shanghai Gesture* was a bordello suffocated by gloom and doom and the punishment of sin.

Lulu Belle, by Charles MacArthur and Edward Sheldon, opened in February 1926 under the "personal direction of David Belasco. " Lulu was played by Lenore Ulric, a daughter of Minnesota who had made a career of playing passionate, dark-skinned women. She was a Spanish señorita, she was the "Saffron Chinese" Lien Wha in *Tiger Rose,* she was Carmen, and finally she was the notorious black prostitute Lulu Belle. She couldn't know that Humphrey Bogart would remember her in 1943 in the film *Sahara,* naming his desert tank the Lulu Belle.

In *Sex* Mae West broke with Broadway moralities and made sin a domestic product. The scenes in the brothel were set not in the tropics but in Montreal, and although the second act moved to Trinidad, the last act brought the story back to Connecticut. And as Margy LaMont, Mae West was unmistakably a New Yorker who talked about a moniker, a joint, a dump, a jane, being gypped, giving someone the gate, planting a body under the daisies. She would "chuck the bugger" and "bankroll a kid." Margy talked about sugar daddies and dames, about dolling up, about croaking a guy, and putting on the ritz, about paying the freight, about dirty rats, and dirty liars, and "dirty charity." Margy's goodbye is "blow, bum, blow." When Dashiell Hammett elevated the "private eye" to an American hero in *The Maltese Falcon* (1929), when Sam Spade talked about suckers and chumps, about "taking the fall," and putting in "the fix"—all that language had been set in place by Mae West. West's language came out of the speakeasies, and the jokes she used were the familiar routines of burlesque. Critics might pretend outrage, but audiences recognized lines that had been honed by every top banana in the business. Margy and her "client" talk about the gift he is saving for her after a three-month absence:

Lt. GREGG: Oh, I've got something for you, wait until you see this, wait until you see this.

MARGY: Well, come on and let's see it.

Lt. GREGG: You'll get it, you'll get it. I don't mind telling you I had an awful time saving it for you. Why, all the women were fighting for it.

MARGY: It better be good.

Lt. GREGG: It's good alright. It's the best you could get, but you've got to be very careful not to bend it.

The "it" that couldn't be bent was a feather, but the "business" signaled in the stage directions indicated a more anatomical reference.

West brought the Fleet Street Band into the play, and she chose the songs. Some of them were sentimentally familiar, like "Home Sweet Home," "Bells of the Sea," I'm Sorry Dear," and, for her critics on *Variety*, the "Meditation" from *Thaïs*. Music signalled audiences what she was up to, as when she had sailors dance jigs with other sailors or do steamy tangoes with the women of the brothel. The best of the dirty dancing she saved for herself—a new Charleston called "Sweet Man" (words and music by Ray Turk and Maceo Pinkard, 1925) about kisses as "hot" as TNT, gasoline, and nitroglycerine. She did her famous shimmy to "Shake That Thing" (1926), lyrics by Charlie "Papa" Jackson, who worked with the blues singer Ma Rainey.[11]

All around her, Broadway shows were bringing in black dance and black music as fast as they could. The Ziegfeld Follies hired black dancers to teach showgirls how to move, and in 1927, Ruth Etting danced a "rhinestone shimmy" to Irving Berlin's new song "Shaking the Blues Away." Stylish women like Anita Loos and Ellin Mackay Berlin went to a "local dance parlor" to learn how to do the Black Bottom.[12]

But the rhinestone shimmy and the Black Bottom at the dance parlor were not what Mae West was doing on the stage of Daly's Theatre.

West told reporters that she first saw the "shimmy shawabble" in 1911 in a club for "spades" on Chicago's South Side and that she did the dance the same night in her act, although in deference to her father's discipline she called it a "muscle dance." Songs identified with black singers were part of her signature, songs like "A Guy What Takes His Time," "Easy Rider," and W. C. Handy's "Memphis Blues." She meant audiences to know the black sources of her comedy and attitude.

In a waggish mood, Timony and C. W. Morganstern formed the Moral Producing Company, found two new "angels," and sent *Sex* to preview in New London, Connecticut. Word about the salacious comedy reached the naval station, and a line of sailors snaked around the block. The manager brought in kitchen chairs and sold standing room. John Cort, who owned Daly's Theatre, saw the play in Connecticut, paid off the cast of Earl Carroll's *White Cargo*, and brought *Sex* to 63rd Street on April 26, 1926.[13]

Sex was an amateur effort with echoes of O'Neill's *Anna Christie*. "It was all men's fault—the whole business." A smart woman, however, could find a comfortable life with a man she could manage.[14] But no playwright had ever attacked "respectable women" from the stage. Margy accuses Clara, the "society lady," of being a whore in disguise. "She's one of those respectable dames who . . . is looking for the first chance to cheat without being found out." And later, "I'll bet without this beautiful home, without money and without any restrictions, you'd be worse than I have ever been. . . . The only difference between us is that you could afford to give it away." Margy goes on, "I'll remember this night as long as I live. And if I ever get a chance, I'll get even with you, you dirty charity. I'll get even."* Margy's anger is one of the startling aspects of the play.

Mae West added only one character to Byrne's original script, Agnes, the young whore who yearns to go straight. Margy gently tells her, "Get a grip on yourself. There's a chance of rising to the top of every profession." Underscoring that bit of entrepreneurial advice,

---

* "Dirty charity": a woman who plays at being a prostitute. —L.S.

Margy argues that a woman can survive alone. "Go it alone, Agnes, there's more chance of getting ahead."

Margy follows her own advice, "gets a grip on herself," gives up Clara's son, and goes off with her navy lieutenant. She is a good (enough) woman. She makes no apologies; she is neither saved or reborn. There is no spiritual redemption. There is no transformation or renunciation or reformation. The ethical arithmetic is redrawn—the wages of sin are reduced from mortal transgression to misdemeanor. If you "played your cards right," there is always a chance of "getting away with it." West's ribald good humor carried the show which grossed $14, 000 a week at the end of its first month and $16, 000 a week in its second.[15]

Theatre critics, however, were neither amused nor forgiving. The *New York Times* considered it a "crude and inept play, cheaply produced and poorly acted." *New York World* declared *Sex* "as bad a play as these inquiring eyes have gazed upon in three seasons." *Variety* considered *Sex* "nasty, infantile, amateurish [with] vicious dialog. . . ." Walter Winchell in the *Graphic* called it "a vulgar affair," concluding that the "stench was not the fault of the street cleaning department." The *New York Post* called it "Nasty." The *Daily Mirror* called *Sex* "offensive. . . . [A] monstrosity plucked from Garbage Can to [the] Sewer." *Billboard* wrote that the play was "the cheapest most vulgar low show to have dared to open in New York this year. It is a disgrace." The *Evening Post* called it "crudely vulgar." The *New Yorker* said the play was composed of "street sweepings." The *New York Herald Tribune* wrote that the play concerned "a world of ruthless, evil-minded, foul-mouthed crooks, harlots, procurers and other degenerate members of that particular zone of society." Only the *New York Sun* found some redeeming qualities—"The play has a frantic vulgarity" but nonetheless "unavoidable jollity."

The avalanche of condemnation was not as surprising as the fact that so much attention was paid to so flimsy a play by a newcomer. Audiences, for their part, didn't read the reviews or didn't care. Behind the dirty jokes and the smartmouth lines, they had discovered a "natural" they could trust. *Sex* played to full houses, the only play above Broadway to survive the summer and continue through the fall.

As the new season opened, Broadway chose a new form of sexual titillation in two new plays—*The Captive* and *Virgin Man*—that

THREE PLAYS BY MAE WEST   11

explored the theme of homosexuality. *The Captive* was Arthur Horn-blower's translation of Edouard Bourdet's French play about an affair between two women. It starred the glamorous Helen Menken and a newcomer from England, Basil Rathbone. Opening night at the Empire Theatre was attended by Mayor Jimmy Walker, producer Lee Shubert, playwright Anita Loos, and actress Ruth Gordon. The press was not merely respectful; it was fawning in its praise, finding in the play "an aura of pity and terror that comes close to the Greek ideal." Brooks Atkinson in the *New York Times* wrote that Basil Rathbone acted "with rare dignity and understanding." Helen Menken gave interviews suggesting that young college women see the play to learn how to avoid sexual perversion. At the final curtain, the woman who lured a young wife away from her husband was represented only by a small bouquet of violets left on a table. The word "lesbian" was never uttered. With Broadway feeling itself linguistically pure, Mae West went to work on *The Drag*, street slang for the dress-up celebrations by female impersonators.

The gay subculture fascinated New York society in the 1920s and '30s. Historian George Chauncey writes that "over the course of the decade, gay men became more visible in almost every setting [Times] Square provided, including its streets, burlesque halls, theatre roof gardens, and nightclubs, as well as the 'legitimate' stage." Langston Hughes recalled "it was fashionable for the intelligentsia and the social leaders of both Harlem and the downtown area to occupy boxes at [drag balls] and look down from above at the queerly assorted throng on the dancing floor." The Vanderbilts and the Astors came to watch, along with Broadway celebrities popular in the gay world—Beatrice Lillie, Clifton Webb, Jay Brennan, and Tallulah Bankhead. *Broadway Brevities* in 1932 headlined "Fag Balls Exposed—6, 000 Crowd Huge Hall as Queer Men and Women Dance."[16]

The story of *The Drag* was similar to the story in *Sex* in that, once again, wealth hides corruption. Rolly Kingsbury is a judge's son and a homosexual. He has married an unsuspecting young woman named Claire, thrown over his gay lover, and set his cap to snare a "straight" man. A drag ball at the end of the play offered audiences a gaudy display of cross-dressing, and covered the darker story about Rolly's murder.

West and Timony collected gay actors from a Greenwich Village club. "Word got out she was casting a play about homosexuals ... and those kids really turned it on." West took a waiter's pad and scribbled a casting call for the following night at Daly's Theatre after the final curtain of *Sex* had come down. From the fifty young men who showed up, West chose twelve principals and a crowd of extras.[17] Midnight rehearsals were wildly improvisational as performers were invited to "script" their own dialogue. Scenes were never exactly the same, and the play began to take on alarming dimensions.

Word of mouth about *The Drag* was contagious. *Variety* sent a reporter to Paterson, New Jersey, and readers of the review learned that the play concluded with a drag ball "staged with hippodrome elaborations taking up close to 20 minutes of the third act, without dialogue or dramatic action of any kind. In the playing it is exactly like a revue number, or the floor show of a night club. Some 30 young men take part in this spectacle, half tricked out in women's clothes and half in tuxedos. Half dozen of the boys in skirts do specialties, and the episode takes on the character of a chorus girl 'pick-out' number in a burlesque show."[18]

The Drag had no star; it was meant to be spectacle. "One [of the young men] dressed as an oriental dancer, [with] bare legs and wearing only what amounts to a brassiere above the waist, does a muscle dance; another sings after the manner of female impersonators, and all hands are rouged, lip-sticked and liquid-whited to the last degree. During the whole scene a jazz orchestra plays "hot" music in the background."[19] Female impersonators—Clem and the Duchess—took possession of the story and the comedy; the dialogue was insolent and raw. Clem picks up a taxi-driver:

CLEM: You better wait, you great, big, beautiful baby.

TAXI-DRIVER: I don't get you guys.

CLEM: If you don't you're the first taxi driver that didn't.

TAXI-DRIVER: What do you want me to do?

CLEM: Ride me around a while, dearie, and then come back for her, if you're so inclined.

TAXI-DRIVER: O. K. with me.

At the drag ball, Clem recounts the meeting:

CLEM: So that's how I met this taxi-driver and he's been riding me ever since.

As the moment of the grand ball approaches, the "queens" and "queers" talk about their clothes and their conquests.

DUCHESS: Oh, my goodness, I've got the most gorgeous new drag. Black satin, very tight, with a long train of rhinestones.

CLEM: Wait until you see the creation I'm wearing dearie. Virginal white, no back, with oceans of this and oceans of that, trimmed with excitement in front. You know I'm more the flapper type, not so much like a canal boat.

WINNIE: Fat! I should say not. I'm the type that men prefer. I can at least go through the navy yard without having the flags drop to half mast.

KATE: Listen, dearie—pull in your aerial, you're full of static. I'm just the type that men crave. The type that burns 'em up. Why, when I walk up Tenth Avenue, you can smell the meat sizzling in Hell's Kitchen.

The jazz band was worked into *The Drag* as it had been in *Sex*, this time openly scoffing at Helen Menken's play about lesbians with a song by a gay chorus called "The Woman Who Stole My Gal" and other songs notorious for their special meanings—"How Come You Do Me Like You Do," and "Goody, Goody, Goody."

Gay characters "dish the dirt" and flirt. Winnie says, "So glad to have you meet me. Come up some time and I'll bake you a pan of biscuits." But there are also darker resonances behind the comedy. Clem tells about a "poor queen" taking heroin and morphine "by the barrels," about gays beaten by the police, and about the danger and the sadness of life on the streets.

Previews of *The Drag* set for Stamford, Connecticut, were cancelled when the manager of the theatre thought the subject too risky. Timony got a split week with Minna Daily's Burlesquers in Bridgeport, and then he put up billboards advertising "A Homosexual Comedy" and "The Male Version of *The Captive*." "More Sensational than *Rain*." The reviews were unrelenting. *Variety* wrote "This reporter doesn't believe Mae West wrote it. It has all the earmarks of being the work of a boss hosteler in a livery stable." West and Timony moved the play from Stamford to Paterson, New Jersey, where "burlesque regulars who traditionally gave 'nance humor' a raucous reception" lined up for tickets.[20] There were also middle-class audiences who knew that a Mae West play was a "good time."

If Mae West thought for a moment that the homosexuality of *The Drag* was not so different from the lesbianism of *The Captive*, she badly miscalculated the homophobia of the city police and of theatre critics. When the play opened in Bayonne, New Jersey, the police ordered a seated audience out of the theatre. In New York, the Society for the Prevention of Vice warned Jimmy Walker that if *The Drag* opened, there would be a move to censor all Broadway plays.

On February 9, 1927, with Walker out of the city on holiday, Deputy Police Commissioner Joseph B. McKee ordered the city police to raid *The Captive, Sex,* and *Virgin Man.* The intention, clearly, was to get Mae West wherever they could catch her. If she weren't on the stage in *The Drag,* then the police would close *Sex* even though the play had been running for almost a year. The anti-vice societies were sending a warning to this burlesque dancer, vaudeville hoofer and upstart actress from Brooklyn, daughter of a corset model and a two-bit boxer, that she was not to expect a career as a Broadway playwright.

The police raid itself was like a Buster Keaton comedy. The acting mayor sent a limousine for Helen Menken, the star of a highbrow play. And then he sent a Black Maria to pick up Mae West and the entire cast of *Sex.* Everybody crowded into the van and then tumbled out at the Eighteenth Precinct police station, on West 47th Street in Hell's Kitchen. At night court, West gathered her ermines and told waiting reporters that unlike Menken's "lesbian play," the cast of *Sex* were all "normal." After a night in the Jefferson Market Women's Prison, West arranged bail—$1000 for six principals and $500 each for sixteen others named in the complaint, $14,000 in all.

Though *Sex* was prosecuted, *The Drag* was the play under attack. According to George Chauncey, Mae West had "moved the sort of gay act that had become a part of Times Square's roof garden revues, dramatically expanded it, and transposed it to the legitimate stage." The play "allowed thirty of its performers to put on a 'show' much as they might have at Mother Childs, at a Rockland Palace ball, or in a night-club revue...."[21] The trouble was its timing; Broadway was now under scrutiny and threat of censorship.

Helen Menken announced she would have no more to do with *The Captive,* and the court offered to dismiss all charges against *Sex* if West and the cast would close the play. They refused. Timony and Morganstern obtained a restraining order against police interference, and *Sex* went on, with a booming box office, until May 21, a week before the obscenity trial began.

A grand jury indictment found that Mae West, Morganstern, Timony, twenty actors, and theatre-owner John Cort had prepared, advertised and produced "an obscene, indecent, immoral and impure drama," that the play contributed "to the corruption of the morals of youth," that the content was "wicked, lewd, scandalous, bawdy, obscene, indecent, infamous, immoral and impure." The theatre of litigation was about to begin.

On May 28, 1927, Norman Schloss opened the case for the defense, pointing out what must have been obvious, that *Sex* had already run for 339 performances, that it had been seen by more than 325,000 patrons, including members of the police department and their wives, by judges of the criminal courts, by seven members of the district attorneys' staffs, and by citizens of the city who showed no moral impairment. A Broadway "play jury" had previewed the show, and the belated prosecution was unreasonable.

The prosecutor, District Attorney Joab Banton, argued with passion that the play was obscene and called a series of detectives who became courtroom actors. Sergeant Patrick Keneally of the Mid Town Vice Squad, recited ribald lines from the play, and imitated the walk and the gestures of the "fairies" on stage. James S. Bolan, Deputy Inspector of Police, testified that Mae West had performed a dance that "suggest[ed] an act of sexual intercourse." He added that the play included a scene in which a young man "goes through with her the business of making love to her by lying on top of her on a couch each embracing the other." "The language they used does not contain the words 'sexual intercourse,' but the purport and tenor of the business and language is to that effect."

When it came time for his rebuttal, Schloss compared *Sex* to *A Tale of Two Cities,* to *Hamlet,* and to the Bible. Timony prayed over his rosary beads, Mae West wore black satin and pretended modest restraint. Barry O'Neill, the leading man, sweated profusely. Newspaper reporters printed as much as they could of what everyone said and did, and readers around the city enjoyed the fun.

Every single upstanding, middle-class businessman was mentioned in *Variety* when it published the names and addresses of jury members—the foreman was a coal dealer, and the remaining men included a printer, a publisher, a contractor, an investigator, a hotel manager, real estate agent, chemist, insurance salesman, retailer, cotton goods dealer, and a lithographer. The jury, on public display, took only five and a half hours to reach its guilty verdict. West and Timony were sentenced to ten-day jail terms. and fined $500 each. Morganstern also received a jail sentence, but charges against John Cort were dropped because the court was concerned that other theatre managers might one day find themselves in jeopardy.

West concluded that time in jail was part of the cost of doing business on Broadway. Even Earl Carroll served time in a federal penitentiary when a newspaper reported that showgirls at a private party played in a bathtub filled with champagne (Carroll swore it was ginger ale). West had herself driven to prison in a limousine, smiling for photographers, carrying armloads of white roses. She spent eight days on Welfare Island, dined with the warden and his wife, and told reporters she wore her silk underwear all the time she was in prison. On her release, *Liberty* magazine paid her $1000 for an interview, and she donated the fee to establish a Mae West Memorial Library in the women's prison. Then she attended a charity luncheon given by the Women's National Democratic Club and the Penology Delinquency Division of the New York Federation of Women's Clubs.[22] If the suffragettes could be jailed in a good cause, if Margaret Anderson and Jane Heap could stand trial for publishing sections of *Ulysses* in *The Little Review,* Mae West could do no less for free speech.

On her release, West told reporters her play was "a work of art," and even if it wasn't exactly art, she calculated, "Considering what *Sex* got me, a few days in the pen 'n a $500 fine ain't too bad a deal." Like Margy LaMont, Mae West had learned "there's a chance of rising to the top of every profession."

Years later, in her autobiography *Goodness Had Nothing to Do with It,* Mae West had different memories of women in prison. The Tombs "was dirty and dismal. . . . The confused, diseased, feeble-minded women were herded like animals. . . . The very young . . . were mixed with foul and decaying old biddies who knew every vice. . . . [The] place was run by . . . ward heelers, relatives, and small-time vote peddlers who were all busy feeding and stealing at the public's expense. . . ."[23]

She went to work on a new play, *The Wicked Age*. Wilva Davis, a young actress from Minnesota, described rehearsals that had become the signature of the Mae West style. "Strange characters who had put money up kept coming in with Mr. Timony. We got the impression they were big-time gangsters. And that was funny because Mr. Timony prayed a lot. One minute he'd be living it up with these rough characters. A few minutes later he'd be off in the corner somewhere saying his beads."[24]

In *The Wicked Age* Mae West was Babe Carson, a role like the one she had written for herself in *The Ruby Ring* and *The Hussy,* but the flapper was always an imperfect fit. When the play opened, *The New York World* called her "pudgy," and *Variety* kept sniping at her burlesque past. But even in a weak play, West was practicing the one-liners that tickled audiences and outraged the press. She was getting good at them.

FLAPPER: I was up in the Count's room alone last night. Did I do wrong?

BABE: How do I know? Don't you remember?

West tried to change the lead actor, but he took the dispute to Actors Equity, and when it ruled in his favor, she closed the play. *The Wicked Age* opened and closed after nineteen performances.

With undiminished zeal, West went to work on another script about a lady named Diamond Lil who worked the Bowery in the 1890s. Jack Lindner sued over the copyright, charging the play was based on his script *Chatham Square*.[25] *Variety,* always eager to embarrass her in public, noted that Lil was a black prostitute from Chicago who got her name by the diamond implanted in her front tooth. Lindner's play gave Mae West a setting in the 1890's, an age of buxom showgirls like Lillian Russell and the hefty damsels of Billy Weston's "Beef Trust." Once again she was handling a "drama of the underworld," and Diamond Lil, black or white, was the role of a lifetime.

Owney Madden, bootlegger and part owner of Harlem's Cotton Club, was one of the backers; he may even have been one of the "big-time gangsters" Wilva Davis remembered at rehearsals of *The Wicked Age*. George Raft, once a tango dancer at Texas Guinan's El Fay Club, was Madden's driver, sent every night in a bulletproof black Packard to pick up his boss's "take" in a brown paper bag.

Variety may have considered Broadway the home of art and aesthetics, but the street was everywhere a cross-section of gangster and socialite, a mix of people brought together by Prohibition. Ethel Barrymore played the Palace "between engagements." The Marx Brothers brought slapstick to Broadway in *Cocanuts*. Charles MacArthur, "the golden boy of the Algonquin set," had just written the sleazy *Lulu Belle*. Black pianist Lucky Roberts listened to a young "ofay" named George Gershwin to see if he was as good at the keyboard as people said. Babe Ruth was the "king" of baseball. Jack Dempsey was king of the prize ring. Tourists and bankers, musicians and performers rubbed shoulders at the Cotton Club. Sex was talked about as loosely as bootleg liquor.

Mae West earned her first good reviews in *Diamond Lil*. *Billboard* acknowledged she "does a much better job . . . than she did with her previous offerings." The *Times* agreed: "She is a good actress, is Miss West." John Colton, author of *Shanghai Gesture*, congratulated her, and West admitted, "I enjoyed my success with no false humility."[26] In the midst of that success, Mae West began to rewrite *The Drag*. It may have been unquenchable egotism, the stubborn refusal to let the Broadway establishment and the police shut her down. It may have been her affinity for the subject of gay life. In any event, *The Drag* was probably the only play Mae West ever seriously rewrote, and when it was finished and retitled *The Pleasure Man*, it was a stronger, more dramatically astonishing play than anything she would write thereafter.

The revisions were intended as an end-run around the censors; West changed the lead character from homosexual to heterosexual, making him a "masher," a "stud," a seducer of young women. Like Hammerstein's *Showboat*, which opened the same year, the scene was the backstage of a vaudeville theatre—the world of acrobats and hoofers, dancers and comics. But she kept the female impersonators and the drag ball at the end of the play. Hammerstein's gentle lyrics about life upon "the wicked stage" had little to do with Mae West's play. The singer, for one thing, was not a girl at all but a sister in drag.

The Pleasure Man was staged with a string of dressing rooms cut open to the audience so that dialogue passed quickly between characters and across story lines. Rodney Terrill ("Call me Rod") is the matinee idol who seduces willing wives and innocent showgirls. A young girl named Mary Ann has become pregnant and pleads with him to remember his promise to marry her. Terrill hardly remembers her name. She has a back-alley abortion, and dies at the end of the play. Her brother, the house electrician, castrates the Pleasure Man, killing him. The word for the deed is never spoken. The avenging brother is led off to prison declaiming that his punishment of the Pleasure Man was more fair than any court might devise.

Most reviewers assumed The Drag and The Pleasure Man were still the same play, but that is not entirely an accurate reading. The crudest jokes were eliminated, and The Pleasure Man was a better comedy built over a more deeply felt melodrama. Rehearsals began when the curtain came down on Diamond Lil, and lasted from eleven-thirty until two or three in the morning. West handed the cast scraps of paper with notes, and actors improvised until they had their scenes. The Pleasure Man was kept close at hand, previewing in September, 1928, at the Bronx Opera House, and then at the Boulevard Theater in Jackson Heights, Queens.

Some reviewers considered The Pleasure Man good theatre, "the second act stands out as a masterpiece, a real slice of stage life." The Jewish Tribune found the play "much livelier and more amusing theater than many of the more decent and ambitious plays." The reviewer of the Evening Post, who was not much put out by the female impersonators, wrote that "the main theme of the play is comparatively clean. It is, briefly, that a rake seduces a young girl, attempts seduction of two others, attacks a man's wife, gets drunk, and is finally murdered in a manner heretofore not suggested on the Broadway stage save in Chee Chee. So far as the plot goes, it is most decent. . . ."[27] Chee Chee was one of those awful Broadway mistakes, a satire on Gilbert & Sullivan's Mikado in which the wife of a petty bureaucrat saves him from a fate worse than beheading.

It was not the story of The Pleasure Man, but the jokes that were astonishing. "The huge audience of Queens high life, interspersed with a number of Broadway people too anxious to wait for [The

Pleasure Man] to come to town, roared over words and allusions which your correspondent would hesitate to use in conversation with Tammany Hall."[28]

1st BOY: I hear you're studying to be an opera singer.
2nd BOY: Oh, yes, and I know so many songs.
1st BOY: You must have a large repertoire.
2nd BOY: Must I have that, too?

The play was riddled with allusions to gay encounters:

STAN: Have you had your cream-puff this morning?
PARADISE: Oh, I always eat early—You know it's the early bird that catches the worm, dearie.

Mrs. RIPLEY: Ugh! Such people. I can't understand them. They're so queer.
Mr. HEATHERINGTON: Yes, my dear—extraordinarily queer. I think queer is the word.

Asked "What kind of act do you do?" Bird of Paradise responds, "Oh, I get down on my knees, and sing . . . Mammy. . . ." The laughter that followed every exchange signaled that Mae West's jokes, and most burlesque jokes, made audiences accomplices to outlaw allusions.

Although the play was intended to be outrageous, the police did not interfere with *The Pleasure Man* at the Bronx Opera House."There was no criticism of or objection to this play during such presentations covering a period of two weeks from any source whatsoever. Public officialdom, the press, the laity, and clerics were as silent as the tomb with respect thereto." The District Attorney asked that one song be eliminated, which was done, and the play continued in the Bronx for eight performances."[29]

But when *The Pleasure Man* opened at the Biltmore Theatre on Broadway on October I, the play was raided. The police waited until the final curtain. The *Evening Sun* reported that at least a third of the audience, in response to whispered warnings, "gathered at the stage door alley, passed cigarettes and the latest rumors, and waited to see the actual collision of the actors and the law. This extra act was by far the best of the evening." The *Daily News* reported that actors "in fantastic female attire, smothered in powder and with blackened eye lashes, carmine lips and rouged cheeks, were allowed to change into prosaic masculine attire. . . . Several skirted male actors fainted." Some were taken in police vans, some in commandeered taxis, and others were led on foot, while several thousand absorbed spectators were jamming the streets near by, held back by a horde of police." And a few newspapers, apparently in concert with the police, carried the story that Stan Stanley, who played the role of the stage manager, had been arrested in Toms River, New Jersey, on "an odoriferous story told by two sailors."[30]

Mae West hired Nathan Burkan, an attorney who specialized in theatrical cases, to obtain a temporary injunction. Equity warned the cast they risked prosecution if the temporary injunction were revoked. "Equity will wash its hands of the matter and consider no appeals," but the entire cast showed up for the Wednesday matinee. The house was packed, some to see the show and some to see if the play would be raided. In the middle of the matinee, "Lieutenant James Coy raced down the aisle. He called for the houselights to be turned up, and ordered the cast under arrest . . . the actors gave catcalls, booed and gave the police the raspberry. One of the drag queens delivered a speech about police oppression."[31]

The police intended the second raid to be bruising and humiliating. Fifty-four actors, still in stage makeup and dresses, were herded into vans and taken to the West Forty-Seventh Street police station. West appeared after the last curtain of *Diamond Lil,* ready to play the final scene. The police sergeant asked whether she had written the play. "Don't ya read ya noospapers?" she answered. "Are you going to provide bail for all these people?" "Somepin' of the sort," she replied. Then she made her exit, the photographers' lights flashing and the company applauding.[32] By morning, West and Timony had contacted four different bail bond agencies and put up bail for the principals and the cast—fifty-nine people in all.

The Pleasure Man had a Broadway "run" of one-and-a-half performances, hardly time to earn the avalanche of vitriolic reviews it received. *Billboard* called it an "abomination," "prostitution of the rankest sort," "an attempt to capitalize on filth and degeneracy."[33] The *Evening Post* called the play "such filth as turns ones stomach even to remember." The *Sun* said, "No play in our time has had less excuse for such a sickening excess of filth." Even George Jean Nathan called the play a "Harlem drag, the kind the police peremptorily raid."[34] The homophobia of reviewers was so great that few of them would even mention the "surgical mutilation" of the seducer. Only a female reviewer, Thyra Samter Winslow, in the *Jewish Tribune,* found the play funny." I hate to admit this but I must acknowledge my shame—I enjoyed *Pleasure Man.* [The play] is full of a curious native wit and some rather keen observation ."

When the trial of *The Pleasure Man* was postponed, West took *Diamond Lil* on tour. *Lil* played eighteen weeks in Chicago, its heterosexuality so explicit that a salacious imitation called "Frankie and Johnnie" was closed by the police. In Detroit the police threatened to close *Lil,* and a temporary injunction was secured until a court hearing could take place.[35] Police raids and court hearings were by then becoming routine.

The Pleasure Man went to trial on March 13, 1930, two years after its opening in New York. *The People vs. Mae West et al.* charged the principals with "unlawfully advertising, giving, presenting and participating in an obscene, indecent, immoral and impure drama, play, exhibition, show and entertainment" at the Biltmore Theatre. Detectives had taken court stenographers to performances because no script was ever produced. The prosecution argued in court that scenes dealt with "sex, degeneracy and sex perversion," a misdemeanor according to New York statute. The management of the Biltmore and the Moral Producing Company were indicted. The defendants, it was alleged, "did unlawfully, wickedly and scandalously, for lucre and gain, produce, present and exhibit and display the said exhibition show and entertainment to the sight and view of divers and many people, all to the great offense of public decency."

The prosecution told the jury that the question was "what took place on stage on October 1st, 1928." "What was [the] play? On what did it depend for its box office appeal?" The prosecution answered its own question: "It was a deliberate attempt to capitalize on . . . the speeches, manners and obscene jokes of a large number of male degenerates." The jokes and the "voguing" by the gay actors constituted the prosecution's evidence, along with the salacious and censurable allusions.

The trial of *The Pleasure Man* was even more sensational than the trial of *Sex*. For one thing, the police were better at the parts they played. Lt. James Coy of the Vice Squad wore a snug brown suit with a canary yellow tie and matching handkerchief in his breast pocket. Describing what he had seen, McCoy placed his hands on his hips, looked over his shoulder and said "They behaved in a very effeminate manner." Defense attorney Nathan Burkan asked if Coy had ever been a chorus boy, and spectators howled with laughter. Irene Kuhn of the *Daily News* reported that Coy had his own kind of outrageous language. Nothing ever happened, everything "transpired." The cast was never dressed, they were "attired." When asked by the defense attorney how he could see such small details Coy replied that the stage was very "illuminous." Burkan asked if Coy would sing the ballad "The Queen of the Beaches" so the jury could determine whether beaches rhymed with peaches, as the defense claimed, or ditches, as Coy testified.[36]

Chuck Connors, who appeared in *The Drag* and toured with *Diamond Lil,* was asked about lines that had been cut from the play, like one that noted there was "not a dry seat in the house." The District Attorney asked Connors if gay men wore brassieres, kimonos or "adopted the mannerisms of women" backstage. He was asked to explain the "peculiar significance" of the jokes between the German acrobats, who peered down each other's baggy trousers. He was asked "Are you married or single? Who do you live with?" Connors, equal to every question, answered that he lived with his mother. Alan Brooks, who played the *The Pleasure Man,* swore he never understood how he was killed in the play.

After fourteen days of testimony, the jury failed to reach a decision, and the indictments against twenty-four defendants (thirty-four other had already been removed) were dismissed. Defending the play in which she never appeared cost West $60,000. On the day she walked out of the courtroom, she must have felt a thrill something like Babe Ruth's after hitting sixty home runs in a single season in 1927—"Let's see some other son of a bitch do that."

Mae West tried one more Broadway play, *The Constant Sinner* (1931). It closed after sixty-four performances, and West decided the only money to be made was in Hollywood. In 1932, she blazed across

the screen for Paramount in "Night After Night" with her old friend
George Raft, who was building a Hollywood career as a Valentino
look-alike. She wrote her own dialogue, and her signature one-liners
were sharper than ever. By 1935, she was the highest paid woman in
the United States, and William Randolph Hearst, who tried to keep her
name out of his newspapers, was the highest paid man.[37] To the
hatcheck girl's admiring "Goodness, what beautiful diamonds," came
the Mae West quip, "Goodness had nothing to do with it, dearie."

Sex, *The Drag* and *The Pleasure Man* were improvisational scripts,
like jazz, spun out of what historian Ann Douglas has called the "nig-
ger keys," the "slurred notes and split sounds" of outlaw life.[38] *Sex*
was a raw practice piece, pitiless in its treatment of whores and police
and respectable women who "sin on the side." But the play was full of
energy, and it was funny. *The Drag* and *The Pleasure Man* made West
the Joan of Arc of gay audiences. "All the chorus boys [in those days]
were gay. But the producers never gave speaking parts to homosexuals!. . . . So I helped a lot of gay boys along. I gave them parts."[39] The
dialogue marked West as an accomplice in forbidden games. The
slang, excoriated by the press for its vulgarity, was always accurate.
Most important, West was always there to bail out her cast when her
scripts got them thrown into jail.

Gay actors were her "sisters" on the road. "They were all crazy about
me and my costumes. They were the first ones to imitate me in my
presence."[40] She brought the gay cast of *The Drag* home to meet her
mother, Matilda. "They'd do her hair and nails and she'd have a great
time. When her mother was dying, Mae brought gay actors to the hos-
pital. "They would always make her laugh."[41] She kept gay actors
working—five actors from the cast of *The Drag* remained in the production of *The Pleasure Man*, and Chuck Connors, who was in *The
Pleasure Man*, toured with her in *Sex*. She used gay actors as rehearsal
doubles in *The Constant Sinner*. She gave old timers like Ed Hearn of
The Pleasure Man small parts in almost all her Hollywood films, and
helped female impersonators like Ray Bourbon, who appeared in
Catherine Was Great (1944), throughout his career. Just as boxers came
to Mae West when they needed a new match or a new manager or a
few bucks, gay actors or Mae West impersonators knew her as a friend.

After she finished the filming of "Myra Breckenridge" in 1970, Mae
West went back to the plays she had written in the 1920s—not to *Sex*

or *Diamond Lil*, but to *The Drag*, and *The Pleasure Man*. At the Masquers Award Dinner in 1974, she sang a song written for the original production of *The Pleasure Man* and got a standing ovation. In 1975, she rewrote the entire script as a novel and looked for new backing for *The Drag*, hoping a tour would lead to a film with George Segal.

In spite of considerable evidence of her lifelong affection for the gay plays and for gay actors, some critics have found the plays only cheap exploitation of the subject of homosexuality. Theatre historian Kaier Curtin wrote that West simply "cashed in." Her "persistent, mercenary attempts to exploit gay transvestites in the 1920's stirred neither public tolerance nor compassion. It reinforced the stereotyping of gay men as vulgar, sex-obsessed effeminates who wear women's clothing at drag parties." Curtin quoted the *Morning Telegraph*, which had written that *The Pleasure Man* was "a menace to the theater, its performers and the theater-going public."[42]

More recently, Marybeth Hamilton agreed that "the aim of *Pleasure Man* . . .was to convey to the audience that these men were . . . degenerates, who, even offstage, when not performing, adopted the mannerisms of women." West "specialized in raunchy plays that retailed 'dirt' to the Broadway public, and her interest in female impersonators was clearly exploitative." "She was unquestionably exploiting them. . . ."[43]

Curtin and Hamilton see West as a shark among the pilot fish, but Richard Helfer argues that West's sympathy for gay characters was "astounding for the times."[44] George Chauncey connects the grand sweep of Mae West's performances with her early admiration for Bert Savoy.[45] And certainly it's hard not to hear Savoy's lines behind the lines West wrote for herself on the stage. When asked, "How did you spend the afternoon?" Savoy answered, "Well, Margie and I went to a matinee and I met a lovely fella in the lobby." "Was he a New York boy?" "No, he was a college boy." "How could you tell?" "He had a Yale lock in his pocket." When Mae West read the line, it was tougher. "Is that a gun in your pocket or are you just glad to see me?" She knew gay humor to be as bold as it was clever.[46] Her association with gay comedy was noted long ago, when George Davis wrote in *Vanity Fair* in 1934, "I can pay you no greater tribute, dear lady, than to say that [my love for you] has healed the wound in my heart caused by the death [in 1923] of the one and only Bert Savoy. I love you, Miss West, because YOU are the greatest female impersonator of all time."[47]

West's descriptions of her own motives are unreliable, but they sometimes offer clues to what she was about. When she was writing *The Drag*, she said, she was moved by "some mysterious, subconscious drive. I was . . . writing a play that could only make trouble. . . ."[48] But the subject that preoccupied her in *The Drag* and in *The Pleasure Man* was not so much homosexuality [which she understood better than most] as sexual instability and the ways in which sexual identities are transformed.

In *Sex*, the "society lady" has the making of a prostitute. In *The Drag*, Rolly Kingsbury throws over his gay lover for a "straight" man. In *Diamond Lil*, West herself says "some of those big guys, when you get to know them, ain't worth nothing as lovers." But sexual instability was most fully developed in *The Pleasure Man*, where Rodney Terrill, the sexual athlete, the stud who has ravished an innocent girl, is really bisexual. Terrill is derided as a "male milliner." In a joke her audiences would have understood, he appears onstage like a prima donna with a Japanese valet who lights his cigarettes and sprays the room with an atomizer. The allusion was to Julian Eltinge, the famous female impersonator who played "The Fascinating Widow" and kept a valet alluded to in the press as "a little Jap." Terrill's bisexuality is underscored when West compares him with Clara Bow, Eleanor Glyn's "IT" girl, who possessed "an inner magic, an animal magnetism."[49]

STANLEY: How do you get these women? What's the attraction?

TERRILL: It is charm, poise, personality, capital IT, IT—It's a gift—it can't be acquired. It is my magnetic attraction—all the women fall for me, I can't keep them away.

Terrill's villainy is defined not by his seduction of a young girl but because he is a chameleon. He is not what he seems. Paradise recognizes the duplicity. "I always knew you were a rotter . . . don't try to scare me—what I know, I know, and that's that." "If you're a man, thank God, I'm a female impersonator."

In the strange ethical architecture of the gay plays, Paradise and all the "queers" are the world's innocents. They do not lie about who they are. Their fantastic gowns and "disguises" confirm their identity. The "straight" world is disguised and the gay world is "straight." The ethical paradox at the heart of *The Pleasure Man* was not lost on Mae West's gay audiences, although it seems to have been lost by most readers.

Closely read, the gay plays hold intimate and tender stories. If you listen to Agnes in *Sex*, she can break your heart. The sad little whore who wants to go home is certain that virtue can be reclaimed. "If he really loves you it won't matter to him what you've been. . . . It's the kind of a wife you make that counts." Anna Christie believed the very same thing—"Loving you has made me—clean. It's the straight goods. Honest!" but Anna Christie found that love could not to be trusted. Like Laura in *The Glass Menagerie*, Agnes suffers a small "impediment," her virtue is damaged, and she finds that love does not cure pain. Like the "poor queen" in *The Drag* who jumps out of the window because "she's sensitive of what she is," Agnes dies of shame. Behind Mae West's rowdy stories are the sad stories. Clem and the Duchess dream of divine entrances and exits, but they remember the "poor queen taking heroine and morphine by the barrels."

At the heart of *The Drag* is the story of David Campbell's love for Rolly Kingsbury, which is told without ridicule or embarrassment. "We loved each other. I worshipped him. We lived together. We were happy . . . in our own way. No normally married couple were happier than we were." West never made light of the deep feelings of gay men for each other. If one is not taken in or swept away by the drag scenes, a close reader will find that the gay plays contain the only love stories Mae West would ever write.

Bird of Paradise, the man dressed as a woman, is the ethical center of *The Pleasure Man*. Paradise plays Portia, the woman dressed as a man, who begs mercy for those who stand before the bar of justice. Paradise asks the audience to pity Mary Ann, dying of an abortion. He cradles her across his knees as she dies, and says, "You poor kid, you had an awful fall. Like happens to all us poor girls." Paradise plumbs the grief that hides behind jokes about infidelity—"You may be mistaken about your wife—why not give her a chance? None of us are perfect. . . . We all make mistakes, you know." The man in drag is Mae West's Madonna.

Critics speculate about Mae West's sexuality. "Was she a lesbian? a nymphomaniac? a transvestite? Did she have . . . a touch of color in her blood?"[50] Perhaps, in her egoist's fantasy, the gay world offered endless images of herself. Or perhaps the answer lies in the plays themselves, where identity may be framed upon sexuality, but sexuality plays across a multitude of passions. Ramona Curry writes of Mae West as "a multivalent image," an image of "sometimes contradictory readings."[51] In Mae West, sexual identities are revealed at will. None of the masks she created is the final word.

In 1950 the artist Willem de Kooning painted a series of grotesque and compelling sirens, the faces sometimes abrasive and ugly, sometimes sad and vulnerable. He wrote, "Art never seems to me peaceful or pure. I always seem to be wrapped up in the melodrama of vulgarity."[52] Finding in women that which was both ferocious and hilarious, de Kooning painted a "quirky" oil sketch on paper and called it MAE WEST. In the melodrama of vulgarity, Mae West changed the way the world saw women, and the way women saw themselves. She changed the way sex was treated on the stage. In de Kooning's paintings and in Mae West's plays, in the ferocious and the hilarious mix, art and political revolution came together.

Notes

1. Lotte Lenya, foreword to *The Threepenny Opera*, Bertolt Brecht, Grove Press reprint, New York, 1964, p. v.

2. Ibid., p. 105.

3. Jon Tuska, *The Films of Mae West*, Citadel Press, Secaucus, New Jersey, 1973, p. 22.

4. Marion Spitzer, *The Palace*, Atheneum, New York, 1969, pp. 50–51.

5. George Eels and Stanley Musgrove, *Mae West, A Biography*. William Morrow & Company, New York, 1982, pp. 35–36.

6. Tuska, p. 24.

7. Tuska, pp. 30–31. Also Marybeth Hamilton, *When I'm Bad, I'm Better: Mae West, Sex and American Entertainment*, HarperCollins, New York , 1995, p. 47.

8. David Stenn, *Clara Bow: Runnin' Wild*, Penguin Books, New York, 1990, p. 79.

9. Ibid., p. 81.

10. Mae West, *Goodness Had Nothing to Do With It*, Prentice Hall, New York, 1959, p. 61.

11. Sandra Leib, *Mother of the Blues: A Study of Ma Rainey*, University of Massachusetts Press, Amherst, 1981, p. 133.

12. Mary Ellin Barrett, *Irving Berlin: A Daughter's Memoir*, Simon & Schuster, New York, 1984, pp. 61, 63.

13. Eels and Musgrove, p. 60.

14. Eugene O'Neill, "Anna Christie," Act I, scene I, p. 72; in Alvin S. Kaufman & Franklin D. Case, eds. *Modern Drama in America*, Vol. I, Pocket Books, 1982.

15. Eels and Musgrove, p. 64.

16. George Chauncey, *Gay New York: Gender, Urban Culture and the Making of the Gay Male World*, 1890–1940, Basic Books, New York, 1994, pp. 309–10.
17. Eels and Musgrove, p. 65.
18. Richard Helfer, "Mae West on Stage: Themes and Persona," City University Ph.D. dissertation, 1990, p. 134.
19. Ibid.
20. Eels and Musgrove, p. 66.
21. Chauncey, p. 313.
22. Eels and Musgrove, pp. 73–74.
23. West, p. 87.
24. Eels and Musgrove, p. 74.
25. Helfer, p. 257.
26. Tuska, p. 40.
27. Helfer, p. 174.
28. Ibid.
29. Ibid., pp. 172–73.
30. Ibid., p. 176.
31. Eels and Musgrove, p. 87.
32. Ibid., p. 86.
33. Tuska, p. 46.
34. Helfer, pp. 174–75.
35. Tuska, p. 50.
36. Eels and Musgrove, pp. 91–93.
37. June Sochen, *Mae West: She Who Laughs, Lasts,* Harlan Davidson, Inc., Arlington Heights, Illinois, 1992, p. 81.
38. Ann Douglas, *Terrible Honesty: Mongrel Manhattan in the 1920s,* Farrar, Straus, New York, 1995, p. 358.
39. West, p. 84.
40. Ibid., pp. 91–92
41. Eels and Musgrove, p. 64.
42. Kaier Curtin, *"We Can Always Call Them Bulgarians": The Emergence of Lesbians and Gay Men on the American Stage,* Alyson Publications, Boston, 1987, pp. 137–38.
43. Hamilton, pp. 64, 141, 143.
44. Richard Helfer, *"The Drag:* Mae West and the Gay World," *Journal of American Drama and Theater,* 8 (Winter, 1996), 66.
45. Chauncey, p. 312.
46. My special thanks to Eric Concklin for sharing with me a 1923 recording of Bert Savoy on the Vocalion label, and for his help throughout the editing of these plays.
47. George Davis, "The Decline of the West," *Vanity Fair* (May, 1934), 46, 82.
48. West, p. 83.
49. Stenn, p. 82.
50. Hamilton, p. 254.
51. Ramona Curry, *Too Much of a Good Thing: Mae West as Cultural Icon,* University of Minnesota Press, Minneapolis, 1996, p. 146.
52. Harry F. Gaugh, *Willem de Kooning,* Abbeville Press, New York, 1983, pp. 42, 48. Also Notes to Exhibit, Metropolitan Museum of Art, 1995.

SEX

A
COMEDY
DRAMA

(1926)

THE CAST

Margy LaMont, a prostitute
Rocky Waldron, a pimp
Manly, a thug
Curley, a pimp
Dawson, an officer of the law
Agnes, a prostitute
Red, a prostitute
Flossie, a prostitute
Jones, a client
Lieutenant Gregg,
    an English naval officer

Captain Carter, an officer
Condez, host of the Cafe Port au
    Prince
Clara Stanton, a wealthy woman
Jimmy Stanton, her son
Robert Stanton, her husband
Marie, the Stantons' French maid
Jenkins, the Stantons' butler
Policeman

First Man, Second Man, Waiter

The action takes place in Montreal's red light district; a cafe in Trinidad; and in a wealthy home outside New York City. The role of Margy LaMont was played by Mae West.

Act One.   Scene One. An "apartment" on Caidoux Street in
                                 Montreal.
               Scene Two. The same.

Act Two.   Scene One. Trinidad, the Cafe Port au Prince.
               Scene Two. One week later.

Act Three. Scene One. The Stanton residence.
               Scene Two. The same, the next day.

The copyright script of *Sex* is dated July 24, 1926, three months after the play opened at Daly's 63rd Street Theatre on April 26th. The cover page shows Mae West as author, but the play was originally attributed to Jane Mast, a pseudonym that was a combination of Matilda West's middle name and the first two letters of Mae West's given and sur- names. The script was hastily typed—it contains a profusion of errors and inaccuracies.

The script offers no description of the set. In several places stage direc- tions have been added where none appear.

SEX

ACT ONE

Scene One

An "apartment" MARGY shares with the blackmailer ROCKY on Caidoux Street, in Montreal's notorious red light district. Night. The curtain rises in the middle of a conversation between ROCKY and MANLY, with CURLEY off to the side.

ROCKY: You ought to be lousy with coin. You ain't depending on any particular lady friend for your jack. What's the matter, ain't the police giving you fifty-fifty on the graft you collect?

MANLY: Aw.

ROCKY: Don't try to tell me—

MANLY: Keep your shirt on—take a tip, old man, and watch your step.

ROCKY: What the—

MANLY: Who's the swell dame you been running around with the last week? Some class to you, picking up a jane at the Ritz—the police have got you spotted.

ROCKY: What do you know?

MANLY: The last one you picked up, she's the kind'll squeal.

ROCKY: I'll take the chance.

MANLY: Yeah? What's the lay?

ROCKY: What's it to you?

MANLY: That's enough.

ROCKY: Are you trying to shake me down?

MANLY: I'm giving you a tip straight.

ROCKY: You'll not get any of my money.

MANLY: Your money? *(Laughs.)*

ROCKY: Yes mine. And you stop butting into my affairs.

MANLY: Your affairs? Say you're none too safe here yourself—get that and get it straight.

ROCKY: Well, it'll take more than a low down graft collector like you to tell it to me.

MANLY: Yeah? Alright. If I can't collect I'll send someone in who will.

(Exit MANLY.)

ROCKY: Can you tie that, Curley?

CURLEY: Let him squawk. He's looking for a meal.

ROCKY: Come on, snap into it. Get some duds on and come up to the Ritz with me.

CURLEY: Not tonight, Rocky I'm broke.

ROCKY: With the British Fleet in the harbor—what's wrong? Agnes holding out on you—you should worry—Montreal is full of janes glad to supply the bank roll for a pretty kid like you.

CURLEY: I'm kinder used to Agnes, I'd hate to change now.

ROCKY: Ain't you the kind-hearted dearie.

CURLEY: Well I got no kick coming, I've got it pretty soft, Agnes don't hold out on me.

(Enter AGNES.)

ROCKY: Hello, Agnes.

AGNES: Oh, there you are Curley, I thought I'd find you here.

CURLEY: Alright dear, I'll be right with you.

AGNES: Where's Margy?

ROCKY: In her room, I guess she's awake.

(Exit AGNES.)

CURLEY: I'll see you later Rocky. *(Opens door.)* Here comes Dawson.

(Enter DAWSON.)

DAWSON *(Enters):* Hello.

(Enter AGNES.)

ROCKY: Hello Dawson.

CURLEY: Hello Dawson.

AGNES: Hello Dawson.

CURLEY: I'll be around tomorrow Rocky. Goodnight. *(Exit CURLEY and AGNES.)*

DAWSON: Business must be good the way you got this dump all dolled up.

ROCKY: Don't call this joint a dump.

DAWSON: I met Manly outside and he said you were a pretty tough customer.

ROCKY: Yeah?

DAWSON: If you think you can run this joint without giving [it] up, you've got another think coming.

ROCKY: Look here, Dawson, I'm a pretty good sort of scout, but I don't like being hounded by a guy like Manly.

DAWSON: Cut the argument and pay up.

ROCKY: Pay up? Hey Margy! Margy!

MARGY: What do you want?

ROCKY: Come out here. Pay up.

MARGY *(Enters)*: Well, what's all the noise?

ROCKY: Dawson wants [his] commission.

MARGY: Commission? Is that all he wants? Let him try and get it.

DAWSON: Now look here—You listen to me.

MARGY: Just a minute, I don't want any unnecessary noise around here. I had a pretty busy night last night and my nerves need quiet. *(She lights a cigarette.)*

DAWSON: What do you think this is? An ash can? Don't try to pull that wise stuff on me. You been getting away with murder.

MARGY: I don't see why I should pay for the privilege of working. You got about all you're going to get out of me.

DAWSON: Well, if that's the way you feel about it, we'll see how far you get.

MARGY: Don't slam the door on the way out.

(Exit DAWSON. Door slams.) He did.

ROCKY: Looks like he's going to start something.

MARGY: Well, he can start it and I'll finish it. How many times have I told you to keep him out of here?

ROCKY: Well, I didn't ask him to come up. Where are my collars? *(Exits. Calls from offstage:)* Hey Marge, where are my collars? Marge, come on and find them for me.

MARGY: Find them yourself, they're your collars.

ROCKY: Why don't you leave things where I put them? *(Enters.)* You didn't even put buttons on my shirt.

MARGY: What do you think I am, your wife? The trouble with you, you've been spoiled. Too many janes been waiting on you. Here's one jane don't fall for that stuff.

ROCKY: Is that so?

MARGY: If there's any waiting on around here, I'm the one that's going to get it. I'm a jane that craves service.

ROCKY: Ain't you funny.

MARGY: Don't wise crack at me, because I'm about ready to give you the air.

ROCKY: Give me the air? Give me the air? You can't get away with that so easy.

MARGY: No?

ROCKY: Not after what I've done for you.

MARGY: What did you ever do for me?

ROCKY: Say, who meets the guys and steers them down here to you? Me. Who's the business head of this here dump? Me. Who raised your price? Me. And you want to know what I did? I started you didn't I? Yes, and I didn't only start you, I made you, get me, I made you.

MARGY: You made me what I am today, I hope you're satisfied. I'll admit you're a great guy and all that.

ROCKY: You do admit I'm a great guy.

MARGY: Oh, without question. But just the same, I'm getting tired of you and this dump.

ROCKY: Not good enough for you, eh?

MARGY: Oh, I'm going somewhere where I can play around with the heavy sugar daddies and see life and get something for it, instead of sitting around here night after night waiting for your cheap bunch.

ROCKY: Gee, getting high brow. Want to play rich. You're alright where you are.

MARGY: Think so?

ROCKY: Getting some fool ideas about bein' decent, eh?

MARGY: Suppose I am.

ROCKY: Baby, you'll never be anything but what you are. So that's that.

MARGY: If a jane like Nan Chalmers can do it, I certainly can.

ROCKY: You mean that gal that used to live next door?

MARGY: Yes. She had a guy she thought she was in love with and thought she needed and then she got wise. Now she's married to an old guy, and she's got a mansion up near Boston and a limousine and diamonds and everything she wants.

ROCKY: And wait until the old gink finds out what she is. Watch him unload her.

MARGY: How's he going to find out?

ROCKY: Easy kid, easy. Plenty of nice people ready to spill the good news.

MARGY: But suppose he really loves her?

ROCKY: Don't make me laugh. It can't be done. Anyway, his friends and family won't stand for it. Listen, you lose this idea about being decent. Stick to your trade, kid, you were made for it. Rocky wouldn't steer you wrong.

MARGY: No, Rocky wouldn't steer me wrong. Rocky's just a wise guy, at least he thinks he is. Anyway my mind's made up and that's that. What's the idea of dolling up? You look like you have a heavy date. Meetin' the society dame Manly was talking about? The one you picked up at the opera?

ROCKY: You can't tell, maybe yes, maybe no.

MARGY: Well good luck to you—you'll need it.

ROCKY: She knows a nifty guy when she sees one. I'm class, babe. Just look at that figure.

MARGY: Take it to her and let her look at it. I'm tired of looking at it.

ROCKY: There's plenty of dames ready to take me in.

MARGY: White ones? Just take the tooth brush and park the body some place else.

ROCKY: Where are you going tonight?

MARGY: I don't know.

ROCKY: What time are you coming back?

MARGY: I don't know. Maybe I won't come back at all.

ROCKY: Now don't pull that stuff on me, because you aren't going to get away from me so easy. You're mine and you belong to me. You try to get away from me and I'll plant you under the daisies.

MARGY: What are you trying to do? Scare someone? Just because you croaked a guy and got away with it don't think I'm afraid of you. You know if I start talking, I can put a rope around that lily white neck of yours.

ROCKY: You wouldn't dare squawk on a fellow for that. Besides, I know you too well. You haven't the heart to turn anyone up. If I thought you had, I'd finish you now. I won't get any more for killing two than I will for killing one.

MARGY: Don't be too sure about that. Now I'm going to give you a little inside information—I'm going to leave you the first chance I get.

ROCKY: What are we doing, telling jokes to each other? Get that idea out of your head about leaving me, because if you did, I'd go get you. Lose this idea about being decent. You're just what you are and that's all you ever will be. There's only one thing about you to hold a guy, and outside of that you're merely nothing. Want to give Rocky a little kiss before he goes, you beautiful thing you?

MARGY: Go kiss your society dame.

(Enter AGNES.)

ROCKY: Thanks. *(Exits.)*

MARGY: Hello kid.

AGNES: Margy, I just wanted to give you some more money to keep for me. There's five there.

MARGY: Alright, I'll put it with the rest.

AGNES: I don't know what I'd do if it wasn't for you. You can't trust anyone.

MARGY: Good motto, Agnes. Trust no one and you'll never be gyped.

AGNES: I wonder what Curley would do if he ever found out?

MARGY: What, that you are putting a little away for yourself? Don't suppose I hand over the day's receipts to Rocky.

AGNES: No, it ain't only that. I'm planning to go away as soon as I have enough.

MARGY: Going where?

AGNES: Back home.

MARGY: Home? Do you think you can get away with it?

AGNES: Why not? They think I'm working for a living.

MARGY: Well ain't you?

AGNES: I manage to send them a few dollars once in a while.

MARGY: Listen Agnes. They'll find out and then it will be worse than this for you.

AGNES: Home. It seems like years since I've been there.

MARGY: You've spilled the tale about the old folks and the little white cottage so often, kid, I can almost see the place. What's the use of breaking their hearts as well as your own?

AGNES: But I can't go on. I—Oh, Margy, I wasn't meant for this sort of thing.

MARGY: If I was as dissatisfied as you are I'd join the Salvation Army.

FIRST MAN *(Knocks. MARGY opens the door):* Hello Margy.

MARGY: I'm sorry, but I'm not entertaining tonight.

FIRST MAN: I come down extra to see you. Can't you help a fellow out?

MARGY: I'm sorry.

FIRST MAN: But listen girlie—

MARGY: Good night.

FIRST MAN: Jees. *(Closes door.)*

(Church bells. AGNES cries.)

MARGY: Well, what's the matter?

AGNES: Those bells, every time they ring it seems as if—Oh I—can't stand it Margy, I can't stand it. Back home the little old church—

MARGY: Don't give me that church business again. You'll have me going back to the old homestead.

AGNES: Oh, Margy, if you'd only understand.

MARGY: I understand that you got to get a grip on yourself or you'll never get anywhere.

AGNES: Anywhere in this life?

MARGY: Why not? There's a chance of rising to the top of every profession.

AGNES: Profession? You call this—Oh Gawd.

MARGY: Yes, I said rising to the top of my profession. Why not? Others do it, why can't I? Why can't you? When I think of the dames riding around in swell limousines, buying imported gowns, living at the swellest hotels, terrible looking janes, too. You know if I have to I can put on the ritz, too. Course I don't pull that stuff around here, not at these prices. And there's nothing the matter with you. You're a pretty refined kid. Come from good folks, at least you say you do. It's all a question of getting some guy to pay for the certain business, that's all.

AGNES: Oh, that's what you mean to do?

MARGY: That's what I'm going to do. I'm sick of this town and everything in it.

AGNES: Yeah, and how are you going to find the rich man?

MARGY: Advertise for him in the daily papers. Tack a sign up around the town for him. Say, either you're so wise we can't catch up with you or you're the original Dumb Dora.

AGNES: Oh, I see what you mean.

MARGY: Oh, you do.

AGNES: I'm sorry I made you angry, Margy. You've been pretty good to me and when I get back home—

MARGY: When you get back home, old girl, you'll be buying a through ticket back here, mark my words. They won't let you go straight. They'll hold you up as an example. I tried it. I know.

AGNES: You're wrong, Margy, and maybe some day—

MARGY: Yeah, and until that some day comes, I'm satisfied to be wrong. Going out tonight?

AGNES: No I'm staying in with Curley. I feel I'm kinder doing him wrong, leaving him like this, and that's what's holding me back.

MARGY: Curley?

AGNES: Yes, he'd be lost without me.

MARGY: The lost and found department will take care of him alright.

AGNES: I loved him Margy in the beginning and—

MARGY: Loved him in the beginning, and you thought you couldn't live without him, and then you found out you couldn't live with him. That's the trouble with women like us. They have a tag on them. Go it alone Agnes, there's more chance of getting ahead.

AGNES: I'll leave Curley enough money—

MARGY: Let the big bum go to work.

AGNES: But he ain't very strong, Marge.

MARGY: Would be tough on that guy if he had to get a job for himself. Well you run along to your Curley, I've got to fix this dress up.

AGNES: Alright, goodnight Marge.

MARGY: Good night.

(RED and FLOSSIE knock.)

MARGY: Open up that door and let's see what this is. *(AGNES opens door.) (Enter RED and and FLOSSIE.)*

AGNES: My goodness, it's fighting Red.

RED: Say, I want to talk to you!

MARGY: Well, shoot, what is it?

RED: I want you to lay off my man.

MARGY: Which one?

RED: Sailor Dan from Kansas.

MARGY: Sailor Dan from Kansas? Never heard of him.

RED: Oh, yes you have.

MARGY: I'll tell you whether I have or not. Hey Aggie, over on that table you'll find a little book.

AGNES: No, it ain't here.

MARGY: Red, you look in the second drawer, and Flossie give us a cigarette. *(AGNES takes things out of the drawer.)*

Hey, just the book, just the book. Sailor Dan from Kansas . . . oh, sailor Dan from Kansas. Yeah Sailor Dan from Kansas, flat feet, asthma, check came back, oh, baby, I'll make you a present of that bird. He's yours.

RED: Well, you better.

MARGY: Now, don't be a girl like that.

MARGY: Say Floss, do you still go around with Oklahoma Jack?

FLOSSIE: Oh, he got married.

MARGY: Yes, but you didn't answer my question.

RED AND FLOSSIE: Well, the nerve of her—*(Ad lib and exit.)*

AGNES: Good night, Márge.

MARGY: Good night. *(Exit AGNES.)*

(A knock.):

MARGY: Come in.

JONES *(Enters):* Well, well, if it isn't the beautiful blonde mamma they're all raving about. I always did like blondes. I don't care how they get that way, just so long as they're blondes.

MARGY: Sorry, but you'll have to go.

JONES: You don't mean to tell me you're going to give me the gate? Oh, mamma, you don't know what you're missing.

MARGY: You wouldn't fool me?

JONES: If I go now, can I come back later?

MARGY: Yeah, you can come back.

JONES: In one hour I'll be back to the girl I left behind me. Oh, baby, I've got something you want.

MARGY: You wouldn't fool me?

JONES: Listen kid, Jones is my moniker, clean underwear and everything. Over the river. *(Exits.)*

(Phone rings.)

MARGY: Hello, hello. Oh hello there, kid, how are you? Great, great. Where are you? Where? Oh the Tremaine Cafe. Who's with you? Who? Oh, and how! Yeah. Oh, in about fifteen minutes. Well, say, I've got to get dressed. Yeah, alright. Goodbye kid.

GREGG *(Knocks and enters):* Hello, Marge. How are you?

MARGY: When did you get in?

GREGG: Oh, I got into port this morning. Couldn't think of spending my shore leave with anyone but you, old gal. Warm in here. Mind if I take my jacket off?

MARGY: Sorry, but I'm not entertaining company tonight, Gregg.

GREGG: Oh, don't consider me company. Just treat me as one of the family. I'm back with three months pay and aching for a good time. You and I'll have plenty of sport.

MARGY: I'm in no mood for sport, Gregg.

GREGG: Oh, you're out of sorts. Anything on your mind?

MARGY: You wouldn't understand.

GREGG: I'd hate to say you're not telling the truth, but you are out of sorts. I'll just play a tune on the jolly old music box, that'll cheer you up a bit.

MARGY: Gregg, if you want to do me a favor, you'll get out of here as quick as you can.

GREGG: Now, you don't mean that.

MARGY: Do I look as if I were kidding?

GREGG: What's the matter? Some of the neighbors' kids been stealing your marbles?

MARGY: What is that supposed to be—one of your English wisecracks?

GREGG: No, no. It's rather clever though. Don't be angry with me, old dear. I didn't mean any harm, just couldn't resist the temptation of a bright remark. Oh, I've got something for you, wait until you see this, wait until you see this.

MARGY: Well, come on and let's see it.

GREGG: You'll get it, you'll get it. I don't mind telling you I had an awful time saving it for you. Why all the women were fighting for it.

MARGY: It better be good.

GREGG: It's good alright. It's the best you could get, but you've got to be very careful not to bend it.

(Produces the feather of a bird of paradise.)

MARGY: What a bird, what a bird! How did you know I wanted one?

GREGG: Oh, I know your little weaknesses.

MARGY: You know too much. Where did you get it, honey?

GREGG: Away down south.

MARGY: Won't I burn the janes up when I wear this!

GREGG: Now you're happy, suppose you spill the trouble.

MARGY: Oh, you wouldn't understand.

GREGG: Never can tell, old gal.

MARGY: I'm sick of this town and everything that goes with it. Damn him.

GREGG: Oh the gentleman friend, eh?

MARGY: Gentleman—hell. You're the first one to ever call him that!

GREGG: Well of course, I never met him. Why don't you chuck the bugger? Leave him and travel around a bit. You'd soon forget him. Good lord, gal, I've forgotten a hell of a lot in the same way. I'm serious about this travelling around. It would be good for you. But maybe you don't care for travelling.

MARGY: The way I feel now I'd take a trip to hell if I could get a return ticket.

GREGG: Oh well, I don't expect to go as far as that at present. But seriously speaking, you could make a lot of money travelling around with me. All the gals who are following the fleet are getting rich, and besides they see the world and its ceilings.

MARGY: Sounds good. I'll think it over.

GREGG: Oh it's a sweet existence. I wish I were a gal. You know I'd love to meet up with you in every port I go into. And I could help you a lot by dropping a word here and there among the boys.

MARGY: Sort of an agent.

GREGG: Oh, I wouldn't put it like that. But maybe you and I could hit it up together, eh?

MARGY: What are you trying to do, set yourself in for a home?

GREGG: No, no.

MARGY: Never mind. You wouldn't be the first.

(Knock. MARGY opens the door.)

SECOND MAN: Hello dearie, don't you remember me?

MARGY: No, I don't remember you.

SECOND MAN: What, you mean to say you don't remember me?

MARGY: No, you yellow-bellied piece of cheese, I don't remember you!

SECOND MAN: Yellow-bellied? I thought you said you didn't remember me?

(GREGG shuts the door hard.)

MARGY *(to GREGG)*: What are you doing?

GREGG: Locking up.

MARGY: What's the idea?

GREGG: These interruptions are damned annoying. We don't want to be disturbed. I expect to be here for a long time.

MARGY: Well, you're out of luck.

GREGG: Just exactly what do you mean?

MARGY: I'm going out.

GREGG: I'd hate to be disappointed. I put myself out a lot to come and see you, I don't mind telling you.

MARGY: That's your hard luck. Here's your jacket.

GREGG: Oh, I say.

MARGY: Come on. Put it on.

GREGG: You can't really mean that, you know.

MARGY: No, I'm just exercising my lungs.

GREGG: Well, of course, if you insist. Just to show you I'm not a bad sort, I'll take you down to the Black Cat Cafe and spend the money I was going to spend here.

MARGY: Alright, only I'll let you take me to the Tremaine instead.

GREGG: Anywhere you say, old dear.

MARGY: Take that key out of the door. Put it on the outside.

GREGG: But I say old dear, it's a hell of a trick to lay on a fellow.

(MARGY takes his arm and they exit together.)

CURTAIN

Scene Two

Later that evening. The same room. Lights dim. ROCKY leads CLARA, his "society dame," into the apartment. He looks around suspiciously.

ROCKY *(Enters):* Oho—Oho. Alright, come right in. I thought maybe some of my friends were parked around here. I'm good natured and they take advantage of it.

(CLARA enters.)

CLARA: It's rather dark in here.

ROCKY: Just a minute and I'll light up. *(Lights come up.)* There we are.

CLARA: What an interesting place you have.

ROCKY: Oh, the diggings ain't so bad. Sit down and make yourself comfortable. You're going to be right at home here, you know.

CLARA: I feel very much at home already.

ROCKY: Let me take your wraps.

CLARA: Thank you.

ROCKY: Sit down and make yourself comfortable. Nothin' swell about this joint, but you can do as you please, and there's no one to put a damper on the works.

CLARA: It's so wonderful here in Montreal, I'd like to stay here forever.

ROCKY: Is this your first visit to the town?

CLARA: Yes.

ROCKY: Well I'm going to fix it so you won't forget it as long as you live. Where is your home?

CLARA: My home is in Connecticut.

ROCKY: You're fibbing to me, but it's alright. I can stand for almost anything from a woman as beautiful as you are.

CLARA: You do say the nicest things.

ROCKY: Thanks. When are you going to tell me your real name?

CLARA: I have told you. Clara Smith is my real name.

ROCKY: A two-year-old would know that was phoney.

CLARA: What's in a name? I'm here with you.

ROCKY: That ought to be enough for any man.

CLARA: You have the most persuasive ways.

ROCKY: So you won't tell me what your real name is?

CLARA: You must not ask me so many questions. I'm here to enjoy myself.

ROCKY: And believe me, you're going to have the time of your young life. We'll start off with a little drink, that's always a good start for any party. How about it, Clara dear?

CLARA: Clara dear?

ROCKY: You must get used to me getting familiar like.

CLARA: You do say the cutest things.

ROCKY: Thanks. How about that drink?

CLARA: Yes. I believe I would enjoy a drink.

ROCKY: You'll enjoy this alright, pure Canadian Club, and it's got a kick like a mule. Drink.

CLARA: This is so thrilling. I love it because it's so . . . unconventional.

ROCKY: It's worse than that. There's nothing like sneaking away and stealing a march once in a while, is there?

CLARA: It's wonderful!

ROCKY: I knew you'd love a thrill so I'm going to give you one. Do you know what street this house is on?

CLARA: No.

ROCKY: It's on Caidoux Street. You've heard of Caidoux Street, haven't you?

CLARA: I don't believe I have.

ROCKY: Well Caidoux Street is the most notorious street in Montreal. It's in the heart of the red light district.

CLARA: How perfectly thrilling.

ROCKY: I knew that would strike you right.

CLARA: It's such a departure from the usual course of life! So daring!

ROCKY: Anything for a thrill, dear. A new sensation, eh? I bet you get plenty of them on these little trips, eh?

CLARA: Anything to get away from the dull, monotonous routine of my daily existence. Always doing the same thing in the same way.

Seeing the same people day in and day out almost drives me insane. Yes, I do enjoy a little fling once in a while. It sort of breaks the monotony.

ROCKY: I'm sure lucky to have met you, and it's me that knows it.

CLARA: You say the most wonderful things.

ROCKY: Not half as wonderful as I'd like to say to you. But I suppose after you leave Montreal I'll never see you again. What a beautiful soft hand you have. Gee, this is funny. Here I am falling in love with a married woman, and when you get back home and meet your husband, I fade right out of the picture. You'll forget you ever met me, and I'll be here in Montreal just pining away.

CLARA: Don't be foolish. You're certainly not falling in love with a woman almost old enough to be—well, anyway, you know, is much older than you.

ROCKY: What's age got to do with it? You're wonderful. You need someone like me, someone to cheer you up and say nice things to you. Someone who understands you. Someone who would really appreciate you.

CLARA: Yes, I know I do. I'm neglected too much. You see, I'm married to a tired businessman who gives all his time to making money, and who's years my senior. I have everything that money can buy, every luxury, but the one thing I need most of all—love. Of course you understand.

ROCKY: Let's have another drink. I know just how you feel, dear.

CLARA: Dear? Oh don't make it quite so strong. I'm not used to being petted in that way, my dear boy. You think we are quite safe here?

ROCKY: Why, honey, what do you mean?

CLARA: I mean safe from intrusion. You know, in such a notorious district I'm afraid the police may come in.

ROCKY: Don't worry about that, honey. After you drink this next drink you won't give a rap if the whole Montreal police force comes in.

CLARA: But suppose they did come and there was a scandal? Think of my poor husband.

ROCKY: What's a husband or two among friends? Wrap yourself around this. Atta girl. A few minutes from now and you won't care for a whole flock of husbands.

CLARA: Wasn't that drink terribly strong?

ROCKY: Of course not. Come on over here, babe, and let's get together. Now, I'd like to be around you all the time. Can't you take me back home with you?

CLARA: Why, you silly boy, how could I? My husband would find out.

ROCKY: Couldn't I play chauffeur to you or some other excuse to be around you? I'll promise you a new thrill every day, babe.

CLARA: You say the sweetest things.

(They kiss.)

ROCKY: Come on, let's have another drink.

CLARA: No, I think I've had too much already. I'm not used to drinking so fast—I feel sick.

ROCKY: Right over there babe. Help yourself.

(Exit CLARA to bathroom. After a pause she reenters.)

CLARA: Oh dear, I'm sick, I feel terrible.

ROCKY: Come here, dear. Is my baby feeling sick? Sit down and I'll give you something that will fix you fine. Just this one drink is what you need.

CLARA: No, no, I don't want any more.

ROCKY: But dear, you must take this one, it's just what you need. It'll fix you proper. I'll take good care of you, babe.

CLARA: You say the nicest things.

ROCKY: That's the way—you'll be perfect in a moment.

CLARA: I hope so.

ROCKY: I know so.

CLARA: I'm getting so dizzy—everything is just blank—I feel like I'm in space.

ROCKY: Feel like you're passing out?

CLARA: Oh dear—I—I—

(CLARA faints. ROCKY leads her staggering off toward the bedroom.)

AGNES *(Outside):* Margy Margy. *(She enters.)*

MARGY *(Enters with GREGG in conversation):* Oh hello, kid.

AGNES: I thought I heard someone in here, Margy.

MARGY: Wait till I light up. Maybe Rocky's back.

GREGG: Then maybe I'd better go.

MARGY: I'm paying the freight on this joint, and what I say goes. Come on and have a drink with us Agnes. Agnes lives across the hall. Her idea of a good time is listening to the church bells ring and having a good cry. She's all right when you know her. Sit down.

GREGG: Anything you say. You're the boss.

MARGY: You bet your sweet life I am. Anything I say around here goes. Ain't that right, Agnes?

AGNES: Yes.

MARGY: Take off your jacket and stay.

GREGG: On the level? Here take this. *(Gives her money.)*

MARGY: What's this for?

GREGG: Saves you the trouble of taking it while I'm asleep.

MARGY: You're thoughtful, anyway.

GREGG: I always go the easiest way about everything.

MARGY: What a man, what a man . . . *(They kiss.)* Pardon me, pardon me while I go down to the English Channel. *(They kiss again.)* Now to show you I'm a good sport, I'll have a drink.

GREGG: That's a jolly good idea.

MARGY: That is, if the boy friend hasn't made love to it.

GREGG: This boy friend seems to be sort of a necessity.

MARGY: Not a necessity. A luxury. Where are you going?

AGNES: I'm afraid that Curley might miss me.

MARGY: Do him good.

AGNES: If you don't mind I'd rather—

MARGY: Goin to crab the party?

AGNES: I'd like to. Good night, Margy.

MARGY: I told you her idea of a good time, didn't I?

GREGG: I think she's jolly considerate—three's always a crowd.

MARGY: So long as you're satisfied I don't care. *(They drink.)*

GREGG: Cheerio! You know, Margy, we go on quite a trip from here. Panama, Cuba and Trinidad, and I was thinking how wonderful it would be if I could meet you there. You know, what we were talking about, following the fleet. I wish you'd do that.

MARGY: Trinidad? What kind of a jungle is it?

GREGG: It's an island just north of South America.

MARGY: Oh, where the parrots and the monkeys come from?

GREGG: It's a place where you can live cheap. Why down there you can get a room and bath, a wife and a bottle of liquor for two dollars.

MARGY: It must be bum liquor.

GREGG: It's a place where a girl like you would make a fortune. Say, think it over. All the girls down there are half breeds or a bit off-color. It's the place for a girl like you. You'd coin money.

MARGY: I'll think it over, old dear. I promise you I will, on my word.

GREGG: I wish you would, you don't know how much I want you. Damn you, you don't know how much I want to be with you. You know every time I go to Montreal I spend my shore leave with you, and I could do the same thing any place we go to. *(They kiss.)* Where are you going?

MARGY: I'm goin' to put on a good hot tune and have a little dance.

GREGG: By Jove, you're certainly showing me a good time!

MARGY: Baby, you're goin' to write this night down in your diary in red ink. *(They dance.)*

GREGG: I'm good on swimming, but short on stepping.

MARGY: Have another drink.

GREGG: God girl, you're beautiful, you've got the kind of beauty that makes a savage out of a man. Make him feel as though he'd like to take you in his arms and tear and crush you.

(CLARA groans offstage.)

GREGG: What's that?

MARGY: What's what?

GREGG: I thought I heard someone groan.

MARGY: Oh, you're the greatest guy for hearing things. (*CLARA groans again. MARGY opens door of bedroom and looks inside.*) Well I'll be damned.

GREGG: What's up?

MARGY: He's pulled something. (*GREGG follows MARGY to bedroom door.*)

GREGG: Who is she? One of your lady-friends?

MARGY: I'll bet it's that society jane.

GREGG: This is hardly the place for a society woman. Is she drunk?

MARGY: He's given her the works.

GREGG: He's what?

MARGY: Given her the works.

GREGG: He's given her what?

MARGY: He's doped her. Don't you understand English?

GREGG: Doped her. This is awkward.

MARGY: A fine mess the dirty rat left on my hands. He's given her enough stuff to kill a mule.

GREGG: You don't mean to tell me there's a possibility of the woman dying?

MARGY: Sure there is. That's why he made a quick getaway. Quick, get her off the floor.

(*GREGG carries CLARA to the chaise lounge. MARGY exits to bathroom.*)

GREGG: Don't let her die, old thing, she's a fine looking woman.

MARGY (*Enters with bottle*): If this don't bring her round, it's lillies for her.

GREGG: That gentleman friend of yours must be a nice playmate.

MARGY: Don't talk. Rub her hand and rub it good.

GREGG: He was a generous dog, he gave her plenty of the stuff while he was about it. How could he do this? He gave her enough to kill her.

MARGY: Because he's a rat and always will be. Hold her head back while I . . .

GREGG: I think she's coming to.

MARGY: Get some cold water and bathe her face. *(GREGG exits. To CLARA.)* Come on and take this. *(GREGG enters with glass of water. To GREGG.)* Don't spill it all over her.

GREGG: She's bloomin' lucky to be among those present.

CLARA: Where am I? Where am I?

MARGY: You know damn well where you are.

CLARA *(Coming to)*: Oh, I'm so sick.

MARGY: That's what you get for fooling around like this. You came here for a thrill. You got one, but not the kind you expected. Serves you right.

GREGG: I say, old dear, don't you think you're rather rough on the poor thing?

MARGY: Rough on her? She ain't getting half what she deserves. She's one of those respectable society dames who poses as decent, and is looking for the first chance to cheat without being found out.

GREGG: Well, old dear, you can't blame her. All of us are looking for a little party at times.

DAWSON *(Enters):* Hello, Marge.

MARGY: Oh, hello.

GREGG: Pardon me, old thing, I think you're intruding.

MARGY: Lay off you fool, he's a cop.

GREGG: Oh, a Bobby.

DAWSON: Officer of the law. It sounds better. What's coming off here? Manly said he saw Rocky coming out of here with a grip in his hand.

MARGY: That ain't a crime, is it?

DAWSON: He said Rocky was in a pretty big hurry, so I thought I'd come up and see what all the haste was about.

MARGY: Had a date, perhaps.

DAWSON: Yeah? Who's the dame?

MARGY: A lady friend of mine.

DAWSON: A lady friend of yours? Don't look much like the sort of company you keep. That looks more like your speed over there.

GREGG: Thanks for the compliment, old thing.

DAWSON: Save your comedy till you get back to the fleet. You have a variety of friends, haven't you? This one looks like she was all in. What's wrong with her? Is she sick?

MARGY: She's not feeling well.

DAWSON: Too bad, poor thing. Stop stalling. Come clean. What's the game?

MARGY: No game that I know of.

DAWSON: What's this woman doing in your place?

MARGY: Paying me a visit.

DAWSON: Don't look much like she's enjoying her visit. Well, if you won't tell me what the play is, maybe she will. Hey you—what are you doing with this pair of crooks?

GREGG: Pardon me, old thing, we may be a bit loose, but we're not crooks.

DAWSON: That's enough from you. Well, out with it now. What's the idea? What are you doing here? Do you know what kind of house you're in?

CLARA: Why—I—I—

DAWSON: The truth, lady. It's the best way out.

CLARA: Why, sir, I was lured here.

DAWSON: By whom?

CLARA (Pointing to MARGY): By that woman there. She brought me here. She told me a pitiful tale, then she gave me something to drink. After that I don't remember. My jewels—they are gone!

MARGY: She's a dirty liar!

DAWSON: You shut up.

MARGY: No I won't shut up! She's lying to you do you hear? She's trying to make me the goat. But she can't do it! She's ashamed to tell you why she came here, but I will. She came here with Rocky. She came here with him so that he could make her!

DAWSON: Wait—you needn't tell me what she came here for. I know.

GREGG: Pardon me—

DAWSON: You stay where you are. We're going on a little sightseeing tour and you're going to be one of the party. Now you women get your wraps.

CLARA: You're not going to arrest me, are you?

DAWSON: I'm going to take you to headquarters for further investigation.

CLARA: No, no, don't do that please! The publicity would ruin me! Isn't there some way I could fix this with you?

DAWSON: Well, perhaps.

CLARA: I understand. *(She hands money to DAWSON.)*

MARGY: No you don't. This dame is going to take her medicine even if I have to go to jail.

DAWSON: You mind your own business or *you will* go to jail. I'm on to this game; Rocky's been up to his old tricks again. If I take you two, it means I get Rocky. You won't want him in jail, because you know what he'd do to you when he got out. Come on Miss, I'll see you safely out of the district. And as for you, you better take a little tip and blow. Montreal is getting a little hot for you. That's just a hint, and you'd better take it.

MARGY: Just a minute *(She faces CLARA.)* You were almost dead when I found you in this room. I brought you back to life, and you try to frame me to save yourself. I don't count, I suppose, because I'm what I am, but I'll tell you something. I'll remember this night as long as I live. And if I ever get a chance, I'll get even with you, you dirty charity, I'll get even.

CURTAIN

ACT TWO

SCENE ONE

The Cafe Port au Prince in   Trinidad. The scene begins with musical numbers. The company sings "Sailor's Sweetheart," followed by solo choruses and specialty dances. The entire company dances the finale. Onstage, CONDEZ, sailors.

JONES *(Entering)*: Oh señor Condez.

CONDEZ: Cómo está usted señor?

JONES: I thought this affair was going to be over at the Casino.

CONDEZ: No, no, no, no, señor, I told you the Cafe Port au Prince. You like it?

JONES: And who is giving the affair?

CONDEZ: We are giving this in honor of the boys of the fleet.

JONES: Some fellow to give an affair like this. I think I'll stay a while.

CONDEZ: Sí, sí. There is a table some place.

JONES: Thank you, I'll sit over here.

(Musical numbers "Bells of the Sea," "I'm Sorry, Dear." Soprano and baritone solos; "Castles in Spain," tango by sailor and one of the fleet women.)

(Enter GREGG and MARGY, who are greeted by JONES.)

JONES: Hello there, lieutenant. Sit down and have a drink. I've been looking for you. Say, isn't that the baby from Montreal? *(MARGY turns.)* Well, well, if it isn't the beautiful blonde mamma from Montreal.

MARGY: Well, if it isn't the loud-speaking papa. Who is your friend, Gregg?

GREGG: Name is Jones.

MARGY: Jones?

JONES: Yes, you remember me, baby.

MARGY: How could I ever forget you?

JONES: That was some wait you gave me that night in Montreal. If the milkman hadn't spilled the milk on me I'd have been waiting there yet. Now baby, when I got back I rapped on the door . . . *(GREGG stops him.)* Say what are you trying to do, high hat me? *(Turns to MARGY.)* Now listen baby, give us a kiss and we'll call it quits.

GREGG *(Stopping him again)*: Now take it easy.

JONES: What is she, private property?

GREGG: No, but don't get personal.

JONES: Yes, but I'm your friend. Gee, if I were only a lieutenant I might stand some chance with her. *(Turns to MARGY.)* Now listen, kid, I'm different and I work fast.

MARGY: Now don't give me that business.

(Song, "Myilenberg Joys," and dancing. Applause.)

(MARGY sings "My Sweet Man." Much applause.)

(MARGY sings and dances to "Shake That Thing." Applause.)

CONDEZ: Ladies and Gentlemen, there will be dancing in the main ball room. There we will have señorita Carmentina and señor Bollontino, entertainment extraordinaire. *(Applause and ensemble exits.)*

JONES *(Starting for ballroom)*: Baby, you'd make a bull dog break his chain. *(Sees Captain Carter. Drunk sailors exit.)* Oh, here comes the Captain.

CAPTAIN CARTER: Ensign—Lieutenant. How do you do, Miss Lamont. Having a good time?

MARGY: Yes, indeed.

CONDEZ: Capitan, Cómo está usted?

CAPTAIN CARTER: Hello, Condez.

CONDEZ: Siéntese aquí Capitan y Usted teniente aquí.

CAPTAIN CARTER: Thank you. Thank you.

JONES: Fix up something for the Captain.

CONDEZ: Sí, sí, oh waiter, clear the table, and give the Captain the best in the house.

(Enter JIMMY STANTON.)

Stanton! Usted conoce a el Capitán, verdad?

JIMMY: Hello captain, how are you?

CAPTAIN CARTER: Oh Stanton, come and sit down.

CONDEZ *(Rushing to MARGY):* Señorita, that is the young millionaire señor Stanton! He is son of the Stanton U.S.A. He is—what you call him—inspector for his father's plantation. He is a very fine gentleman and he is very wealthy. Ah—sí, sí, tiene mucho dinero, y ojálá tenga la oportunidad de conocerle señorita. Perdone, regreso después.

CAPTAIN CARTER *(Crossing to MARGY):* Miss Lamont, may I present Mr. Stanton.

MARGY: Yes, you may.

CAPTAIN CARTER: Mr. Stanton, Miss Lamont. Mr. Stanton, Lieutenant Gregg.

JIMMY: How do you do?

(Exit CONDEZ and JONES.)

CAPTAIN CARTER: Pardon me lieutenant, just a moment. *(Exit CAPTAIN CARTER and GREGG.)*

JIMMY: Now don't think me foolish, but I don't suppose you remember going up the gangplank on the ship leaving Cuba for Trinidad?

MARGY: Cuba for Trinidad? Oh yes, yes.

JIMMY: You were talking to a young naval officer.

MARGY: Naval officer? Yes, yes.

JIMMY: Oh, I shall never forget it. I just stood in the middle of that gangplank like a big sap, and forgot they were waiting to pull it up—and you glanced at me. There was a certain look in your eyes.

MARGY: Certain look? What kind of a certain look?

JIMMY: I don't know, but I only hope you don't look at any other man that way.

MARGY: You silly boy.

JIMMY: And just now I asked the Captain here who you were. I told him I thought I'd met you in New York. He said that your name was Miss LaMont, and that he didn't know very much about you except that you were beautiful, and he expected that every man on the ship would want to dance with you. Then I told him that here was one man who did want to dance with you—and then we were introduced.

MARGY: Oh, I see.

JIMMY: I had to get acquainted with you some way, didn't I?

MARGY: And just what was it about me that attracted you.

(Music. "Always.")

JIMMY: Oh, I—I don't know, just everything. Your eyes, they're so marvelous—they're heavenly and yet again—I'm afraid of them. And your hair—and the way you smile. You know, you are just perfect to me. *(He gets up to dance)* May I? *(Asking for the dance and a kiss. GREGG enters rear on parapet, smoking. He watches them silently.)*

MARGY: You may.

(They kiss and waltz off toward ballroom. GREGG shrugs and saunters off. Music swells.)

CURTAIN

Scene Two

(One week later. Lobby of hotel where JIMMY is staying. Musicians playing "Stars and Stripes." Curtain up on second chorus.)

(Enter JONES and GREGG.)

JONES: What is the idea of running away from the fun, Gregg?

GREGG: Oh, you don't have to follow me, old fellow.

JONES: What, leave you alone on your last night in Trinidad? I should say not.

GREGG: You'd do me a great favor if you'd slip along and let me have a word with her alone.

JONES: What, is she stopping here? Some class to her. So that's the kind she is, hey? Never mind, old fellow, we'll find a way to show her up.

GREGG: Has it ever occufred to you that a girl may be wanting to go straight?

JONES: Straight? Don't make me laugh.

GREGG: Anyway, she's off the game and she's off me since she met this Stanton.

JONES: He's that rich guy, isn't he? She'll get enough out of him to lay off and live comfortable ever after. Come on, Gregg, I'm going over to the Casino.

JIMMY *(Entering from hotel left):* Hello! Well, well, where have you been keeping yourself? I haven't seen you in the last few days.

GREGG: I've been around here. I've been rather busy.

JIMMY: Getting ready to leave? What is your next port?

GREGG: We leave for the States in the morning. It's my last trip as a naval officer.

JIMMY: You don't mean to say—

GREGG: Yes, my last trip. I've sent in my resignation.

JIMMY: Well, good luck, old man.

GREGG: Thanks awfully.

JIMMY: I'm leaving for the States myself in the morning. While you're there, I'm just a short way out and I'd be very glad to have you spend a weekend with me. I'll show you the finest golf course in Westchester.

GREGG: Golf—that's very interesting. I used to be considered quite a golfer myself.

JIMMY: Is that so? What do you go around in?

GREGG: About 80.

JIMMY: That's too good for me. Won't you join me in a little walk?

GREGG: In a few minutes. *(JIMMY exits rear. GREGG turns to Waiter.)* Oh, Waiter, let me have a pencil.

WAITER: Yes, sir.

GREGG *(Writing on card)*: Give this card to Miss LaMont, please.

WAITER: Yes, sir.

GREGG: Remember. *(Exit.)*

(A waltz plays softly offstage. Enter MARGY. Waiter gives her card and exits.)

JIMMY *(Entering from rear):* Here I am.

MARGY: Why, dear, I thought you were down at the ball at the flagship?

JIMMY: You wouldn't go, and I wouldn't go without you.

MARGY: I wasn't feeling well.

JIMMY: If it's alright now, can't we still go?

MARGY: I'd rather not.

JIMMY: Dear, I'm going to leave for the States in the morning. When are you going to promise to marry me?

MARGY: Why, we've only known each other a week. You don't know anything about me, who I am, or what I am.

JIMMY: You're the sweetest girl in the world, and that's all I want to know.

MARGY: You're just a big boy out of college, and you don't know what you're talking about.

JIMMY: I do know what I'm talking about. But it's funny.

MARGY: What's funny?

JIMMY: When Dad sent me down here to see how his plantation was running, I didn't want to come. I didn't have any idea I was going to bring back the most wonderful wife in the world. *(MARGY turns her head away.)* Why, dear, you're not married already?

MARGY: Oh no, dear, no.

JIMMY: Then it's all settled.

MARGY: Nothing's settled, only that you go back home, and you'll promise to think of me sometimes, won't you?

JIMMY: I don't want to rush you honey, but I'm leaving tomorrow and you'll say yes—? I always get what I want, and I want you. *(Taps bell.)*

MARGY: Why, what are you doing?

(Enter waiter.)

JIMMY: Celebrating our engagement.

WAITER: Yes, sir.

JIMMY: Bring us a bottle of Pol Roger.

WAITER: Yes, sir. *(Exits.)*

JIMMY: Just think of it. Tomorrow we'll be on our way home. Home, isn't it glorious?

MARGY: What would your folks say?

JIMMY: They'd love you because I do.

MARGY: I'm not so sure about that.

JIMMY: Yes they would. You're adorable and I love you so much.

WAITER *(Enters with champagne)*: Yes, sir.

JIMMY: Thanks, waiter. I'll pour it myself.

WAITER: Yes, Sir. *(Exits.)*

JIMMY *(Lifting glass):* Here's to the future and the dearest girl in the world. I'm crazy about you Margy. There's not another girl like you.

MARGY: Let's be serious.

JIMMY *(He drinks)*: Alright now, we're very serious. *(JIMMY drinks several drinks more.)*

MARGY: Not so fast, dear, take it slow. *(She starts to drink.)*

JIMMY: You little darling, what do you know about drinking?

MARGY *(Chokes)*: Here in the tropics, wine goes to your head, and I want you to know what you're doing.

JIMMY: Alright, now we are serious.

MARGY: Suppose you found you'd made a mistake in me?

JIMMY: I'm not making a mistake.

MARGY: Suppose I'm not all you think I am?

JIMMY: Are you trying to frighten me? You can't do it. All I know is that I love you and you're going to be mine. Are you satisfied?

MARGY: Yes I am.

JIMMY: Then it's yes?

MARGY: Yes.

JIMMY: Hurrah, I'm the happiest man in Trinidad!

MARGY: Honey, not so loud. *(They kiss.)* You do love me don't you dear? Tell me, I want to hear you say it again.

JIMMY: I love you more than anything in the world—I love you—love you. *(MARGY pushes him away. JIMMY is smashed.)* Why dear, I'm sorry, you were right. Wine does go to your head in the tropics, I didn't realize. But say you love me and we leave tomorrow?

MARGY: Yes, dear, I'll go. *(He kisses her hand.)*

JIMMY: I'm off to arrange for the staterooms and I'll take care of everything.

(Exits.)

MARGY *(Starting after him)*: Dear, dear . . . Damn it.

AGNES *(Enters)*: Margy, Margy.

MARGY: Agnes, Agnes—You poor kid, I thought you went home.

AGNES: I did, but you were right. They wouldn't let me come back.

MARGY: What? Your folks?

AGNES: When I got back home, Mother was dead. If she had lived it might have been different. But the others—

MARGY: They forgive you but they won't let you forget—Oh what's the difference? *(Pats AGNES on the back.)*

AGNES: And when I got back to Montreal, Curley was—

MARGY: What, another jane?

AGNES: No, an overdose of morphine.

MARGY: You poor kid. But what brought you here?

AGNES: I heard you were following the fleet and doing well—And I thought travelling around would help me to forget.

MARGY: But you didn't—

AGNES: No, it's all too much—My—Mother—*(Cough. AGNES is crying.)*

MARGY: You poor kid—Come on over here and have a drink. Pull yourself together. *(Offers her a drink.)*

AGNES: Thanks. *(Drinks.)* I been trying to get a chance to talk to you, but the gobs said you were ritzing it.

MARGY: So that's what they think?

AGNES: I wanted to tell you that I saw Rocky before I left and I'm afraid that he—

MARGY: I don't want to hear anything about that rat.

AGNES: Gee, you must have caught that rich guy you were talking about in Montreal!

MARGY: Kid, I could have caught a dozen had I been so inclined.

AGNES: And you didn't?

MARGY: No, I did not. I guess I've been saved up to try and forget.

AGNES: Margy, you're in love with someone.

MARGY: How did you guess?

AGNES: Who?

MARGY: A clean boy, Agnes, and he loves me and wants me to marry him. A boy that believes I'm straight.

AGNES: My Gawd, that's wonderful. What are you going to do?

MARGY: I'm sending him back to his folks. Sometimes I feel that I should tell him the truth.

AGNES: Don't do that—don't do that—What he don't know won't hurt him.

MARGY: You mean I should marry this boy and pretend—No, I can't. That's what's worrying me.

AGNES: Margy, this is your chance! Suppose you tell him, what good would it do? If he really loves you it won't matter to him what you've been, but for God's sake get out of this life—just look at me—I'm a wreck—my health is all gone—and I'm nothing—*(She coughs.)*

MARGY: Come on, pull yourself together, you're all to pieces.

AGNES: Sometimes I wish I were out of it all.

MARGY: Come, Aggie, brace up, I've never seen you as bad as this before.

AGNES: Marge, promise me you'll do it, promise me you'll marry him, you must! God, if I had your chance nothing in the world would keep me from it. Don't be a fool, it don't matter what you were—it's the kind of a wife you make that counts.

MARGY: Maybe you're right.

AGNES: I *am* right! *(Coughs.)*

MARGY: Come on, I can't let you get away like this. Let me get you a room and some clothes, and get these rags off of you.

AGNES: No Marge, what would they think of you if they saw me here—

MARGY: The whole hotel is down at the ball on the flagship.

AGNES: No Marge, I got to go—I got to walk—I got to think—I may see you later—But I got to go—I got to go—*(Exits sobbing.)*

GREGG *(Enters right):* Hello, Marge, I knew they'd all be down at the ball on the flagship, and I thought this would be a good chance to have a word with you alone. You look pretty well set here.

MARGY: Yes, he thinks I'm a tourist. It's a lot different when they don't know. You've something to say to me, Gregg.

GREGG: Yes, that's why I'm here.

MARGY: I know it wasn't just the right thing to do leaving you like this.

GREGG: It's a bit beyond me old dear, but there's something else I wanted to talk to you about—The fleet's leaving port in the morning, and it's my last trip as a naval officer, then I'm going out to Australia.

MARGY: Australia, that's pretty far, isn't it?

GREGG: Yes, but it's a place where a fellow and a girl can start a new life out there.

MARGY: I see.

GREGG: You see what I mean? We could hit it off together.

MARGY: No Gregg, I'm through.

GREGG: You don't understand. I mean we'll get married.

MARGY: Thanks, Gregg.

GREGG: I'm not so bad, Marge.

MARGY: Why you're the best old scout I ever run into. Sometimes I wonder why you're where you are.

GREGG: It's a long story, the same old tale, though. Decent folks over in old England, father's a clergyman, I'm the black sheep—it's not only girls that drop out of the City Directory, old dear. What do you say to my little idea?

MARGY: No Gregg, I couldn't do it.

GREGG: Why I've got plenty to live on, a beautiful little white cottage, a garden, and a church—

MARGY: My God, you sound like Agnes—I'm sorry Gregg. Two weeks ago I'd have thought that over, but now—I can't.

GREGG: I guess I know.

MARGY: What do you mean?

GREGG: That youngster I see you walking around with every night since you struck Trinidad. Young Stanton, isn't he?

MARGY: It's just been kind of a dream, Gregg.

GREGG: I thought so. You've changed since you met him.

MARGY: You don't understand, Gregg.

GREGG: Oh, I'm no fool. Only don't singe your wings, old dear.

MARGY: Singe my wings? Don't make me laugh.

GREGG: Marge, the body doesn't mean a thing—but when it's the heart, it hurts.

MARGY: What do I know about a heart? To me every man is just an asset.

GREGG: Yes, and for this one chap you're giving up everything—and you say you know nothing about a heart? Why, Marge, ever since Montreal you've been mine, and I've been yours, all of me, every bit of me. There was a time I could share you with other men, but not now. Why, the thought of it drives me mad, almost. Tell me, do you really want this other fellow? Do you really love him?

MARGY: I guess I do.

GREGG: So that's it. And all the time I thought you were only making a play for his money.

MARGY: No Gregg, I couldn't roll him, of all men. From the moment I met him I knew.

GREGG: What do you mean?

MARGY: I'm beginning to see things different, Gregg, since I met that boy. He made me feel ashamed. He asked me to marry him.

GREGG: Haven't I asked you the same thing? Hasn't every officer in the fleet offered you the ring? And a dozen rich traders asked you to the altar?

MARGY: Yes, but he was the first one who asked me while he was sober.

GREGG: And you said yes?

MARGY: I'm beginning to see things different, Gregg. Why ever since I've been old enough to know Sex I've looked at men as hunters. They're filled with Sex. In the past few years I've been a chattel to that Sex. All the bad that's in me has been put there by men. I began to hate every one of them, hated them, used them for what I could get out of them, and then laughed at them, and then—then he came.

GREGG: But what about when you said you loved me? When you held me in your soft arms and kissed me and told me you loved me? Do you think you can get away from me as easy as this. To walk into another man's life and tell him the same things. Then all the beautiful things you told me you didn't mean?

MARGY: You don't understand, Gregg. When I held you in my arms and kissed you, when I felt your strong, warm body close to mine I wanted you, I needed you, I loved you more than any man I'd ever known. Don't you understand Gregg? I loved you in that one way. But this is different. It's a clean, wonderful love I have for this boy. I'm sorry, but I can't help it. God, it's good to be in love this way even if I have to pay for it with tears.

GREGG: All I can say is, don't be looking for heartaches. If this fellow really loves you, I suppose that's all there is to it. But remember if ever you want me, I'm yours, all yours.

MARGY: Don't talk to me that way Gregg. I suppose I shouldn't be doing what I am to you—but I can't help it.

GREGG: But you know your positions are pretty far apart. Why, that boy's folks are real folks. They're aristocrats. Tell me, are you sure that it's really love that's drawing him to you?

MARGY: I'm sure.

GREGG: Oh well, whenever you want me you'll know where a word reaches me. What I said about Australia goes. It's a long way and far between, but it's a place where a fellow and a girl can start a new life.

MARGY: Gregg, don't leave me like this. You've given me the chance. I'm not ungrateful, but it's . . . things just happen, that's all, that we can't explain.

GREGG: It's alright Marge, we all have to float with the tide.

(The "Meditation from Thaïs" is heard playing softly on the flagship in the bay. Jimmy enters and goes to Margy.)

JIMMY: I've arranged everything, we leave tomorrow.

(Noise offstage of suppressed shouts and murmurs as though a town were awakening to a catastrophe. The only distinguishable word is "Overboard!")

MARGY: What's that?

JIMMY: They're crowding down at the docks. Let's go see!

MARGY: No, no, wait.

JIMMY: Don't be nervous, you're all upset.

MARGY: Go, see what it is.

JIMMY: I'll find out. *(Calls offstage.)* What's going on down there?

OFFSTAGE VOICE: One of those fleet women jumped into the bay! *(Music and voices swell and fade. MARGY nearly faints.)*

JIMMY: Nothing to worry us, dear. Just one of those poor wretches that follow the fleet.

(Music and voices swell to a crescendo.)

CURTAIN

ACT THREE

SCENE ONE

(The Stanton residence. A richly appointed room. Onstage, ROBERT STAN-TON and JENKINS, the butler.)

MARIE *(Enters with a vase of flowers)*: I'm taking these to the young lady's room, sir.

STANTON: Yes, yes, go ahead Marie. See that everything is ready Marie.

MARIE *(Exits):* Yes sir.

STANTON: They ought to be along any minute. *(Exits.)*

MARIE *(Enters):* If he would only keep his watch in his pocket. It hasn't left his hand since Mr. Jimmy went to the station to meet the train.

JENKINS: Well, any man would be anxious to meet his future daughter-in-law.

MARIE: Yes, when he don't know very much about her.

JENKINS: She's evidently very wealthy. Mr. Jimmy met her while she was touring the world.

MARIE: Yes. She travel all alone, no chaperone.

JENKINS: Oh, the days of chaperones are past. Wealthy orphan, no doubt. Marguerite LaMont is her name.

MARIE: Marguerite LaMont. That sounds like a French name.

JENKINS: Mr. Jimmy calls her Margy.

MARIE: Short for Marguerite. French descent, no doubt. All Mr. Stanton he worry about is what church she belong to.

JENKINS: I haven't any idea.

STANTON *(Enters):* When they arrive, Jenkins, call me. I'll be in the library.

JENKINS: Yes, sir.

STANTON: I'm going to lose a couple of hours sleep as it is—I have to get up early to be at business. *(Exits.)*

MARIE: If he were not at his desk at nine A.M. to the minute, the world would come to an end.

(An auto horn is heard.)

JENKINS: System, my dear, that's what makes a man successful. *(Exits.)*

JIMMY *(Enters with MARGY)*: Home at last, darling. By Jove, it was hard work to get you to come out here. Take this to Miss LaMont's room, Marie, and wait just a minute. Well, darling, how do you like it?

MARGY: This is the first case of cold feet I ever had.

JIMMY: Why, darling? Mother and Dad are just a pair of peaches. You'll love them, you can't help it.

MARGY: That part's alright. I know I couldn't help loving your dad and your mother, but the question is, how about me? Am I the kind of a girl they've pictured for their only son? You know, parents are funny.

JIMMY: Mother and Dad are just crazy to meet you. I've talked to them about you ever since I came back from Trinidad. Let me take your wraps. *(To MARIE and JENKINS)* Take these also. Marie and Jenkins you may go. *(Exit MARIE and JENKINS. Enter CLARA.)*

JIMMY: Oh, there you are, Mother. I've been looking for you. Mother, this is Margy. *(CLARA and MARGY recognize each other—and pause.)*

CLARA: How do you do.

JIMMY: I hope you'll like each other.

MARGY: Well, we'll understand each other anyway.

(Enter STANTON.)

JIMMY: Oh, Dad!

STANTON: Well, son?

JIMMY: Margy, this is Dad.

STANTON: Well, well, so this is the young lady that Jimmy's been raving about ever since he came back from Trinidad! Why he's been going around with his heart in his fist.

JIMMY: Oh, Dad. You're telling tales now.

STANTON: I'm going to show you right up! Margy—of course I'll call you Margy?—you've certainly worked a great change in my boy. He used to read nothing but the sporting news—but now, he reads the furniture ads, isn't that right, Clara?

CLARA: Yes.

STANTON: I hope you're going to like it out here, Margy.

MARGY: I'm sure I will.

STANTON: You've never been to our little town before?

MARGY: This is one place I've missed.

STANTON: Enjoy travelling, don't you? Jimmy says you are a regular globe trotter. Well, you'll find everything here. We've got everything they've got in the big cities, parks, YMCA buildings, churches—er—which one do you attend?

MARGY: One's as good as another to me.

CLARA: Naturally, I presume—travelling so much.

MARGY: Yes, naturally, when in Rome do as Rome does, or again when in Trinidad follow Trinidad's customs, or Montreal—

CLARA: I've visited Montreal myself, Miss LaMont.

MARGY: Why, you don't say—we can compare notes.

STANTON: You two girls'll have a lot to talk about. Jimmy I'll bet Mother's just dying to get acquainted, and here's your old talkative Dad not giving her a chance.

CLARA: I would like a few minutes alone with Miss LaMont.

STANTON: Come on Jimmy—we'll let the ladies talk, and we'll drink to their health.

JIMMY: Alright, Dad.

STANTON: Then we'll let you ladies take a drink to our health. *(Exit JIMMY and STANTON.)*

MARGY: What's your idea?

CLARA: You certainly don't intend to marry my son.

MARGY: That's your idea.

CLARA: I'll not let him make such a mistake. I'll tell him what you are.

MARGY: Suppose he should ask you how you know what I am?

CLARA: I'll tell him everything. Everything that happened during my visit to Montreal.

MARGY: No, you won't. You haven't the nerve. If you did, I'd have a better opinion of you. You wouldn't sacrifice yourself for anyone. Your pride's what you're thinking of.

CLARA: I'm thinking of my boy's welfare. He certainly is deserving of a better fate.

MARGY: I know my past is nothing to rave about. I'll admit he deserves a better life, yes, and he deserves a better mother, too.

CLARA: How dare you speak like that?

MARGY: How dare I speak like that? Who are *you?*

CLARA: I'll not permit a woman of the streets to talk to me like that.

MARGY: Say, you've got a nerve putting yourself on a pedestal above me. The things I've done, I had to do for a living. I know it was wrong. I'm not trying to alibi myself. But you've done those same things for other reasons.

CLARA: Stop—

MARGY: No, I won't stop. I'm going to dig under the veneer of your supposed respectability and show you what you are.

CLARA: I'll not listen.

MARGY: Oh, yes you will. You've got the kind of stuff in you that makes women of my type. If our positions were changed—you in my place, and I in yours—I'd be willing to bet that I'd make a better wife and mother than you are. Yeah, and I'll bet without this beautiful home, without money, and without any restrictions, you'd be worse than I have ever been.

CLARA: No, no—.

MARGY: Yes, you would. You'd do it and like it.

CLARA: For God's sake stop it, I can't endure any more—

MARGY: Now you're down off your pedestal. You're down where you can see—it's just a matter of circumstances. The only difference between us is that you could afford to give it away.

CLARA: I'm not considering my feelings. It's the welfare of my boy.

MARGY: I've thought of his welfare, perhaps more than you have. I didn't want to come here. I told him from the start that I wasn't the woman for him, but he wouldn't listen.

CLARA: But you have no right to expect him to marry you.

MARGY: I don't know. He could do worse by marrying some little tart who'd wear my colors after she was married to him, some jane who would take a little trip to Montreal. I've had my share of men. They all look alike to me except one—him.

CLARA: I can understand your viewpoint, but even if this marriage was to take place, you could never live down the sins of the past. People would talk.

MARGY: They'd talk anyway.

CLARA: Yes, but we are governed to a great extent by what they say and think.

MARGY: Let them talk. We love each other and that's all that matters.

CLARA: Don't say he loves you. It's ridiculous—he is a boy, scarcely out of his teens. You are perhaps the first woman he has ever come into close contact with. It's only natural that you should attract him with the physical attraction that a woman has for a boy so young.

MARGY: All I've been is a physical attraction to men. I'm sick and tired of being that sort of thing. Now I want a man whose love goes beyond that.

CLARA: If you should get married, you'd find out just how far it goes.

MARGY: Well, I'll find out before. Here.

CLARA: What do you mean?

MARGY: You know what I mean. You're a pretty wise gal yourself.

CLARA: You don't mean that you'd use my home—

MARGY: Well, you used mine.

CLARA: But—

MARGY: We'll at least know where we stand.

(Enter JIMMY and STANTON.)

JIMMY: Dad and I think you've had enough time to get acquainted. Mother, don't you just love her?

MARGY: She's just crazy about me.

CLARA: Yes, son, she's—very—interesting.

STANTON: And trying to keep her all to yourself. Now that's a shame. But you wait until after business hours tomorrow. I'll take charge of Margy. You'll have to tell me all about your travels and your experiences. I'll warrant you had a lot of them, didn't you?

MARGY: I'll say I did.

STANTON: Well, we'll have a lot of time to talk that over. I must be going.

JIMMY: Dad, you're not leaving us?

STANTON: Well, son, you know I get up early, and it's pretty late for me. Margy'll excuse me, I know.

MARGY: Of course I will.

STANTON: I'm so glad you're here, child. You'll be such good company for Mrs. Stanton. Won't she, dear?

CLARA: Yes—yes—indeed.

MARGY: That's so sweet of you, Mrs. Stanton. You don't know how I appreciate your feelings toward me.

CLARA: Thank you. I presume you've a great deal to say to each other. I'd only be intruding. When you are ready to retire Miss LaMont just ring for the maid. She'll show you to your room.

MARGY: Thanks.

STANTON: My goodness. It's past my hour for retiring.

JIMMY: Dad always goes to bed early. He hasn't been up as late as this in six months.

STANTON: I'm the first one up in this house. Have to catch an early morning train to get to the city. You'll forgive me, I'm sure. Besides you and Jimmy have a lot to say to each other.

JIMMY: Well, now Dad . . .

STANTON: Don't make any excuses. I was a youngster once myself. And say Jimmy, if Margy should feel like a bite, you'll find a little spread all ready on the dining room table.

JIMMY: Thanks Dad. I—I never did think of asking Margy—

STANTON: Jimmy even Cupid has to have his dinner. Make yourself at home, child. Get acquainted. If there's anything you want and you don't see it, just ask for it.

MARGY: You're awfully good, Mr. Stanton.

STANTON: I want you to like Jimmy's folks, child.

MARGY: Thanks—why I'm sure—

STANTON: I'm sure that you will, and I'm going to see that you do.

MARGY: Good night, Mr. Stanton.

JIMMY: 'Night, Dad.

(Exit STANTON.)

MARGY: Your dad is a prince.

CLARA: You'll pardon me, I'm sure.

MARGY: Surely.

CLARA: When you are ready to retire, Miss LaMont, Jimmy will ring for the maid. She'll show you to your room. Good night.

JIMMY: Good night, mother.

MARGY: Good night, Mrs. Stanton.

(Exit CLARA.)

JIMMY: You'll have to learn to call her "Mother," you know.

MARGY: Say Jimmy, that'll be the hardest job I ever tackled.

JIMMY: Why—don't you like Mother?

MARGY: There's no question to it.

JIMMY: I'm so glad. It's wonderful to have you here with me, dear.

MARGY: Yes Jimmy, it's been a wonderful night.

JIMMY: I was afraid you didn't mean what you promised in Trinidad—I had such a hard time getting you here. You didn't know what sleepless nights I've had thinking of you and being afraid—

MARGY: Afraid of what?

JIMMY: That maybe you—you found out that you didn't love me after all, and perhaps met some other fellow and—oh, hang it, Margy, a man thinks up all kinds of things when he's in love with a girl.

MARGY: You weren't sure of me?

JIMMY: How could I be, with you so far away, but now tonight, you're in my own home—I'm content for the first time in months. You do love me, don't you?

MARGY: Love you? Jimmy I never knew what it was all about until I met you.

JIMMY: And we'll be married soon, won't we?

MARGY: Do you really want to marry me?

JIMMY: Why, of course—what do you expect?

MARGY: You see, I've been kind of worried too, I thought maybe some other girl—

JIMMY: There's no other girl in the world for me, save you.

MARGY: And why just me?

JIMMY: I love you.

MARGY: Why do you love me, Jimmy?

JIMMY: I love you because you're different, you fascinate me, you draw me to you, you're wonderful and I adore you.

MARGY: Come on over here, dear.

JIMMY: I've been telling you what I like about you. Now you tell me what you like about me. Tell—

MARGY: There's so many things about you that I like—but I never did like bright lights.

JIMMY: I'll turn them down. (He dims the lights.) There, is that better? Now, tell me what you like about me!

MARGY: I like your ears.

JIMMY: You like my ears? (MARGY strokes his face.) Who do you think came into the office today?

MARGY: Who, dear?

JIMMY: Lieutenant Gregg.

MARGY: What did he want?

JIMMY: When I left him in Trinidad I told him where I lived and asked him if he ever came to New York to spend the weekend with me, so of course when he came to the office I asked him out.

MARGY *(Undoing his necktie)*: Take that thing off.

(JIMMY removes tie. MARGY examines it, and lets it fall.)

MARGY: Very pretty, what size collar do you wear?

JIMMY: Fifteen and a half. *(They kiss.)* God, I've never kissed anyone like that before—

MARGY: You have.

JIMMY: I swear I haven't.

MARGY: You have. *(They kiss again.)*

JIMMY: I'll ring for the maid.

MARGY: Can't you show me to my room?

JIMMY: Yes, dear—Good night, dear.

CURTAIN

Scene Two

(The next morning. JIMMY runs out, picks up necktie and returns to bed-room. His father enters, dressed for the day's business. He fills his flask. JIMMY reenters, fully dressed, but very nervous.)

STANTON: Hello, Son, I didn't know you were up. Why didn't you breakfast with me?

JIMMY: Why—I don't know—I—

STANTON: I suppose you're so happy that you can't even sleep in peace.

JIMMY: Dad, you like her, don't you?

STANTON: Of course I like her. Any man would have to like her. She's a fine girl. You're just like your old Dad, a good picker.

JIMMY: I'm so glad.

STANTON: Yes, but I can't let your happiness make me late for business. I'll take the train and you can come down later in the car.

JIMMY: Must I go into the city today?

STANTON: Yes, Son, I need you about the Hoyden affair. Sorry to take you away from Margy, but you can leave as soon as we settle with Hoyden.

JIMMY: But can't you let that go till later? That deal is practically closed. He'll be in today, you really don't need me. Besides that Lieutenant Gregg is coming in.

STANTON: Lieutenant Gregg? Who's he?

JIMMY: He's that English officer that came into the office yesterday. He's coming in on the next train.

STANTON: Well, alright, Son, perhaps I can let you stay. Say good morning to Margy and tell her that I hope she slept well.

JIMMY: I will, thanks.

(STANTON exits.)

MARIE *(Entering from right. She sees JIMMY)*: Good morning, monsieur.

JIMMY: Oh Marie, have you seen Mother?

MARIE: Oui monsieur, she's not feeling very well, sir. She's having her breakfast in her room.

JIMMY: What's the matter with Mother?

MARIE: A bad headache, I think sir. *(Exits left.)*

(JIMMY exits right, JENKINS enters from left as MARGY comes on from back room.)

MARGY: Good morning, Jenkins.

JENKINS: Good morning, Madam. *(Crossing over.)* Does Madam wish anything?

MARGY: No, if I want something I'll ring.

JENKINS: Very well, Madam. *(Exits right.)*

MARGY: I don't like this Madam business.

JIMMY *(Entering from right)*: Margie.

(He goes over to her on the divan with a worried look and kisses her.)

MARGY: What's the matter, you look worried.

JIMMY: Mother's not feeling very well this morning.

MARGY: That's too bad. What's the matter with her?

JIMMY: Oh, I guess it's her nerves again.

MARGY: Is there anything I can do? Er—has she been saying anything about last night?

JIMMY: No, but she seems upset. I imagine it's about last night—I wonder if she—I wonder if she knows about last night—you and I. Oh dear, why did you let me go to your room. It's the thing I've been fighting against ever since I met you.

MARGY: Perhaps I'd better not stay here?

JIMMY: What do you mean—what do you mean?

MARGY: Well, your mother isn't feeling well—and you're all upset—

JIMMY: Why—Margy—

MARGY: You want me to stay?

JIMMY: Want you? I want you always, always. Oh, don't you understand—I love you, love you. I realize it now more than ever. To lose you would be to lose every bit of happiness out of my life—I couldn't live without you.

MARGY: Jimmy, you're mad.

JIMMY: Yes, mad about you dear. We'll get married at once—

MARGY: Married!

JIMMY: Margy—of course—there was never any other thought in my mind. You hold everything in the world for me. We'll be happy together, you and I. *(Holds her in his arms and kisses her.)* Why dear, I couldn't leave you out of my sight long enough to join Dad at the office today.

MARGY: You should have attended to business and—and—

JIMMY: And what?

MARGY: You've got me so nervous, Jimmy, I don't know what I did want to say.

JIMMY: There, I forgot about Lieutenant Gregg again. I've got to go meet him at once. I can't think of anything but you, you see?

MARGY: But why did you invite him here?

JIMMY: I think he's a fine fellow. He seemed very much interested in you. He asked how you were feeling.

MARGY: Oh, he's a wonderful man and all that, but I wanted to be alone with you, dear.

JENKINS *(Entering from left):* The car is waiting, Mr. Stanton.

JIMMY: Very well, Jenkins.

(Exit JENKINS.)

(JIMMY rises and kisses MARGY.)

I won't be long, sweetheart.

MARGY: Hurry back, dear.

(JIMMY exits.)

(MARGY rises and after looking off at JIMMY leaving, makes several ludicrous attempts to rearrange the furnishings of the room. The result is a garish display of taste.)

CLARA *(Entering from right):* Good morning, Miss LaMont.

MARGY: Oh, good morning—I—was just making a few changes here—to kind of suit myself.

CLARA: So I see.

MARGY: I thought that thing would look better over here and this thing would look better over here. *(She is wiping her hands on a brocade.)*

CLARA: Well—well—hmm—

MARGY *(Holding up the brocade):* Oh, what's this thing supposed to be?

CLARA: Oh goodness! That "thing" is supposed to be a brocade from Marie Antoinette, Queen of France.

MARGY: Oh, is that what that thing is supposed to be?

CLARA: And this thing is supposed to have been worn by Madame DuBarry when she used her wiles on King Louis XV.

MARGY: What a break that jane got! I remember reading about that boy.

CLARA: Oh, my nerves, my nerves.

MARGY: Jimmy said you weren't feeling very well, and I was going in to see how you were, but I thought I had better not after the argument last night.

CLARA: Yes, I forgive you for taking the attitude you did. I realize I was quite harsh with you, but you didn't understand my feelings in the matter.

MARGY: No, and I guess you didn't understand mine.

CLARA: At first I thought you came here in a spirit of revenge.

MARGY: Say, I didn't have any idea I was going to meet you here. I should say not! But that was a pretty mean trick you pulled on me that night in Montreal. After the story you told, I could have done time.

CLARA: I'm sorry, but I have a clearer understanding of your problem now.

MARGY: I'm glad you have. Of course we all make mistakes.

CLARA: Yes, I've made mistakes, too. I only caught myself in time. You don't know the agony, the mental suffering I've endured on account of that Montreal affair.

MARGY: I don't know how you ever fell for that guy. Of course with me it was more business than anything else.

CLARA: It was my first and last experience of anything like that. I swear to you from that night to this I've given all of my love, every one of my thoughts to my husband and boy. God, what a lesson it was to me, my nerves go to pieces at the very thought of it.

MARGY: Don't worry about the past. That's my motto. Always think of what you're going to do tomorrow.

CLARA: And what are you going to do tomorrow? You hold my boy's future in your hands. Some day he'll find out—and then, don't you see what it'll be?

MARGY: He loves me and it won't matter.

CLARA: Oh, yes it will matter. He'll never forgive you for deceiving him. He'll hate you and you'll both be miserable.

MARGY: I—I—don't believe it.

CLARA: Those things can never remain a secret—Some day they will come to life, and even though he did love you well enough to forgive, what would it be for him, dreading the very meeting of every man he sees thinking that perhaps his wife—Oh, don't you understand it would be enough to madden him, and you, how would you feel? You would never know a moment of peace.

MARGY: You're certainly not drawing a pretty picture.

CLARA: Yes, but I'm drawing a true picture. Tell me you'll give him up, please. (MARGY turns her head away. MARIE enters dressed for the street.) Oh Marie, are you going out?

MARIE: Madame said I could—the others have all gone on ahead.

CLARA: Oh yes, yes, I'd forgotten, our neighbor's cook—you're all invited to her wedding. My nerves are in such a state, I don't remember.

MARIE: If Madame wish me to remain—

CLARA: No, you go, but call up the druggist, and tell him to send over the nerve prescription Dr. Gordon left for me.

MARIE: Oui, Madame.

CLARA: Has Jenkins returned from the station?

MARIE: I think not, madame. (Auto horn offstage.) I think it is the car now. (MARIE exits and returns later followed by JIMMY and GREGG dressed in civilian clothes. MARIE exits again.)

JIMMY: Come right in, lieutenant.

GREGG: Thanks, awfully.

JIMMY: Mother, this is Lieutenant Gregg.

CLARA: How do you do Lieutenant Gregg. *(CLARA and GREGG recognize each other, but before GREGG gets a chance to admit it, MARGY jabs him. JIMMY notices nothing. GREGG and CLARA falter in their greetings.)*

MARGY *(To Jimmy):* Oh dear—

CLARA: You'll pardon me, Lieutenant Gregg, but I'm not feeling well. I'll see you later.

GREGG: I'm sorry to hear you're indisposed. It's quite alright, I quite understand.

JIMMY: Mother isn't quite herself today.

MARGY: No, she's not feeling well.

JIMMY: Now, dear, that the lieutenant is here I'd like to show him around the place. Won't you join us?

MARGY: Honey, I don't feel that I'd care to go out today. You go.

JENKINS *(Entering from right):* Your mother would like to see you, Mr. Stanton.

JIMMY: Pardon me, I'll be right back. *(Exit JIMMY and JENKINS.)*

GREGG: Isn't that the woman from Montreal?

MARGY: Of course it is. Who did you think it was?

GREGG: I wasn't quite sure. I was just going to ask her when you started all this sort of business. *(He indicates the jabs she had given him.)*

MARGY: That's all I need around here, just one bright remark from you.

GREGG: But doesn't he know?

MARGY *(Going over to the piano):* No, he doesn't know.

GREGG: Aren't you going to tell him?

MARGY: No I'm going to let you tell him. *(She plays "Home Sweet Home." GREGG watches her, smoking silently.)*

GREGG *(At end of piece):* That doesn't sound a bit like you, Marge.

MARGY: It's not supposed to be me. *(Starts to play blues number, stopping just long enough to answer him.)*

GREGG: That's more like you, Marge, You're looking beautiful, Marge, more beautiful than ever.

MARGY: Yeah?

GREGG: You're not saying how I look?

MARGY: You're looking alright.

GREGG: There was a time I looked rather good to you.

MARGY: You look the same to me now.

GREGG: But how do you like me in civilian clothes?

MARGY: They look alright. But I think I like the uniform better.

GREGG: Why?

MARGY: I don't know, I guess it's because I'm so patriotic.

JIMMY *(Entering):* What is my little sweetheart doing? Entertaining?

MARGY: Not tonight, dear.

JIMMY: Won't you change your mind and join us, dear.

MARGY: No, you two run along and hurry back, dear.

JIMMY: Alright. Come along lieutenant, we'll go.

GREGG: You don't care to come, too?

MARGY: No, I don't care to come too.

GREGG: Will you be here when I get back?

MARGY: I'll be here when you get back.

(Exit JIMMY and GREGG. Enter JENKINS.)

JENKINS *(Sees CLARA entering):* Have I permission to go to the wedding?

CLARA: Yes, you may go.

JENKINS: Thank you, madam.

(Door bell rings. JENKINS exits and returns with a card on a salver.)

CLARA *(Looking at card)*: Show the gentleman in. *(JENKINS exits and returns ushering in ROCKY WALDRON. JENKINS exits.)* And you have the impudence to come back here!

ROCKY: Your little boy friend is broke again.

CLARA: I refuse to give you any more money.

ROCKY: Then I park the body here until you do.

CLARA: I can't let you stay here.

ROCKY: I'd be a handy man to have around the house. That husband of yours is an old gink. A young chap like me isn't to be found everywhere.

CLARA: You must leave.

ROCKY: Be reasonable. You don't want to lose a home like this and a husband with plenty of jack.

CLARA *(Rising)*: But I can't let you have any more money.

ROCKY: You can't bluff me, Clara. You play a bum poker hand.

CLARA: I can't let you stay here. You must go. My husband, my boy. Oh for God's sake, please go, go.

ROCKY: I don't mind taking a little jewelry with me. What a nice new collection you have. That husband of yours does like to drape you in gems. By the way, what did you tell him you did with the others?

CLARA: I told him they were stolen.

ROCKY: Well, tell him the same thing about these.

(CLARA is standing by the door to MARGY's room. ROCKY makes a grab for her, and CLARA picks up a gun from a table. She is about to shoot him, but MARGY enters and takes her gun, hiding it behind her own back. ROCKY is astonished by MARGY's entrance.)

ROCKY *(To MARGY)*: You? What are you pulling here?

CLARA: He threatened to tell my husband about Montreal unless I gave him money.

MARGY: Don't my little pet know that blackmail is against the law?

ROCKY: It's none of your business.

MARGY: Yes, but I'm going to make it my business. You know you're not in Montreal now, dearie. No to be exact you're just three hundred fifty-four miles from there. You're in the States now, get out your little map. Rocky Waldron, alias Gentleman Jack, wanted for several things including murder.

ROCKY *(To MARGY)*: So that's what you're pulling! If you think I'd let you get away with it . . . You're mine, you belong to me! *(He starts at her. MARGY drives a chair between him and herself.)*

ROCKY *(To CLARA)*: You stopped my allowance in Montreal but it's going to start again here. You're going to come across with that jack. We're going to blow this town right now.

(MARGY goes to telephone.)

ROCKY *(Back to MARGY)*: What are you going to do?

MARGY: Make a reservation, dear. Now, just where would my little pet care to spend his next twenty or thirty years? I know a beautiful place down South dear, called Atlanta, where I know they're waiting to welcome you with open arms.

ROCKY: You think so?

MARGY: Or maybe you don't care for the warm climate? I could very easily arrange a beautiful trip up the Hudson. Where you get free tonsorial visits. In other words the closest haircut you ever had. And Baby, the classiest suit of clothes, you know, sort of zebra effect. I can just see it draped on that perfect figure of yours.

ROCKY: Who do you think you're kidding? You trying to waste my time around here—why I'd—

(MARGY brings the gun out on him. He recoils in fear. She takes receiver off phone.)

MARGY *(Calmly)*: Hello, police headquarters, yes please hurry. *(To Rocky)*: Mmmm—I can just see it draped on that perfect figure of yours. Hello, police headquarters? This is the Robert Stanton residence, Boulevard Road, yes, will you kindly send someone here immediately, yes, to take a desperate character. Yes, please hurry, thank you.

ROCKY: So you'd turn me up after all I've done for you?

MARGY: After all you've done for me? A fine thing you did when you left this woman on my hands. If she hadn't come to, I'd be in jail yet.

ROCKY: I'd have come back, I'd have got you out.

MARGY: Yes you would. Yes you would.

ROCKY: Come on Marge, you're not going to turn me up. Why they're on my trail now. That's why I came here. I just wanted more jack to make a get away. Please don't turn me up.

MARGY: Alright rat. I'll give you a chance. Escaped convict 3844. I've got a pretty good memory, haven't I? Why, if I didn't have a certain amount of refinement, I'd kick your teeth all over this floor. Now blow bum, blow. Not that way, you ought to know better than that. Come on, come on. *(ROCKY exits hastily.) (To CLARA:)* Where do you keep this thing? *(She indicates the revolver.)*

CLARA: Just put it on the table.

MARGY *(She writes on a pad on the table and hands CLARA a piece of paper)*: Now any time your little boyfriend should forget his promise and come back, a little phone call will put him right where he belongs.

CLARA: Thank you very much. When he threatened to tell my husband about Montreal I thought about my boy and everything. I picked up that gun and I would have shot him.

MARGY: You must never do that. You must never shoot anyone.

CLARA: Oh, why did I do it? I went mad. *(Door bell rings.)* Oh, the police are here. What are you going to tell them?

MARGY: Now don't worry, I know how to handle those babies. *(Exits to door.)*

POLICEMAN *(Offstage)*: Alright Mike, you stay outside.

VOICE *(Offstage)*: Look out Al, he's desperate.

POLICEMAN *(Entering with MARGY)*: What's the trouble, lady?

MARGY: I'm very sorry, officer. But there has been a slight mistake on our part.

POLICEMAN: Why, the report at headquarters was to come and get a desperate character.

MARGY: Yes, he was desperate, in the beginning, very desperate, wasn't he, Mrs. Stanton?

CLARA: Yes, he was very desperate. You see, we ladies were all alone. The servants have gone to a wedding.

MARGY: Yes, the butler and the maid, they had a friend, a cook. And she just got back from her honeymoon and is going to be married tonight.

CLARA: Why, she hasn't had her honeymoon yet—

MARGY: Oh, I don't know how it is, but I will make those mistakes. Yes, she's going to be married tonight and tomorrow night she's going to have her honeymoon. I will do those things. And you see, we ladies were here alone. And this man, he came in, and he wanted money, he wanted carfare, he was going some place. And of course we ladies, we felt that we didn't dare to give it to him. And then he became very annoyed, oh very angry. But after a while he cooled off and he began to see things our way, and he left. I don't think he'll be back, in fact I'm sure he won't. *(She starts to flirt with officer in her attempt to make him believe her.)* So you see, officer, a slight mistake and very sorry to have troubled you, really.

POLICEMAN *(Starting to exit)*: It's alright lady, no harm done. *(Stops. Comes to MARGY.)* I beg your pardon. Haven't I seen you some place before?

MARGY: I beg pardon?

POLICEMAN: Haven't I seen you some place before?

MARGY: Well, I've been some place.

POLICEMAN: Don't you remember me?

MARGY: I can't say that I do.

POLICEMAN: Sailor Gordon?

MARGY: Do you mind stepping out here for just a minute? *(Starts to exit.)*

POLICEMAN: Coitenly.

(They exit together. CLARA stands and looks out after them thoughtfully. After a few moments, MARGY returns. She cannot look CLARA in the face, and goes to her room in silence. JIMMY and GREGG enter.)

JIMMY: Mother, has there been any trouble here?

CLARA: Why no, Son, why?

JIMMY: I saw Warren and he said he saw some officers coming in here.

CLARA: Yes, they were here but they had the wrong place, darling.

JIMMY: I'm so glad. We certainly did hurry to get here, didn't we Lieutenant?

GREGG: We whizzed, what?

JIMMY: Mother, where's Margy?

CLARA: Up in her room.

JIMMY: Mother, you haven't been saying anything to offend her have you?

CLARA: Of course not, Son.

(MARGY enters dressed to go away and carrying a bag. They all turn and stare at her.)

JIMMY: Why, dear, what's the matter?

MARGY: I'm leaving, dear.

JIMMY: You're leaving? Why?

MARGY: Do you remember that last night in Trinidad?

JIMMY: How could I ever forget it?

MARGY: Do you remember the woman that threw herself into the bay?

JIMMY: Why yes, of course. But what has that got to do with us?

MARGY: I was no better than she.

JIMMY: What are you saying?

MARGY: I was one of those women.

JIMMY: You? Why that's not true!

MARGY: Ask Gregg.

(GREGG turns away, too ashamed to look at him.)

JIMMY: I can't believe. . . . *(He sits down, heartbroken, and puts head in hands.)*

MARGY: Mrs. Stanton, I'm giving back your boy. I'm sure you'll teach him to forget me.

CLARA: But you are not going back to that life?

(GREGG appeals to her mutely to remember his feeling for her. She looks at him and smiles.)

MARGY: No, I'm going straight—to Australia. *(Holds out hand to GREGG.)*

FINAL CURTAIN

THE DRAG

A HOMOSEXUAL COMEDY IN THREE ACTS

(1927)

THE CAST

Dr. James Richmond, a physiciann
Barbara Richmond, his sister
Clair, his daughter
Judge Robert Kingsbury
Rolly Kingsbury, his son, married to Clair
Jessie, a maid
Parsons, a butler
Allen Grayson, a civil engineer
Marion, a matron
David Caldwell, an outcast
Clem Hathaway
Hal Swanson, called "The Duchess"
Winnie Lewis
Rosco Gillingwater
Taxi-Driver
Billy Mack, a boy
Inspector

Detective, guests and musicians at the drag ball

The action takes place in New York City at the homes of Dr. James Richmond and of Rolly Kingsbury.

Act One.		Afternoon. The library in the home of Dr. Richmond.
Act Two		The same, later that afternoon.
Act Three	Scene One.	Evening. The drawing room of Rolly Kingsbury's home.
	Scene Two.	The same in the early hours of the next day.

THE DRAG

ACT ONE

(Afternoon. The library in the home of DR. RICHMOND, New York City. The room is large and roomy, comfortably furnished in subdued richness, the kind of room a tired business or professional man would use as a haven of rest. Center entrance leading to general entrance. Door right leading to Doctor's office. Stairway left or doors, leading to other parts of the house. Windows overlooking a courtyard with a few potted plants. At rise, DR. RICHMOND's sister, AUNT BARBARA, a kindly faced woman in her fifties, is dressed conservatively yet not unfashionably. She is arranging magazines and books on a desk in the center of the room. DR. RICHMOND, a dignified, calm-looking man, is seated behind the desk.)

BARBARA: Do you want this book?

DOCTOR: Yes—The Ulrich book I've been so eager to get.*

BARBARA: I'm glad you've got it!

(Gives him a side-long glance.)

I never heard of such outlandish diseases in my life.

DOCTOR *(Turning pages of book)*: There are many, many ills that science has not yet discovered Barbara, to say nothing of being able to cure them.

---

*Karl Heinrich Ulrichs, a German writer of the 1860s, who used the word "invert" to describe homosexuals as possessing "a woman's spirit in a man's body."

BARBARA: Brother, why should you give your whole life to trying to find out things that no one else knows anything about?

DOCTOR: Why, every physician owes something to medical science. Old Hippocrates, the Greek founder of medicine himself, did his bit when he formed the school of physicians, and it's up to the rest of us to do our share.

BARBARA: That's no reason why you should give your whole life to it. You always were bad enough, but now—since Clair is married—it's the only thing in your life. You used to give your daughter a thought once in a while—

DOCTOR: But Clair's happy now.

BARBARA: How do you know?

DOCTOR: Why shouldn't she be? Married to Rolly Kingsbury, son of Judge Kingsbury, from one of the finest families. The judge and I were boys together—chums since childhood.

BARBARA: To hear you two quarrel—

DOCTOR: We never quarrel—just differences of opinion—just differences of opinion.

BARBARA: So long as you're satisfied, I'm sure I am.

(Sighs. DOCTOR looks at her.)

DOCTOR: I wouldn't know what to do without you. Ever since Clair's mother died, you've been sister and mother to the little one—and—no, I guess I wouldn't know what to do without you.

BARBARA (Sighs): I guess you wouldn't get along very well.

DOCTOR (Thoughtfully.): I haven't been fair to you. I never thought of it just like that before. Now I'm seeing it. I'm afraid I've kept you from marrying.

BARBARA: That's not such a hardship for me.

DOCTOR: Why—

BARBARA: A woman's never certain what she is marrying.

DOCTOR: How's that?

BARBARA: Men—you never know about them till you get them and then it's generally too late—better not to know.

DOCTOR *(Laughs)*: We know that Clair's pretty certain about what she married, no question there, is there?

BARBARA: I'm not so sure.

DOCTOR: Now, now! Rolly is one of the best chaps—he's never been up with a single scandal—for a young man as rich as he is—why, Barbara, he never even associated with another woman—Clair has been his life—

BARBARA: I've been looking over this—Ulrich book as you call it.

DOCTOR: Now—

BARBARA: All I say is, you doctors get away with murder.

DOCTOR: Barbara!

BARBARA: I mean in the printed matter you read. Surprised they let it go through the mails.

DOCTOR: A work of science—

BARBARA: Science is a good name for it.

DOCTOR *(At phone)*: Since when have you taken it into your head to read—*(Indicates magazines.)*

BARBARA: I've read everything else in the place a dozen times.

DOCTOR *(Picks up telephone)*: Central—give me Irving 9200.

BARBARA: What now?

DOCTOR: Keep you out of further mischief.

BARBARA: Oh I don't—

DOCTOR: Hello, hello! Gordon and Mason, publishers? This is Dr. Richmond speaking. Send me some late issues of the medical journal and—you might send the Buffalo Bill series—

BARBARA: Don't bother—I read the Buffalo Bill series when you were a boy.

DOCTOR: Never mind the Buffalo Bill series, but send some love stories, regular love stories.

BARBARA: Love stories, brother, at my age?

DOCTOR *(At phone)*: Send them over as soon as you can. Good-bye. *(Turns to BARBARA.)* No more of those books for you, Barbara.

BARBARA: Isn't science proper reading?

DOCTOR: What some people don't know, my dear, don't trouble them.

BARBARA: In other words, it's a good thing one half of the world doesn't know how the other half lives, eh?

DOCTOR: Excellent—in most cases.

BARBARA *(Crosses to table right—picks up the Ulrich volume)*: Now this book—

DOCTOR *(Takes book from her and places it on table center)*: Yes, but you wouldn't understand.

BARBARA: I'd rather not.

(Enter Maid.)

Yes, Jessie?

JESSIE: Two gentlemen to see the doctor.

BARBARA: Patients?

JESSIE: I think so.

BARBARA: These are not the doctor's office hours, Jessie, you know it. Tell them to come back between seven and eight.

DOCTOR: How unkind! You don't know but that they need me. Jessie—show them in.

JESSIE *(Stops, plainly heeding BARBARA above the doctor)*: Yes, Miss.

BARBARA: Tell them to come back.

JESSIE: Yes, miss. *(Starts to exit.)*

DOCTOR: Jessie! *(Nods to her).*

BARBARA: You never will think of yourself. *(Looks toward center.)* What's the use! *(DOCTOR exits rear.)*

JESSIE *(Enters followed by DAVID and CLEM)*: This way, please. Come right in.

(DAVID looks worn, tired and haggard as in great trouble.)

BARBARA: These are not the doctor's office hours. Have a seat, the doctor will see you presently.

CLEM: The doctor's office hours don't mean a thing to me, dearie, as long as I get this one off my chest. *(Crosses to DAVID.)* Calm yourself, honey, calm yourself, All you need is a jab in the arm and you'll be all right. Oh! *(Business.)* Oh! *(BARBARA exits.)* Queer old thing, she looks like the pig woman that squealed. If I had to look at her much longer, I'd need the doctor myself. *(Looking around room—sits in chair left.)* Oh, what a gorgeous place!

JESSIE *(Offstage left)*: I tell you, you can't go in.

TAXI-DRIVER *(Off left)*: I want to know if they're here.

CLEM: My God! That brilliant taxi-driver. I forgot all about him.

TAXI-DRIVER *(Enters)*: Do you boys want me to wait?

CLEM: You better wait, you great, big, beautiful baby.

TAXI-DRIVER: I don't get you guys.

CLEM: If you don't, you're the first taxi-driver that didn't.

TAXI-DRIVER: What do you want me to do?

CLEM: Ride me around a while, dearie, and then come back for her, if you're so inclined.

TAXI-DRIVER: O.K. with me. *(Exits.)*

CLEM: Rough trade, Davy.* Well, so long, kid. I hope he's a gorgeous doctor and does you good. *(Exits rear.)*

DOCTOR *(Enters from rear)*: It is not my office hour, but I am at your service.

DAVID: You are very kind, doctor.

DOCTOR: My friend, what can I do for you—you look ill.

DAVID: I am ill—in body and soul.

---

*Slang for heterosexual men who sometimes engage in gay sex.

DOCTOR: I am versed in bodily ills, my friend, but the soul is a little out of my line, I'm afraid.

DAVID: If you can't help me, no one can. *(Covers face with hands.)* It is so hard to tell you.

DOCTOR: Are you a drug addict?

DAVID *(Rises, paces floor, stops at table):* If it were only that—if that were all—I'm one of those damned creatures who are called degenerates and moral lepers for a thing they cannot help—a thing that has made me suffer—Oh, God!—Doctor, I can't explain.

DOCTOR: Tell me everything—This perversion of yours—is it an acquired habit or has it always been so?

DAVID: Always, from the earliest childhood. I was born a male, but my mind has been that of a female, Why, as a child I played with dolls—I even cried when they cut off my curls. As I grew older the natural desires of a youth were unknown to me. I could not understand why women never interested me. I was attracted by my own sex. How was I to know it was wrong, when it seemed perfectly natural to me.

DOCTOR: Go on!

DAVID: I soon realized that I was not like other men. I sought those of my own kind as companions. I realized that we were outcasts. I suffered. I rebelled. I fought with myself—but it was stronger than I. Then I gave in. Why not? I was what I was. There were others like me. Oh, we all fight in the beginning, but it was no use.

DOCTOR: What seems right to the normal man in the matter of sex, seems wrong to you?

DAVID: As wrong as our desires seem to those others. *(Pauses.)* In time I met another like me. *(Rises, paces floor.)* How can I tell you? *(Pause.)* We were attracted to each other. We loved each other. I worshipped him. We lived together. We were happy. The curse didn't seem to matter so much. We lived our own life . . . lived it in our own way. No normally married couple were happier than we were. Then—he married. *(Sits on divan.)*

DOCTOR: Married?

DAVID: He didn't want to, but his family demanded it of him. He owed it to them. To his name. Don't you understand?

DOCTOR: Yes.

DAVID: We drifted apart. It almost drove me mad. And then—somehow his wife didn't hurt me as much as—

DOCTOR: As what?

DAVID: He has found another—a man—a normal man. He loves him. It's maddening.

DOCTOR: But, come, pull yourself together. There must be some way out of this.

DAVID: I've tried to find it. I've tried doctor. I can't! I've thought of death—I haven't the courage to kill myself—I wish I had . . . I love him . . .

DOCTOR *(Glances at the book):* We can only reach this subject through the mind.

DAVID: I came to you because we all know you are trying to find a way. Doctor, there is not one of us that would not be like other men. Comes a time when our burden is too heavy and—there is only one way.

DOCTOR: Don't talk like that. One man is born white, another black—neither man is born a criminal. A difference in a man's mind, and you are the greatest sufferers. We'll get you into physical shape—get this worry out of your mind.

DAVID: I've tried and tried—

DOCTOR: Ever try athletics?

DAVID: I loathe them.

DOCTOR: How about sports—baseball, football, racing—

DAVID: They don't interest me.

DOCTOR: Come, I'll give you something to quiet your nerves and then we'll see what we can do.

DAVID: If I only could forget—can't you understand, doctor—Oh, I think of him and that other. *(In anguish, covers face and sobs.)* I'm going mad!

DOCTOR *(Looks at DAVID):* You're all in pieces. Come, pull yourself together. *(Tries to brace him up. DAVID rises and nearly collapses.)* Get a grip on yourself. *(DAVID staggers—grasps chair for support.)* Come, come— *(Leads DAVID toward office rear.)* Don't go to pieces on me— I'll give you something to steady your nerves. *(Helps DAVID out rear.)*

(Re-enter BARBARA with JUDGE KINGSBURY.)

BARBARA: He must be in his private office, Judge. Patients come here any hour of the day or night, makes no difference to my brother. He's at their beck and call.

JUDGE: That's why he's a great man.

BARBARA *(Crosses to divan and sits):* Even great men have to eat and sleep once in a while.

JUDGE: As bad as that?

BARBARA: Worse—Tell me—how about it?

JUDGE: Clair?

BARBARA: Yes, none of the rumors have reached her father. No use troubling him. Any truth in them? You'd find out if any one could.

JUDGE: You asked me to, and I did. I'm as fond of Clair as if she were my own child, and as for Rolly, my son, no one could be dearer.

BARBARA: What have you heard?

JUDGE: Nothing to it. Just idle gossip. This young man, Grayson, is a very promising civil engineer employed by a concern that is putting up some additional buildings to the Kingsbury iron works. Business takes him to Rolly's home quite frequently, and young Grayson has taken Clair to the theatre on several occasions when Rolly's been engaged elsewhere.

BARBARA: I had an idea that Rolly left business matters in the hands of his managers. Never knew him to take such an active interest in his business before.

JUDGE: But he does. He's as interested in the great Kingsbury iron works as any of his fathers before him. And it's taken a great burden off my shoulders.

BARBARA: I'm glad of that. Glad too, that this young Grayson and Clair aren't—well—that everything's all right. I've heard stories, nasty ones, Judge Kingsbury, very nasty ones.

JUDGE: Gosh! Why Rolly's very fond of Grayson. If any one's interested in Grayson, I'd say it's Rolly and not Clair.

BARBARA: I suppose it's all right, but, I don't like it. *(Glances right, rises.)* I guess you'll have to wait—seems to be engaged with his patient. *(Rises, crosses around desk to left.)*

JUDGE: I'll wait.

BARBARA: Waiting's the most we can do sometimes.

JUDGE: Now, Barbara, just what is the trouble? Something is wrong? Is it this gossip about Clair?

BARBARA: Not alone. Seen Clair lately?

JUDGE: Not within the past few days.

BARBARA: For a bride of less than a year, she's looking mighty unhappy.

JUDGE: You imagine that.

BARBARA: Judge, I raised that girl. Her mother died when she was five—there's very little that goes on in Clair's heart or mind that I don't understand.

JUDGE: Now, what should be wrong?

BARBARA: If I knew that, I wouldn't have to worry wondering what it is. *(Re-enter DOCTOR.)*

DOCTOR: Hello, Judge, How's the old man?

JUDGE: Come begging as usual.

DOCTOR: What it this time?

BARBARA: Look out, brother, he'll want you to cut someone up, or find out which way a bullet got into someone's brain or how it got out or—I'll get out before you get into it. *(Exits. JUDGE looks after her.)*

JUDGE: She should have married twenty-five years ago.

DOCTOR: It's taken you a pretty long time to find that out.

JUDGE *(Bristling):* Do you mean that I—

DOCTOR: All a judge thinks of is his law. Everything he does is measured by the law, and when he gets through measuring there is nothing left to measure.

JUDGE: That's silly.

DOCTOR: It's a fact.

JUDGE: It's nonsense! What do you know about law?

DOCTOR: And what do you know about fact? You base everything on theories—hypothesis. When it comes to facts, you're groping.

JUDGE: And what is your whole profession, but theory?

DOCTOR: Theory nothing, we work on fact.

JUDGE: You theorize before you find the fact . . .

DOCTOR: I believe we're arguing, Bob.

JUDGE: I believe we are, Jim.

DOCTOR: At least we're agreed on that. Have a cigar—and now, what are you after? *(JUDGE takes cigar.)*

JUDGE: I want you to testify in some insanity proceedings. Fellow as crazy as—

DOCTOR: How do you know he's crazy?

JUDGE: That's what I want you to find out.

DOCTOR: How can I call anyone insane?

JUDGE: If a man's insane—

DOCTOR: How do I know he is? Isn't sanity or what we call insanity the state of a man's mind—his viewpoint? When he differs from the course laid down by the rest of us, we call him crazy or a genius. And then, we say, all geniuses are insane. And perhaps he thinks the rest of us are crazy.

JUDGE: That's nonsense. A thing is or it isn't. Right is right, my friend, wrong is wrong. You won't argue that point, will you?

DOCTOR: Yes, I will. What you think is wrong may be perfectly right to another man—

JUDGE: Jim, you're overworking. You don't know what you're talking about. *(Sits in chair left of table right.)*

DOCTOR: I know what I'm talking about *(Rises, crosses around to center.)* I've got a poor devil in there right now, whom you'd call a criminal perhaps—a degenerate—an outcast, and yet in his own mind, he's committing no wrong—he's doing nothing save what he should do—his very lack of normality is normality to him. I'd call him—a trick of fate—a misfit of nature—

JUDGE: Nature has no misfits. Look at the trees—the flowers—

DOCTOR: —but how do we know they aren't misfits?

JUDGE: Jim, you're—

DOCTOR: Crazy?—No. Take that poor devil in there—you'd say send him to an asylum—an institution of some sort—even to jail—and yet the man has done no wrong. He's only what he was born to be—a sexual invert.

JUDGE: One of those things!

DOCTOR: Things! Perhaps the word suits them better than any other—neither male nor female, but something of both—Physically a male with feminine instincts.

JUDGE: People like that should be herded together on some desert isle—

DOCTOR: Why?

JUDGE: For the good of the rest of humanity.

DOCTOR: You'd need a large island, Judge. And again, why? What have they done? Their crime isn't one of commission or omission. It is a misfortune for which they are not to blame.

JUDGE: A man is what he makes himself—

DOCTOR: And before that, a man is what he is born to be. Nature seems to have made no distinction in bestowing this misfortune upon the human race. We find this abnormality among persons of every state of society. It has held sway on the thrones of kings, princes, statesmen, scholars, fools! Wealth, culture, refinement, makes no difference. From the nadir to the zenith of man's career on earth, this nameless vice has traversed all the way. It is as strong today as it was centuries ago.

JUDGE: That's unfortunately true—despite all we can do by law to suppress and stamp it out of modern society.

DOCTOR: Yes, despite all you can do by law. You law-makers. You think that four stone walls and a barred window will cure everything or anything. But still you endeavor by law to force a man born with inverted sexual desires, born to make his way in the world with millions of human beings radically different than he is, to become something which his soul will not permit him to become. I'm not discussing those who are deliberately depraved or who have acquired the habit of this nameless vice through bad associations and environment. I am talking about the born homosexual, and that type is not deliberately vicious.

JUDGE: My dear doctor, you are perhaps a little unfair to the law. Consider what would happen if this nameless vice were permitted to go rampant in society. How long do you think it would be before its degrading, pernicious effect would be felt throughout the very foundations of society? The law has forced this vice into a corner, just as it has forced prostitution into shady byways.

DOCTOR: Granted the law has done just that, but what specific good has it done? Has the law made secret prostitution unprofitable? However, the question involved does not concern financial gain. It concerns society socially and it is this: Are we, the majority of people, normal human beings, are we going to declare as outcast and criminal these unfortunates who through no fault of their own have been born with instincts and desires different from ours? Are we who have as our guiding principles in life the virtues of faith, hope, charity and love, going to deny to these miscasts the right to faith in what life has to offer, hope in eternal goodness? The charity of our hearts is the only love which they can ever know. Or are we going to force them into secrecy and shame, for being what they cannot help being, by branding them as criminals and so lead them into the depths of misery and suicide?

JUDGE *(Rises, takes step to center):* I'm afraid doctor, you're becoming a trifle hysterical over the matter. After all, what have you done? You medical men, you scientists, you social philosophers? Not one damn solitary thing, so far as I have been able to learn. You sit back just as you are doing now and gabble about faith, hope and chari-ty—you commiserate with these abnormal creatures, out of the charity of your hearts, no doubt, but you don't lift a finger to relieve the situation. I happen to know that there are approximately five million homosexuals in the United States and of these the greater percentage are born sexual inverts. How many there are in this country that are not accounted for, God only knows. Quite an appalling figure, this, for the United States, and in Europe there are a damn sight more. And yet, you brilliant physicians, you learned doctors who are curing cancer, tuberculosis and other diseases have not bothered to thoroughly investigate what is as vitally menacing to society as any of the more pernicious diseases. Have you five mil-lion cancer cases in this country, or in the world, for that matter? Yet you sit back in your offices and rant and rail against what the law is doing to handle the situation, but can you offer any solution?

DOCTOR: There is a cure for this thing. *(Enter CLAIR.)*

DOCTOR: Why Clair! This is a pleasant surprise. Didn't know you were in the city.

CLAIR: Came in to do some shopping. Rolly is calling for me. Hello, Daddy Kingsbury! *(Crosses to JUDGE.)*

JUDGE *(Kissing her):* Where's Rolly?

CLAIR: He'll be here, shortly.

JUDGE: I'm sorry I can't wait for him. I'll see him tomorrow. You look a little tired.

DOCTOR: You do look a little worn, Clair. Been overdoing it? Too many dances, too many parties? Oh, you young folks never know when to let up.

CLAIR: You're wrong, Daddy. I'm not ill.

DOCTOR: Shopping's peeved you, my dear.

CLAIR: I'm sorry if I seem unpleasant.

JUDGE: That simply could not be, my dear.

CLAIR: If one could thrive on compliments, there'd be no invalids among your acquaintances.

JUDGE: Indeed—indeed.

CLAIR: I'm afraid I missed the mark—But I plead pardon. I am tired. Shopping is a weary job.

JUDGE: Well, I must be running along.

CLAIR: Please don't let me drive you away. I know how dearly you and Dad love an argument.

JUDGE: We've had it.

CLAIR: Oh, and you've no further taste for each other's society.

JUDGE: One can't get too much of a good thing. Jim, how about my insane man?

DOCTOR: You can depend upon me to do my bit. It's all in the law you know.

JUDGE: My compliments to Miss Barbara.

CLAIR: Good-bye, Daddy Kingsbury.

DOCTOR: You don't look well, child. What is it?

CLAIR (Choking): Daddy!

DOCTOR: Why, why—honey—What's the matter?

CLAIR: I can't stand it—I want to go away—to Europe—anywhere—Daddy. I can't go on.

DOCTOR: Why child—Clair, what's wrong? Have you and Rolly quarreled?

CLAIR: No, no, no, no!

DOCTOR: What's wrong? Has Rolly done anything—?

CLAIR: Oh, he's a model husband! I couldn't find fault with him! I just can't go on—I'll go mad if I stay with him—Daddy—I can't make you understand—I'm unhappy. I'm miserable. (Sobbing. DOCTOR tries to comfort her.)

DOCTOR (Crosses to bell): Honey, honey. (Rings bell.) Trust me. What's wrong? What has Rolly done?

CLAIR: Nothing—I just—I—

DOCTOR: Don't you love him any more?

CLAIR: I feel the same toward him. *(Enter JESSIE.)* Jessie, ask Miss Barbara to come here—Tell her Miss Clair is here.

JESSIE: Yes, sir. *(Exits.)*

DOCTOR: Clair, are you sure it's not—may not be—your condition. Goodness child, you can trust your father.

CLAIR: There's nothing the matter with me. It's just that—that—it's something I can't understand myself, something that seems tearing at my heart—keeps me restless, hungry for something—Always wanting something—I don't know what it is—I'm so discontented—so unhappy.

DOCTOR: You've fussed with Rolly. Come, confess.

CLAIR: I tell you no!

DOCTOR: Then what have you to be unhappy about? If Rolly hasn't been at fault? You loved him, didn't you? You love him still?

CLAIR: I suppose so.

DOCTOR: You suppose so! Good land, you suppose so!

CLAIR: I can't explain. I don't know myself what is wrong—If I did, I'd understand, that's the trouble—Don't you see—Dad? Something I sense and feel—something that makes me dissatisfied—not wanting to live, as it were, and I can't name it.

DOCTOR: Good land! What talk! That's this Twentieth Century idea. I'll tell you what's the matter with you. You have nothing to do— Everything is done for you. Servants to fetch and carry—house-keepers to take care of your home—to plan your every meal. Nothing to do but gad around and look for trouble. I'll tell Rolly to discharge some of that staff of servants of his and let you look after your own establishment—

CLAIR: It's not that.

DOCTOR: Then, has some other man been making love to you?

CLAIR: No, of course not!

DOCTOR *(Sits in chair back of desk center):* Whatever it is, the fault is not your husband's. *(CLAIR is over right as BARBARA enters.)*

BARBARA: Hello, Clair—Why, James, not quarreling with your daughter?

DOCTOR: My daughter has taken leave of her senses. I want you to talk to her. Wants to go to Europe—leave her husband or something and she doesn't know why. *(BARBARA looks from CLAIR to DOCTOR.)*

BARBARA: She probably has her reasons.

DOCTOR: If you can discover them, you're doing more than I can do. *(Crosses to rear.)* I've got to look after my patient. *(Turning at door.)* And remember, Clair, no nonsense. We've enough scandal in society as it is. I'll not have you bring my name or the Kingsbury name, for that matter, into the mire. *(He slams into his office. BARBARA turns to CLAIR.)*

BARBARA *(Crosses to Clair):* What's it all about? *(CLAIR sighs.)* Tired of Rolly? Is he too perfect?

CLAIR: I don't know what it is, Aunt Barbara. I'm not tired of Rolly, but somehow, I'm disappointed in him.

BARBARA: You knew him long enough before you married him. You were raised together from the cradle.

CLAIR: You never know a man until you're married to him.

BARBARA: And sometimes, not then. What's he done?

CLAIR: Why nothing. That's just it. Somehow I expected Rolly to be different after we were married. *(Sits.)* I don't know what I expected him to be, but somehow—Oh, I don't know! Sometimes I think I annoy him by just being alive—that I'm a nuisance—he never says so and he's always so courteous. Oh, Aunt Barbara, it's all wrong. Something is crying out in me—I can't understand it. Just as if something were trying to tell me something—and I can't understand. I try and try and try, but it's always the same. Just as if I wanted something—and didn't know what it was.

BARBARA: So that's it. Clair, what do you know about love?

CLAIR: What a question! I suppose I love Rolly, I always did. I never was interested in any other man—when no man ever so much as kissed me, save Rolly.

BARBARA: Sure you're not in love with this—Allen Grayson?

CLAIR *(Flaring up):* Now what do you mean? Mr. Grayson—

BARBARA: Rumor.

CLAIR: Why, Mr. Grayson has never so much as—what nonsense! He's a perfect gentleman. A charming man. Why, Aunt Barbara, he's too fine to make love to another man's wife.

BARBARA: I see. Your husband admires him?

CLAIR: One can't help admiring Allen Grayson. He's a man among a thousand. You'd single him out anywhere. A man bound to do things—a man worthy of trust and confidence.

BARBARA: I see. And you want to go to Europe?

CLAIR: I thought if I could go for a little while, I might feel different.

BARBARA: Toward Rolly?

CLAIR *(Looks at her quickly)*: Why, yes—toward everything.

BARBARA: I see. *(Enter DOCTOR from rear. BARBARA looks at him.)*

DOCTOR: Have you two come to a decision?

BARBARA: Yes. Clair and I have been planning a little trip.

DOCTOR: What—what—are you both crazy? Clair is not going to leave her husband—

BARBARA: The best thing for Clair and her husband is a separation for a while. Ever know that two people can get too much of each other? That's your trouble, Jim, you've had too much of me. That's why I'm going to Europe with Clair.

DOCTOR: I'll talk to Rolly about this—

CLAIR: I don't think he'll mind—But Dad, I'd rather you'd let me tell him.

DOCTOR *(Turns upon her)*: Oh! *(JESSIE enters and announces.)*

JESSIE: Mr. Kingsbury. *(Enter ROLLY. JESSIE exits. CLAIR turns to ROLLY unconsciously, expectant, sensing something amiss.)*

DOCTOR: Hello, Rolly.

ROLLY: Hello—How's everybody? Just finished up at the office. Rather difficult day's work.

DOCTOR: I understand you're building additions.

ROLLY: Yes, we need more room. I don't see why they can't do things without consulting me.

BARBARA: It's your business, Rolly.

ROLLY: Who took care of it while I was under age? Why can't they do it now?

DOCTOR: My dear boy! A man's business is his God in a way.

ROLLY: Then I'm afraid I'm an atheist in that line.

CLAIR: Rolly hates business.

DOCTOR: I suppose you'd rather play polo or hockey and take a chance with your neck, eh?

ROLLY: Oh, land no. I've never sat on a polo pony in my life. I'm afraid of the darn things.

DOCTOR: Yes, I know, your mother coddled you till you thought the wind should stop when you told it to. That's your one fault, Rolly, you've been coddled too much. Get out in the open, take a few bruises, get smashed up, better for you in the end.

ROLLY: Being mother's only child, she always used to tell me it was the dread of her life that I'd turn out to be a roughneck.

BARBARA: Not much chance. *(She speaks with a scarcely perceptible sneer.)* By the way Rolly, I've decided to take a little vacation in Europe, and I want to take Clair with me for company. Think you can spare her a little while?

ROLLY: Why—*(Glancing at CLAIR):* If Clair wants to go. I wouldn't think of keeping her home.

BARBARA: That's settled. Come on, Clair, we'll discuss ways and means—I mean to start before the week's out.

ROLLY: Isn't that rather soon?

BARBARA: Not when you're in a hurry. Come Clair—Rolly you'll wait for her?

ROLLY: Certainly. *(CLAIR and BARBARA exit. DOCTOR turns to ROLLY and explodes.)*

DOCTOR: What the devil's wrong between you and Clair?

ROLLY *(Surprised):* Nothing. Not a thing.

DOCTOR: What are you both hiding from me? Clair's miserable.

ROLLY: Has she said so?

DOCTOR: She doesn't have to. Don't you think a man can see when his own daughter's heart is breaking?

ROLLY: I'm surprised—I thought Clair was very happy. We get along splendidly. An ideal couple, really.

DOCTOR: Then why does she want to run away to Europe?

ROLLY: Aunt Barbara—

DOCTOR: Aunt Barbara detests nothing in the world more than travelling—especially on water. She gets seasick when she takes the boat to Coney Island. It's Clair who wants to go.

ROLLY: That's puzzling. She hasn't said anything to me.

DOCTOR: Really, I've known you since you were a baby. I can't have been mistaken in you. When I gave you my daughter, I thought it would be for the happiness of both of you. You loved each other, at least you thought you did—Well?

ROLLY: There's no woman in my life. Clair's the only girl I ever really knew.

DOCTOR: I don't like the idea of this European trip, but there must be a damn good reason for it. Are you sure there isn't another woman?

ROLLY: Why I wouldn't think of looking at another woman.

DOCTOR (Rises): You tell it well. Watch out. (Crossing to door.) Wait for Clair. I don't like this European trip, I'm going to talk these women out of it.

(ROLLY crosses to table and picks up Ulrich book. Much disturbed, puts it down again. Looks off after DOCTOR. DAVID opens door rear. His coat and vest are off. He half staggers into room.)

DAVID: Doctor—Doctor—It's no use I can't—Rolly!

ROLLY: You—What are you doing here?

DAVID: Rolly—

ROLLY: Why are you here?

DAVID: I couldn't stand it any longer—I came here to see the doctor—I thought—

ROLLY: You came to tell him—

DAVID: It's not so. I didn't tell him I so much as knew you. I came because I thought he could help me.

ROLLY: You fool, he can do nothing for you—For any of us. *(Takes out wallet.)* Here take this—and get out of here.

DAVID: I don't want your money—Rolly please—

ROLLY: Get out of here. I've had enough of you.

DAVID: I've heard all about you and Grayson. He doesn't give a damn for you.

ROLLY: Shut your mouth about Grayson—leave his name out of this.

DAVID: It's true and you know it. He doesn't give a damn for you.

ROLLY: Damn you—you—You—*(Grabs DAVID by the throat and swings him onto divan.) (DOCTOR enters.)*

DOCTOR: Rolly!

ROLLY: Who is this—this mad man—He tried to attack me.

DOCTOR: My poor lad—What's got into you? It may be the drug I've given him—I don't know—poor devil—Thank God, Rolly, you're not what he is—Come, come, my boy—Come—

DOCTOR *(Leads DAVID toward rear exit. DAVID turns and looks at ROLLY.)*

ROLLY: Not what he is—*(Looks after DOCTOR and DAVID and then sinks in chair.)* Good God!

CURTAIN

ACT TWO

(The same room, later that afternoon. PARSONS onstage at rise. Telephone rings. PARSONS answers it.)

PARSONS: Mr. Kingsbury is not at home, sir. *(Writes message on pad.)* Very, well sir, I shall give him the message. *(Enter ROLLY.)*

PARSONS: A Mr. Clem on the phone, Sir. Are you in, Sir?

ROLLY: Yes, Parsons, I'll speak. *(Takes phone.)* Hello there! Where are you . . . Oh, you did. . . . Well yes, I was out . . . just got in. Who is with you? Where are you molls calling from? No, the wife is out. All right, hurry! Oh, it ought to take about ten minutes from where you are now. *(Hangs up—then to PARSONS.)* What time did Mrs. Kingsbury leave today?

PARSONS: Quite early, sir. Madam went out riding with Miss Barbara.

ROLLY: Riding?

PARSONS: Yes, riding . . . Mrs. Kingsbury wasn't feeling very well. She seems rather worried.

ROLLY: Worried, why she has nothing to worry about. Her time's her own. Silly! I'll be in my room. If anyone calls, let me know. *(Exits.)*

PARSONS: Very well, sir. *(Bell rings furiously—PARSONS rushes to door.)* Good gracious! *(Opens door.)*

BILLY *(Rushing in, out of breath):* Where's Black Boy?

PARSONS: Here, here, young man! What do you mean by ringing the bell that way.

BILLY: You ain't heard nothin' yet. Wait until I put a pin in it.

PARSONS: A pin?

ROLLY: Who was that, Parsons?

PARSONS: Master Billy Mack, the boy across the street sir. He wants his dog sir.

ROLLY: All right, he can take him. *(BILLY rushes out for dog. PARSONS stops him.)*

PARSONS: Come here, I'll get him for you.

BILLY: I know where he is.

PARSONS: You can't be running him through the house like you did the last time.

BILLY: Oh, don't be an old crab. *(PARSONS looks at him in surprise. BILLY smiles a little guiltily.)* I won't run him through the house, Parsons.

PARSONS: All right, come on, take him out the rear of the house. *(Door bell rings. BILLY exits, running through library door. PARSONS answers door. Enter CLEM, ROSCO and DUCHESS.)*

PARSONS: Right this way, gentlemen, be seated, I'll tell Mr. Kingsbury you are here, sirs. *(Exits.)*

CLEM: Riding around all day in that goddamn car—I'm so stiff. I'll have to try a couple of splits and back bends to straighten myself out. *(ROSCO and the DUCHESS have seated themselves in rather artistic poses. The DUCHESS takes out powder puff.)*

ROSCO: Say, Clem, did the Duchess ever meet Roland?

CLEM: No, but if she takes out that goddamn powder puff again—she won't be here to meet him.

DUCHESS: Oh, shut up.

CLEM: You've had that thing out forty times in the last twenty minutes. You took it out in front of that cop, too. What the hell do you think—that I want to be locked up with you?

DUCHESS: Oh, wasn't he grand!

CLEM: You wouldn't think he was so grand if he sat your fanny in jail.

DUCHESS: Say—the cops, they like me. They all know me from Central Park.

WINNIE: Ha! ha!

ROLLY: What about you, Duchess?

DUCHESS: Oh, my goodness. I've got the most gorgeous new drag. Black satin, very tight, with a long train of rhinestones.

CLEM: Wait until you see the creation I'm wearing, dearie. Virginal white, no back, with oceans of this and oceans of that, trimmed with excitement in front. You know I'm more of the flapper type, not so much like a canal boat.

DUCHESS: Creation—ha! That old thing. I knew that three years ago. Oh, Annie.

CLEM (*Very angry*): For Chris' sake sit. This big bitch thinks nobody has anything or looks like anything but her.

DUCHESS: Oh, shut up.

ROLLY: Say, how about a little drink? (*Rings bell.*)

CLEM: Yes! How about a little drink?

DUCHESS: I don't mind a little drink once in a while.

CLEM: Why you big Swede. You'd take it through a funnel if anybody would give it to you.

WINNIE: Funnel? That's nothing. I'd take it through a hose. Whoops. (*Enter PARSONS.*)

ROLLY: What will it be, Scotch or Rye?

ROSCO: Rye. (*WINNIE ad libs. CLEM chooses Scotch to be different*).

PARSONS: Yes, sir.

ROLLY (*Entering*): Scotch and Rye.

PARSONS: Yes, sir.

DUCHESS: Say, I was at a party the other night—when was that—last week, one day.

ROSCO: Oh. I heard about that, over at Peter Pan's.

CLEM (*Tells all about party*): It was a great party but the place was raided and when they backed up the wagon, they got all but one and she jumped out the window. That must have been you.

PARSONS (*Enters and serves drinks.*)

DUCHESS (*Goes to piano*): Do you mind?

ROLLY: Go right ahead.

DUCHESS: What will I play?

ROSCO: Play "Humoresque."

DUCHESS: I don't like that.

CLEM: Play "The Woman Who Stole My Gal."

DUCHESS: I don't know that.

CLEM *(Repeats the line 'Don't know that. I don't like that')*: That's what I can't understand. Somebody sits down at the piano. They'll ask you what to play. You tell them, then they play something entirely different. What did you want to ask for?

DUCHESS: Oh, shut up! That one's always giving advice or trying to tell you what to do. Give your mouth a holiday. *(Then he starts to play. WINNIE "whoops." CLEM and ROSCO add comedy to the tune the DUCHESS plays.)*

WINNIE: Beautiful voice! Wonderful voice! Gorgeous voice!

ROLLY: Wonderful! Beautiful touch!

CLEM: You should feel my beautiful touch, dearie. *(Laughs.)*

BILLY *(Rushes in with dog. All pet the dog.)*

PARSONS *(Enters):* Is that your taxi outside by the water plug? If he don't move, the cop will give him a ticket.

ALL: All right, Billy, I'll take care of him.

CLEM *(Rises):* Oh heavens, he ought to know enough to keep away from a fire plug. I'll have to get him a book of regulations.

DUCHESS: Maybe he's in love and can't think.

CLEM: Then you must have been in love all your life.

WINNIE: Whoops.

ROLLY: What, did you come in a taxi?

CLEM: Oh, Rolly, I forgot to tell you about that handsome brute of a taxi driver. Don't get suggestive. We rode in a taxi. *(DUCHESS, ROLLY and ROSCO laugh. CLEM repeats)*: I forgot to tell you, dearie, about this handsome brute of a taxi-driver. Let me tell you. Yesterday, you know Dave, that sentimental moll, the one who used to be crazy about you. Well, she calls me up and asked me to come right over, she's hysterical. Well, I goes over and there was the poor

---

*An insider's joke for audiences who remembered Helen Menken's starring role in *The Captive,* a play about love between lesbians.

queen ready to jump out of the window. Of course, I knew what was the matter. She needed a jab. She's been taking heroin and morphine by the barrels. The trouble with her is she's sensitive of what she is. Now, I don't give a goddamn who knows it. Of course, I don't go flouncing my hips up and down Broadway picking up trade or with a sign on my back advertising it. *(Laughs.)* But of course. I don't pass anything up either, dearie. I'm out to have a good time as well as the next.

WINNIE: You'd be a fool if you did.

ROSCO: What about Dave, what happened to her?

CLEM: Well, I took her to the doctor's. Some doctor on Park Avenue she wanted to go to. I took a taxi and took her over and left her there. I must call her up today and see how she is. So that's how I met the taxi driver and he's been riding me ever since. *(ROLLY has a peculiar expression on his face during CLEM's story.)*

CLEM: Dish the dirt, because you won't be able to dump that bird so easy. *(Bell rings. PARSONS crosses stage.)*

ROLLY *(Looks at wristwatch)*: If it's Mr. Grayson, have him come in. *(To the others.)* Now, be a little careful, no wise cracks.

CLEM: Well dearie, perhaps we'd better be going and leave you alone. I understand how it is. Come on, molls, I suppose my boyfriend's getting nervous waiting out there anyway. *(They take their hats and coats.)*

ROLLY: No hurry. That's that young engineer who is putting up the new structure for the Kingsbury iron works.

CLEM: Now, I must meet him.

PARSONS: Mr. Grayson.

ROLLY: All right. Show him in, Parsons.

DUCHESS *(Takes out powder puff)*: I just love engineers. *(CLEM takes powder puff and throws it in a vase.)*

GRAYSON *(Enters.)*

ROLLY: How do you do?

GRAYSON: How do you do? I beg your pardon, I didn't know you had company.

ROLLY: I want you to meet Mr. Hathaway, Mr. Winnie Lewis, Mr. Gillingwater and Mr. Swanson. *(They acknowledge introduction, shaking hands.)* The boys just dropped in on their way to town.

GRAYSON: I hope I'm not rushing you gentlemen away.

ROSCO: Not at all, we were just about leaving.

WINNIE: Sorry we can't stay longer. We heard so much about you.

DUCHESS: Yes, it's too bad.

ROLLY: I've just been telling the boys about the plans for the iron works, which we were to go over.

CLEM: Yes, I'd love to stay and see your wonderful construction. But we have other plans.

ROLLY *(A bit uneasy):* Sorry you have to go, boys.

CLEM: Don't give us the rush act, dearie. *(All shake hands and say goodbye.)*

WINNIE: So glad to have you meet me. Come up some time and I'll bake you a pan of biscuits.

DUCHESS: Goodbye.

CLEM: Makes you think of President Coolidge, shaking so many hands. *(As they exit. DUCHESS looks around.)*

ROLLY *(To DUCHESS):* Did you lose something?

CLEM: She lost it years ago.

DUCHESS: Oh, shut up. I'm looking for my gloves. *(Finds powder puff in vase and puts it in pocket.)*

ROLLY: Did you find them?

DUCHESS: Yes, I got it. *(Exits and looks at GRAYSON.)*

GRAYSON *(Takes the blueprints from his pocket):* I've completed that corner.

ROLLY: Cigarette, Allen?

GRAYSON *(Takes cigarette—doesn't pay any attention—keeps looking at blue print.)*

ROLLY *(Watching GRAYSON intently.)* Light? *(Lights his own and GRAYSON's cigarettes.)*

GRAYSON *(Feels uncomfortable. Sits left of table, but interests self in blueprint.)*

ROLLY *(Crosses to divan and sits):* Well, what did you think of my friends?

GRAYSON: I didn't see very much of them. I felt I was rushing them out.

ROLLY: Great boys, great boys, I am going on a weekend party and I'd love to have you join us. You'll find the boys rather interesting, I think.

GRAYSON: You think so?

ROLLY: You've never met that particular type before?

GRAYSON: I can't say that I have.

ROLLY: Perhaps you have and you didn't know it.

GRAYSON *(Looks up.)*

ROLLY: Why do you suppose I've had you come here so often? Haven't you noticed the friendship I've had for you since the day you stepped into the office? All I could do was eat, drink, sleep, think of Allen Grayson.

GRAYSON: Why, Rolly, I'd hate to have you think of me in just that way. *(Rises.)* I've always looked at you as a he-man. God, this is— *(Crosses over to left of center, faces left.)*

ROLLY: I *(Rises. Crosses toward him and over to table. Hums song.)* I thought you had some idea of how I felt toward you—my great interest in you.

GRAYSON: Yes, I did think it extraordinary. *(Crosses center, turns and looks at him.)* But what about your wife?

ROLLY: You mean why I married?

GRAYSON: Yes.

ROLLY: That is very easy to explain. Clair's dad and mine were very good friends, it was their one ambition that we should marry. It was practically arranged ever since we were children together and Clair is the same today as the day I married her, if you know what I mean.

GRAYSON: Why, I think that's the most contemptible thing you could do—marry a woman and use her as a cloak to cover up what you are.

ROLLY: I don't see why you should feel this way about it. She's perfectly contented.

GRAYSON: You don't mean to tell me she knows what you are.

ROLLY: No. Clair is just the type of woman that wouldn't understand if she did know.

GRAYSON: How could you play on a woman's innocence like that?

ROLLY: Just why should you take such an interest in my wife? *(Takes step to center.)*

GRAYSON: I just can't stand to see a sweet innocent girl like Clair treated that way.

ROLLY: Oh, I see. *(Takes step toward him.)* I think I understand where your interest lies. After I've given you the hospitality of my home, trusted you with my wife.

GRAYSON: Yes, I am interested in your wife. As for your hospitality, your plans and the great Kingsbury works, they can go to hell. I think you're a rotter. God! *(He throws the plans on the table—starts to go.)*

ROLLY *(Tries to stop him):* Just a minute, Allen.

GRAYSON: Please . . .

ROLLY: Now you can't go like this. You're taking the wrong attitude. Now, let's forget all about it.

GRAYSON: Forget about it. *(CLAIR enters left.)*

CLAIR: Oh, Rolly—Hello Allen. *(Crosses to ROLLY. He kisses her.)*

GRAYSON: Hello, Clair. *(Enter MARION and BARBARA.)*

MARION: How do you do Mr. Grayson?

BARBARA: How do you do, Mr. Grayson?

ROLLY: Hello Marion—Aunt Barbara. Marion, you're quite a stranger, where have you been hiding?

MARION: Not hiding, Rolly, just busy. My husband likes to have me around.

CLAIR: It was just by chance we met. Aunt Barbara and I met her downtown and took her riding with us.

BARBARA: I suppose you're very busy. *(Crosses to GRAYSON.)*

GRAYSON: Yes, rather.

MARION: How are the new buildings coming along?

GRAYSON: Progressing very rapidly.

ROLLY: Wonderful work. Come here Marion. Just look at this, here are the plans.

MARION *(Crosses to table):* What's this?

ROLLY: What's this, Allen?

GRAYSON: That's the outside.

ROLLY: Yes, this is the outside of the housing of the new blast furnace and these are the ground plans of the steel rolling floors.

MARION: It looks like a cross word puzzle to me.

ROLLY: Yes, it would. I think I shall start to dress.

BARBARA: Are you going to take Clair to the opera, Rolly?

ROLLY: Why, no, Mr. Grayson is going to accompany her.

BARBARA: Oh—I see, where are you going tonight, if I'm not too inquisitive.

ROLLY: I have an important engagement in town which I have to keep.

BARBARA: We'll wait and ride together.

ROLLY: Very well. *(Exits upstairs.)*

BARBARA: Clair, doesn't Rolly care for the opera? *(Sits on chair left of center.)*

CLAIR: He's a great lover of music but his time is so occupied with business, he's scarcely has time to go anywhere. If it weren't for Mr. Grayson, I should see nothing but the four walls.

BARBARA *(Meaningfully)*: Hm, hm. *(GRAYSON smiles.)*

MARION: My dear, you're quite fortunate to have an escort so charming.

BARBARA: And a husband so generous.

MARION: What could be sweeter?

CLAIR: Marion will have her little joke, but tell me, are all husbands so very busy?

MARION: My dear, I don't know about all husbands. I only have one and one is enough. He just runs me ragged.

BARBARA *(Crosses over back of table to right rear corner)*: Come, Mr. Grayson, I think we'd better go inside. There is something I want to ask you.

CLAIR: Aunt Barbara is always asking questions.

BARBARA *(At door rear)*: Yes, my dear, I have a curiosity complex. *(Exits. GRAYSON starts to exit.)*

CLAIR *(Looking at wrist watch—to GRAYSON)*: You talk with Aunt Barbara and I shall dress. *(GRAYSON exits left.)*

MARION: What are you going to wear?

CLAIR: I have that pretty black chiffon and I have a new white gown you haven't seen.

MARION: Wear the white one. It reminds me of purity, so becoming to one when one's not out with one's husband.

CLAIR: Marion, you're so clever, but just what do you mean by that?

MARION: Nothing, dear.

CLAIR: Oh, yes you do. I wish I could make people understand how miserable and unhappy I am.

MARION *(Crosses over to her)*: Clair, dear, I'm so sorry. I didn't mean to be rude but you can't expect to be seen in a man's company constantly without causing comment. Why, dear, it's common gossip.

CLAIR: Common gossip?

MARION: Why, don't take it so seriously, of course. I always thought Rolly would be cold and indifferent. I can always tell that by looking at a man. *(Crosses to chair left of table and sits.)*

CLAIR: That's why you've been so successful in your marriage. You've had more experience than I.

MARION: Clair, it's time you should learn.

CLAIR: Oh, Marion, if I only dared to take you into my confidences. *(Crosses to sofa.)*

MARION: I may like to talk, but I don't tell everything I know.

CLAIR: I don't think Rolly loves me.

MARION: Not married a year and doesn't love you any more?

CLAIR *(Sits on sofa right.):* I don't believe he ever did.

MARION: Why Clair. Oh, tell me, when he kisses you, does he give you one of those long warm kisses, like he did when you were first married?

CLAIR: He never gave me a long warm kiss.

MARION: He never gave you any?

CLAIR: Just little short ones, most of the time on the cheek. *(Points to face.)*

MARION *(Rises and takes center):* Then he's a new kind of man to me. *(Turns to her.)* Do you suspect some other woman?

CLAIR: I don't know.

MARION *(Crosses to front of chair):* I'll tell you what to do. When you're ready to retire, put on your smartest negligee. Be sure it's sheer, one you can see through.

CLAIR: I haven't any like that.

MARION: You should have. If you haven't, get one, get one. Put it on and drape it tight around you and sit on the end of his bed *(Sits on chair.)* and cross your legs so, and of course, show as much as you can. Be sure you have a cigarette in your hand. It gives one poise. Then tell the boy a couple of bedstead stories.

CLAIR: I don't smoke and I don't know any stories and I never go to his room.

MARION: Well, when he comes to yours.

CLAIR: He never comes to my room. *(Rises.)*

MARION: What kind of a wife are you?

CLAIR: A wife and not a wife.

MARION: Why, Clair—*(ROLLY enters.)*

ROLLY: Are we ready, Marion?

MARION: I am.

CLAIR *(Crosses to center behind MARION's chair)* It's getting rather late, I think I'll go up and dress.

MARION: When shall I see you, Clair?

CLAIR: I'm spending the weekend at father's. I shall see you in town tomorrow afternoon. Good bye dear. *(MARION crosses to her and kisses her. To ROLLY.)* Tell Aunt Barbara to see me before she goes. *(Kisses ROLLY as she exits upstairs—MARION crosses to rear.)*

ROLLY *(To CLAIR as she goes upstairs):* I don't know what time I'll be home dear. I'll meet you at your dad's. *(She exits. He crosses down to table left.)*

MARION: My, what a busy man you must be. *(Rises and crosses around above divan.)*

ROLLY: Yes, it's damned annoying at times. A fellow doesn't get any time for recreation at all.

MARION: Must be terribly hard on Clair.

ROLLY: Yes, the poor dear, I feel sorry for her myself sometimes, but business must be attended to. *(Crosses to rear—calls off to BARBARA.)* We're ready Aunt Barbara.

BARBARA *(Entering):* Here I am.

ROLLY: Clair wants to see you. She's in her room. *(BARBARA exits upstairs.)*

MARION *(Rises and crosses to rear exit.):* I must say goodbye to Mr. Grayson.

ROLLY: I guess he's busy in the library.

MARION: Well, I *must* see him for a moment. *(She exits into library.)*

ROLLY *(Fills cigarette case):* Parsons, get everything in readiness for tomorrow night. Serve a buffet supper in the dining room.

PARSONS: Will you use the ballroom?

ROLLY: No, arrange this room for the dancing.

PARSONS: Very well, sir, is that all, sir?

ROLLY: Yes, that's all.

MARION *(Entering from library)*: A very interesting man, Mr. Grayson. *(Crosses to front of table.)*

ROLLY: Yes. How is Kenneth?

MARION: He's fine. He wants to know why you and Clair don't pay us a visit.

ROLLY: Yes, we'll come down sometime, glad to.

BARBARA *(Entering down stairs)*: Come on I'm ready. *(MARION joins BARBARA. They cross left.)*

ROLLY *(PARSONS enters.)*

PARSONS: Yes sir?

ROLLY: When Mrs. Kingsbury and Mr. Grayson leave, you can lock up. We won't be home tonight. *(BARBARA and MARION exit left.)*

PARSONS: Very good sir. *(Arranges room. ROLLY puts on coat, pauses, looks rear, then upstairs, then exits left.)*

GRAYSON *(Enters, lights cigarette, goes to piano. PARSONS exits. Lights lower.)*

CLAIR: *(Enters from stairs in evening gown and wraps—she pauses and looks at GRAYSON, crosses and places her cloak on chair—crosses back to GRAYSON then left of center.)*

GRAYSON *(Rises and looks at her)*: You look beautiful in that gown.

CLAIR: Thank you. I'm glad you like it. That's the first compliment you ever paid me, Allen.

GRAYSON: I've never dared, but I've thought them. Your aunt told me you were contemplating a trip to Europe.

CLAIR: Yes, we were planning to go.

GRAYSON: I should like to take a trip myself someday when I've nothing else to think about.

CLAIR: Nothing to think about?

GRAYSON: Nothing to think about but you.

CLAIR: Why, Allen, what are you saying?

GRAYSON: What am I saying? Something I've been wanting to say for a long time. The thing that's been tearing my heart. I've struggled long enough to keep from telling you. From the day I met you, you've been my inspiration, you've been my life. The touch of your hand, the softness of your voice, the very sight of you. God I must have you. *(Kisses her.)*.

CLAIR *(Sobs with an hysterical joy as GRAYSON mistakes it for something else and feeling ashamed of his emotion, turns downstage.)*

GRAYSON *(CLAIR stretches her arms out toward him. He turns and sees her and going over to her, embraces her again):* I need you, I want you, I love you, God how I love you. *(He wraps her in his arms and kisses her passionately.)*

CURTAIN

ACT THREE

Drawing room of Rolly Kingsbury's home. As the curtain rises all the guests of the drag are dancing. At the finish of dance, guests all take seats. The DUCHESS in low-cut black evening gown enters from stairs and crosses to left downstage. PARSONS announces as characters come on.)

PARSONS: Mr. Swanson, as the Duchess.

NO. 1: My goodness here comes the Duchess.

NO. 2: The Duchess!

NO. 3: The Grand Duchess!

PARSONS: Mr. Hathaway, as the Doll. *(CLEM appears at head of stairs and crosses down right.)*

NO. 4: My God that's Clem, the Doll.

NO. 5: Clem, the Doll!

NO. 6: The Doll! *(TAXI-DRIVER makes his entrance.)*

NO. 7: She picked herself a grand taxi-driver.

NO. 8: Taxi-driver!

NO. 9: He's a taxi-driver!

NO. 10: Rough trade, dearie!

NO. 12: Rough trade!

PARSONS: Mr. Gillingwater! *(Rosco crosses down right.)*

NO. 13: Hullo, Rosco.

(WINNIE comes down-stage center. Gives her usual scream.)

NO. 14: My God, where have you been?

EVERYBODY: Hello Winnie—How are you? How are you?

(CLEM discovers the DUCHESS trying to make the TAXI-DRIVER.)

CLEM: Listen, Bargain, if you don't want me to clean out this joint, lay off of Civic Virtue before I knock you loose from that flat beezer of yours. I've got what gentlemen prefer.

TAXI-DRIVER: What is this power I have?

CLEM: It's certainly not your face, but that's for me to know and she to find out, after I'm through—If there's anything left.

DUCHESS: You'll never be like me, Winnie.

CLEM: Sit down, you big Swede!

(Music. "Toe Dance." Enter Hell's Kitchen Kate. A scream is heard.)

WINNIE: My Gawd, if it isn't Kate!

KATE: How do you do, how do you do—Your face is very familiar but I don't know where to put it.

WINNIE: —Don't you remember—I'm the girl that jumped out the window when the wagon drove up.

KATE: —Oh yes, of course—But dearie, you should have stayed with us. We had a grand time—The police were perfectly lovely to us— weren't they girls?

ENSEMBLE: Yes!

WINNIE: They were?

KATE: Perfectly lovely, why the minute I walked into jail, the Captain said—Well, Kate what kind of a cell would you like to have? And I says—Oh, any kind will do, Captain, just so it has a couple of peep- holes in it. I crave fresh air.

WINNIE: My, but you're getting thin.

KATE: I am not. I can at least cling to a man without wearing him out. You're terribly fat.

WINNIE: Fat! I should say not. I'm the type that men prefer. I can at least go through the navy yard without having the flags drop to half mast.

KATE: Listen, dearies—pull in your aerial, you're full of static. I'm just the type that men crave. The type that burns 'em up. Why, when I walk up Tenth Avenue, you can smell the meat sizzling in Hell's Kitchen.

(They share cigarettes. Dance to "How Come You Do Me Like You Do." scream.)

WINNIE: By the way, I saw your husband the other day.

KATE: Which one, dearie, which one?

WINNIE: The bootlegger—and what he told me about you was enough.

KATE: What did he tell you?

WINNIE: *(Whispers.)*

KATE: *(Scream.)* I did not. Anyway I only took two puffs off the horrid old thing—and cigarettes make me deathly sick.

WINNIE: One never can tell.

KATE: Listen girls, let me tell you.

(CLEM sings "Goody-goody-good.")

KATE: My dear, I forgot to tell you about my operations. I've had so many operations I look like a slot machine. I had my face lifted the other day and when I got home I looked in the mirror and it dropped. Why I have a perfect triangle here.

WINNIE: That's nothing—I have one that's zig-zag.

KATE: That's nothing, dearie, I have a gash from here to here. *(Exit.)*

(ROLLY strolls over left. CLEM joins him, leaving the TAXI-DRIVER. DUCHESS crosses over right and joins TAXI-DRIVER. CLEM looks around and see's DUCHESS trying to make the TAXI-DRIVER, rushes over and swings him around to center. The guests all sensing a fight, crowd around. DUCHESS runs off center, followed by CLEM and the guests. (A fight off-stage). After a few seconds, DUCHESS rushes on minus her wig, followed by guests. DUCHESS runs over left. then crosses right. CLEM pushes his way through crowd with DUCHESS's wig. He throws it to DUCHESS.)

CLEM: Take your rag.

(DUCHESS catches wig. Door bell rings off left. Twice, then three short rings. There is a sudden hush—then everybody in hushed tones says "Ooooh!" Lights out.)

NO. 1: Oh, My God, it must be the cops!

NO. 2: My God, the place is pinched!

NO. 3: Don't give your right name, dearie!

NO. 4: The place is raided!

NO.. 5: Don't lose your drawers, dearie!

NO. 6: Don't forget your fan, Flossie!

NO. 7: Ooooh, you're squeezing me!

NO. 8: Take your foot off my face!

NO. 9: Take your face off the floor!

NO. 10: It must be the wagon, let me in first!

NO. 11: I had to stand the last time!

NO. 12: I don't care, I had a gay time!

NO. 13: I had a grand time!

NO. 14: I had a gorgeous time!

(ROLLY has gradually worked his way through center of crowd during repartee.)

ROLLY: Boys—boys—Ssssh—be a little careful—Don't get excited—Everything is going to be fine. I'll fix everything all right.

(The music picks up, pianissimo. Exit number, as the guests all file out center, shaking hands with ROLLY, wishing him good-night. ROLLY stands at center looking off after guests while PARSONS starts to tidy things up. ROLLY turns and sees him.)

ROLLY: Don't bother, Parsons. Let the house go until later.

PARSONS: I wanted to get things straightened before Mrs. Kingsbury returned, sir.

ROLLY: That's all right, She won't be back until Monday.

PARSONS: Very well, sir.

ROLLY: Has everybody gone, Parsons?

PARSONS: Yes, sir, everyone.

ROLLY: Have there been any calls for me, Parsons?

PARSONS: No, sir—Oh, I almost forgot, sir. Mr. Grayson called and said he would not be here, sir. *(ROLLY stands at center, lost in thought and repeats GRAYSON's name, then exits.)*

(PARSONS fixes telephone. Places a couple of chairs, then crosses up back to light switch and turns down lights. There is a pause then a door slam. Another pause, then a pistol shot. Still another pause, then a door slam. PARSONS hesitates, then rushes off upstairs. He returns in a few moments, almost in a state of collapse. The servants rush on.)

SERVANTS: What was it? what was it?

PARSONS *(Too upset to answer, goes hurriedly to telephone)*: Plaza 6606—06 *(Pause.)* Judge Kingsbury—This is Parsons, at your son's home. Something terrible has happened. Come at once. I—can't—explain.

(PARSONS hangs up receiver, staggers back with his hands over his eyes as if trying to blot out the horrible picture he has just seen. Then sinks in chair.)

CURTAIN

SCENE II

(The same, a few hours later. The INSPECTOR is questioning those present, including JUDGE KINGSBURY, CLAIR and PARSONS.)

INSPECTOR *(To PARSONS, who is standing center)*: You say, Mr. Kingsbury had words with Mr. Grayson the night before the murder?

PARSONS: Yes, sir.

INSPECTOR: What were they?

PARSONS: I don't know exactly, sir.

INSPECTOR: You know what it was. If you don't tell now, I'll take you where you will tell.

PARSONS: Well, sir, I don't know exactly, sir, but I think, sir—

INSPECTOR: Don't think, sir, but know, sir. What was it about?

PARSONS: It was about Mrs. Kingsbury, I think, sir.

INSPECTOR: What did you hear?

PARSONS: I was in the hall, sir. I wasn't listening, sir, but I heard, sir, rather indistinctly, but clear enough to understand, sir.

INSPECTOR: Yes, yes.

PARSONS: About the interest Mr. Grayson took in Mrs. Kingsbury— and also, sir, about the hospitality of the home—that is, Mr. Kingsbury's hospitality to Mr. Grayson.

INSPECTOR: What else, what else?

PARSONS: Mr. Grayson told Mr. Kingsbury to go to hell, sir—that he didn't care for his hospitality—he only cared for his wife, sir.

JUDGE: What's this? *(Rises, then sits.)*

INSPECTOR: Have Mr. Grayson and Mrs. Kingsbury ever been alone in the house?

PARSONS: Yes, sir, quite often, sir.

INSPECTOR: How long were they alone at any time?

PARSONS: Not very long, sir. Just until Mrs. Kingsbury would dress for the theatre and long enough to bid her good-night when they returned.

INSPECTOR *(Pause):* Have you ever seen them in an intimate position?

PARSONS: Not very intimate, sir. Just in his arms, sir.

INSPECTOR: How many times have you seen this?

PARSONS: Only once, sir.

INSPECTOR: When was it?

PARSONS: Friday night, sir.

INSPECTOR: What else did he do?

PARSONS: He kissed her.

INSPECTOR: How many times?

PARSONS: I only saw one, sir, but that one was quite enough, sir.

INSPECTOR: Sit down. Don't leave this room, I'll talk to you later. *(Crosses to center. Speaks to CLAIR.)* Sorry, Mrs. Kingsbury, but I'll have to ask you a few questions.

CLAIR: I understand.

INSPECTOR: Why did you spend last night at your father's home?

CLAIR: I intended to spend the weekend there, as my husband informed me he would be away on a business trip and I didn't want to be alone here with just the servants.

INSPECTOR: When is the last time you saw Mr. Grayson?

CLAIR: Friday night. He took me to the opera and then to my father's home. That is the last time.

INSPECTOR: Was Mr. Grayson in the habit of escorting you to the theatre?

CLAIR: Yes, quite often.

INSPECTOR: Did your husband object to it.

CLAIR: No, it was my husband's wish. He was too busy to take me himself.

INSPECTOR: The neglected wife and the attentive lover.

DETECTIVE *(Enters):* Grayson is here.

INSPECTOR: Show him in.

GRAYSON *(Enters. Pauses inside door—looks around at those present):* Why, what is the matter?

INSPECTOR: Rolly Kingsbury's been shot.

GRAYSON: Shot!

INSPECTOR: Yes, murdered.

GRAYSON: Murdered!

INSPECTOR: Yeah, perhaps you can tell us something about it.

GRAYSON: Why this is the first I've heard. I don't know what to say. *(Looks at CLAIR.)* God—this is terrible!

INSPECTOR: Where were you at three o'clock this morning?

GRAYSON: I was at a card game. But, why question me?

INSPECTOR: When was the last time you spoke to Rolly Kingsbury?

GRAYSON: Friday evening.

INSPECTOR: Oh, that is the evening you escorted Mrs. Kingsbury to the opera. The evening you held her in your arms and kissed her. The evening you quarreled with Rolly Kingsbury over his wife.

GRAYSON: That's a lie. I quarreled with him, but it was not about his wife.

INSPECTOR: What did you quarrel about?

GRAYSON: Men can quarrel over other things besides women.

INSPECTOR: Then, what did you quarrel over?

GRAYSON: We quarreled over business matters.

INSPECTOR: Ambitious young engineer—employed by the wealthy Kingsbury iron works—accepts the hospitality of Rolly Kingsbury— is trusted with his young, innocent wife. He falls madly in love with her—a quarrel with Rolly Kingsbury over his plans. He sees dismissal and ambition unrealized—a dream of a wealthy young widow—the great Kingsbury wealth at the tip of his finger—a life's ambition realized. Then Rolly Kingsbury is murdered! Now tell us who killed Rolly Kingsbury.

GRAYSON: Your story is very interesting, Inspector, but I'm sorry, I don't know who killed Rolly Kingsbury.

INSPECTOR: You phoned Rolly Kingsbury, last night.

GRAYSON: Why, yes, Rolly invited me to come here last night to a—party, I phoned him that I couldn't attend. I had a previous engagement.

INSPECTOR *(To CLAIR):* Mrs. Kingsbury, did you know there was to be a party here last night?

CLAIR: Why no—I did not.

INSPECTOR *(To GRAYSON):* When were you invited to this—er—party, Mr. Grayson?

GRAYSON: Friday evening.

INSPECTOR: Before you quarreled with Rolly Kingsbury?

GRAYSON: Yes.

INSPECTOR: Then it was because of the quarrel you refused to go?

GRAYSON: Well—partly.

INSPECTOR: You said nothing to Mrs. Kingsbury about the quarrel or the party?

GRAYSON: No.

INSPECTOR: Why not?

GRAYSON: I assumed Mrs. Kingsbury knew about the party, and the quarrel did not concern her.

INSPECTOR: Can you tell us just why you preferred to go to a card game rather than accept the invitation of a man who was your employer and who was in a position to push you on toward success in your career? Can you tell us that?

GRAYSON: I—I'm afraid I can't.

INSPECTOR: You mean you won't.

GRAYSON: No.

CLAIR: Allen—

GRAYSON: Please, Clair.

INSPECTOR: Things look pretty bad for you Mr. Grayson. *(DOCTOR enters from hall up-stage left.)*

INSPECTOR: Oh, Dr. Richmond—You must have something to tell us.

DOCTOR: Yes, I have and I'll make it very brief.

CLAIR *(Rushes to the DOCTOR. He takes her in his arms.)* Daddy! *(She is convulsed with sobs.)*

DOCTOR: Yes, my child, yes, my child—I know, I understand. *(Goes over to JUDGE.)* Bob, it's all in life. Be calm. *(Turns to INSPECTOR.)* Inspector, there will be no further need for investigation. I have your man. *(The JUDGE jumps to his feet in a fury. The DETECTIVE holds him.)*

DOCTOR: Bob, for God's sake, don't. *(The DOCTOR crosses to the door.)* Come in. *(DAVID enters from hall up-stage left. He is pale and nervous.)*

DOCTOR: This is the madman. The poor, depraved, unfortunate who shot our boy.

JUDGE *(Struggles with detective to get at DAVID):* You killed my boy! You killed my boy!

DAVID: I killed him because I loved him. *(He collapses.)*

JUDGE *(Gazing at DAVID):* A madman, a madman.

DOCTOR: This is the poor, abnormal creature we discussed the other, day.

JUDGE: Take him out of my sight, before I strangle him.

DAVID: Strangle me, strangle me! You Judge Kingsbury—the great supporter of justice—you would crush me, destroy me—but your son was the same as I. Yes, I killed him. I came into the garden—I heard the music, the singing, the dancing—I waited until they were all gone. Then I shot him. When you condemn me, you condemn him. A judge's son can be just the same as another man's son—yes a king's son, a fool's son—Oh! I loved him—

DOCTOR: Inspector, could we be alone for a few moments?

INSPECTOR: Of course. *(To DETECTIVE):* Take your man in the other room.

(DETECTIVE takes DAVID out left and the INSPECTOR follows them out.)

DOCTOR *(After a pause):* Bob, take it easy. I know it's hard. But you must listen—We were boys together. The Kingsbury name has been a great name for generations, without a spot or blemish. The Richmond name, the same. We must fight to keep them so. I don't know how to tell you, how to tell you. *(The JUDGE looks up at him.)*

DOCTOR: Bob, we don't know what we bring into this world. We are blind, deaf and dumb. We can see no faults, no sins, no wrongs in our own, those dear to us. But now we must meet facts face to face. When it's another man's son, you condemn him, it's true, it's true. You've sent many up the river, and you know it, Bob, but when it hits home it's a different story. In this civilized world, we are not civilized enough to know why or for what purpose these poor degenerates are brought into the world. Little did we know that a fine, strong boy, like Rolly, was one of them.

JUDGE *(Looking up slowly, says in a broken voice):* Jim, call the Inspector.

INSPECTOR *(Comes to door):* Yes, sir.

JUDGE: Report this—a case of—of suicide . . .

INSPECTOR: Yes—your honor.

CURTAIN

THE PLEASURE MAN

A COMEDY DRAMA

(1928)

THE CAST

The Theatre Crew

Bridget ⎤
Maggie ⎟ scrubwomen
Lizzie ⎟
Tillie ⎦

Steve McAllister, the manager
Bradley
Bill
Stanley Smith
Ted Arnold
Mary Ann, Ted Arnold's sister
Leader
Call Boy

The Performers

Dolores, a dancer
Randall, her husband and partner

Flo ⎤
Bobby ⎟ dancers in their act
Jewel ⎟
Jane ⎦

Chuck and Joe, dancers

Hermann and Fritz, the Otto Brothers, German acrobats

Paradise Dupont, a female impersonator

Paradise's Four Boys

Peaches, a female impersonator
Bunny, a female impersonator
The Cobra

Edgar, a small-time vaudevillian
Edgar's wife
Lester Queen
Maybelle, a dancer
Four Hoofers

Ripley Hetherington ⎤ dramatic
Mrs. Hetherington ⎦ actors

Rodney Terrill, a voluptuary
Nikko, his Japanese valet

Toto, a wealthy retired performer

Police Chief

Assistant Police Chief

Set in a small Midwest town, *The Pleasure Man* takes place in a theatre and in the home of a wealthy retired performer.

Act One.		A theatre.
Act Two.	Scene One.	Two-tier dressing rooms and a corridor to the stage.
	Scene Two.	The same.
Act Three.	Scene One.	The drawing room of Toto's apartment.
	Scene Two.	The same, two hours later.

THE PLEASURE MAN

ACT ONE

(A Theatre. Enter four scrubwomen, LIZZIE, MAGGIE, TILLIE, BRIDGET, with their mops and pails. Three from one side, BRIDGET from the other. BRIDGET calls to the others.)

BRIDGET: Ah, there ye are, me darlins—Did this actors what wuz here last week leave anythin' in their rooms?

MAGGIE: Picture any o' that tribe leavin' anythin' behind 'em but unpaid bills!

TILLIE: Yis, an' dirty underwear.

LIZZIE: I found somethin'—a piece o' fish left over from the seal act. *(Seeing BRIDGET hold up a piece of cloth.)* What've yer got there, in Heaven's name? *(All gather around.)*

BRIDGET: Ah, that takes yer eye, does it? Well, it's a bit o' ruffle offer one o' thim bally dresses. An' I found a rusty nickel in the room that Scotch comedian wuz in.

MAGGIE: May the Saints preserve us!

LIZZIE: Yer better turn it in to the manager, dearie. The bonnie lad'll likely be askin' fer it the nex' time he plays here.

TILLIE: Sure, he'd say it was a dollar.

BRIDGET: No ma'am, I'm keepin' it fer a heirloom to show me great grand-chillern just how careless those Scotchmen is with their money.

MAGGIE: I wonder what kind o' acts is comin' in this week? I hopes there ain't no animal acts. They mess up the place somethin' terrible.

TILLIE (*At table, dusting*): Yeah, what with this and that, all over the place.

LIZZIE: I hopes there's acrobats. They're so strong an' clean. It's a pleasure to look at their muscles.

(*TILLIE rises, puts chair back.*)

BRIDGET: Oh, ho, me darlin'! So you've been havin' a look too!

LIZZIE: There ain't no harm in lookin'.

BRIDGET: No, but I've knowed o' some lookin' that's led to doin'.

LIZZIE: That was a handsome lad what played in that sketch last week. He reminded me o' me poor dead Mike, Lord ha' mercy on 'im.

MAGGIE: Yus, that wuz becaue 'e waz layin' down most o' the time.

LIZZIE: Ah, gwan wid ya. *Your* Jerry ain't so crazy about work.

MAGGIE: Maybe so. But he's thoughtful an' kind an' allus sees *I* got a good job.

TILLIE: Now ain't that sweet!

BRIDGET: Will you two prima donnas stop bein' so temper'mintal?

LIZZIE (*Comes downstairs*): You're no one to be preachin', Bridget O'Shea. I see you watchin' that good lookin' pianer player. An' what I seen in your eyes—meant no good.

BRIDGET (*Rises*): Let me tell you, Lizzie McSwiggin, When I get so old I can't appreciate a good lookin' man, may the Lord forgive me, then I'll make a box fer meself. (*Drinks.*)

MAGGIE (*Laughing*): Ye ould Divil! Talkin' as if ye wuz sixteen.

BRIDGET: Well, I'll admit I'm older nor sixteen, but I got "it."

TILLIE: Yeah—more than once.

LIZZIE: An' you just after layin' away yer fourth husband.

BRIDGET: It wuzn't my fault he couldn't hold up. Father Reilly says to me, he says, "Bridget O'Shea, you've been rather unfortunate with your husbands." An' I says—Father, unfortunate is no word for it; I never seen men used up so quick.

MAGGIE: Bridget, yer a scandal.

BRIDGET: Oh, I've had me time.

TILLIE: Yeah, with the whole Fire Department.

LIZZIE: Yus, it's showin' on yer.

BRIDGET: I'll slap yer sassy mouth, so I will.

MAGGIE: Ah, she's only risin' yer.

BRIDGET: I'll rise 'er on the end o' me toe!

LIZZIE: Yer will not. Not you an' all yer firemen friends.

BRIDGET *(Dropping her mop and pushing up sleeve):* I'll lick ye wit' me right hand, ye Orange bastard!

TILLIE: Call in yer cops, Lizzie.

LIZZIE *(Swinging her mop):* I'll polish yer upper set wit' this, ye Divil's wench!

MAGGIE *(Shouting):* Howly mother, they're at it agin!

(At the beginning of the argument, the Orchestra enters, takes its place in the pit, and after tuning up, starts to play a number. TILLIE separates BRIDGET and LIZZIE.)

BRIDGET *(Taking LIZZIE's arm, all friendly again):* Say Lizzie, you an' me's as good as anythin' they has on this bill.

LIZZIE: Git hot, girls!

(The four take their positions and dance and sing. CREW enjoy the antics of scrubwomen. STEVE enters.)

STEVE: What the hell do you think this is, a concert?

(Crew scatters to work.)

Snap it up you bozos. Get these lines cleared. Strike this stuff on stage. Clear all the lines and tie off. We've got a big act coming in with six hanging pieces.

BRADLEY: Hey, Steve, is dis thing a production comin' in or just one o' dem things?

STEVE: What do you care? Get these battens off these lines.

VOICE FROM FLIES: Hey, Steve, you'll have to get three more grips.

STEVE: Three more grips? Try and get them. This crew's big enough to handle a circus. So snap into it.

(*General stage noises, some hammering. STEVE takes advance plots from his pockets— calls BRADLEY and Grip to whom he hands the respective lists.*)

This is the light plot of the big act. (*Grip takes it and walks away, looking it over.*) These are the light plots of the entire show.

BRADLEY (*Studying light plots*): I wish these acts would call for some original lighting once in a while. Nothing but blue, amber or green spots. (*Studying Dancing Act light plot*) Say, what the hell is this, a Chinese act? I can't make this out, can you, Steve?

STEVE (*Laughs*): Well, did you ever see anything that an actor laid out that you could understand?

(*LEADER enters.*)

LEADER: Good morning, Mac.

STEVE: Morning—

BRADLEY (*Scrutinizing plot*): Oh, I can make dis out now. Dey got deir own electrician wit' dis act. Dis must be dat bologney's code so nobody kin git wise to his job—some bozo!

STEVE: Yeah, holding down the old job his own way! (*Points off stage.*) Here's some of the acts arriving now. (*Calls to Crew.*) Give a hand to this baggage comin' in.

(*Several Grips exit and return with trunks, etc. They clear stage as BILL enters.*)

Come on, you bozos—get busy with these trunks, snap into it.

BILL (*Crosses to STEVE*): Are you the manager?

STEVE: Yes. Who and what are you?

BILL: I'm the electrician wit' the Dolores and Randall dancin' act.

STEVE: Is the act in yet?

BILL: They stopped off to get sumpin' to eat—they'll be in any time, now.

STEVE *(Calls):* Hey, Bradley, take care of this fellow—he's the electrician on that "Follies" act.

BRADLEY *(To BILL, as STEVE turns and directs something on stage for a moment):* Whatcha bringin' in?

BILL: I got two babies, three olivettes—moon-box and a water and cloud machine. Guess we can use the house bunches, eh?

BRADLEY: Yeah, but don't forget, we don't supply spiders or cables.

BILL: Aw, dat's all oks, I got all dat stuff wit' me. Dis is a regular act. And say, youse guys wants to get an eyeful of dis act.

(Turns to STEVE, who has just crossed to them.)

Listen, boss, you never seen such lightin' in all your young career— Don't care whose acts yer seen—some lightin' on dis act. *(Pompously)* I laid it all out myself, too.

STEVE: Yeah, well, what do you want me to do about it?

BILL: Yeah—dere ain't nuttin' fer youse to do—yer see I used to work at dare Hip* in New York—Why de—

STEVE: Oh,—tell that to Bradley.

BRADLEY: What's dat? a teeayter?

(STEVE crosses to Crew. Crew is swinging trunks, drapes, general crew work.)

BILL: Aw, gee, dat's right, I couldn't expect you to know dat.

BRADLEY: Yeah—but dere's one thing dat I do know. Dis ain't no Hip, and from your bologney I think you're full o' hop. Where's yer union travellin' card?

BILL: I didn't use a card last week. Is der union strong out dis way?

BRADLEY: Yer damn right dey're strong out dis way. Yer gonna use a card dis week.

STEVE: Hey—Stan—where's Stan?

(BILL fumbles in pockets for card he hasn't got. STEVE turns from him, gives ad lib direction of swinging scenery, BILL goes over to some apparatus and is about to haul it out when he is noticed by BRADLEY who shouts at him and crosses to him.)

---

*The Hippodrome. —L.S.

BRADLEY: Hey, lay off o' dat stuff. Where der hell is your card? Tryin' to pull a fast one around here?

BILL: Gee, I can't find it—I ain't got me card wit' me.

BRADLEY: Well, den dere ain't gonna be no act.

(STEVE crosses to them inquiringly.)

BILL: What do ya mean, no act?

STEVE: Just what he said. No union card, no act. That's quite clear, isn't it?

BILL *(With show of bravado)*: No, it ain't. Explain it! explain it!

STEVE: You have all the explanation necessary!

(Crosses stage.)

BRADLEY: Say, you heel, do you want me to get fined a hundred smackers fer lettin' a wise-guy pull in here wit'out a card? Where do you get dat stuff—in der Hip?

BILL: Well, what do yer want me to do?

BRADLEY: Why, join der union—join der union, wise guy—it's der only way yer kin work here.

(Hammering starts. STEVE fretfully looks at watch.)

BILL: Gee, I can't join der union in dis town.

BRADLEY: Well, dat's your grief, Hippy.

(He crosses to crew.)

STEVE: Hey—Stop that noise—Where's Stan?Hey, Stan!

(STAN enters—and pretends to be panting.)

STEVE *(STAN crosses to left)*: What's the matter? What you panting for?

STAN: That ain't panting—that's passion!

STEVE: Say—what's the idea of goin' round with one black and one tan shoe?

STAN: A woman lied to me she said there was nobody home.

(To grip.)

Take yer long line up—change No. 4 over to No. 12.*

(STAN turns to STEVE.)

STEVE: Remember that Prima Donna. She's coming back. I want you to look after her.

STAN: Don't forget I got rheumatism. Hey! shorten that long line—

STEVE: Here—what did you say about swimming? When was it first invented?

STAN: Two Scotchmen came to a Toll gate.

STEVE: Oh—get to work.

STAN: That was a parky lunch last week—*(Ad lib.)*

Say, do you remember dat team o' hoofers—well, neider of dem guys dare go near Chicago, New York or any of the big time yokel-takers.

STEVE: Why not?

STAN: De little one's afraid o' meetin' a wife—yer see he always marries a new dame wit'out shootin' the last one—and de partner, der big bimbo—well he just forgits to marry 'em at all.

STEVE: Cut out that noise over there.

(They don't stop.)

Where the hell are these acts? It's ten-thirty.

LEADER: Yeah, we've always got to wait. You'd think they were Dukes or Earls or maybe Queens . . .

(Enter PARADISE DUPONT tripping lightly.)

Whoops! I've been discovered, Royalty has arrived, dearie.

STEVE *(Crossing to PARADISE.)* Who are you and what you do?

PARADISE: O—Oh! I'm the Bird of Paradise and my four Manly-kins.

STEVE: Well, what do you do?

(Enter STANLEY loaded with props.)

---

*Shades of lighting on the color wheel. —L.S.

PARADISE: Well, for God sakes, what do you think I do?

STEVE: I'm not thinking—I'm asking—

STANLEY *(Downstage):* He chases butterflies on the dewy grass. *(Illustrates.)* And makes delicious fudge on Sundays and holidays. *(Up to table.)*

STEVE: What kind of an act do you do?

PARADISE: Oh, I get down on my knees—and sing a couple of Mammy songs . . . you see I'm a character imperson-eater.

STEVE: A what?

(Enter two boys of Paradise company.)

PARADISE: A female impersonator.

(Boys cross left.)

STEVE: I guessed as much.

STANLEY: Have you had your cream puffs this morning?

(Downstage right.)

PARADISE: Oh, I always eat early—*(To STEVE.)* You know it's the early bird that catches the worm, dearie.

STEVE: Dearie, hell. *(Advances threateningly.)*

I'm Mr. McAllister to you.

PARADISE: Mercy Mac, you're a terrible villain. Don't you dare strike me, or I'll scream.

STEVE: You'd better get your stuff arranged with the leader, third place on the bill.

PARADISE: Oh Mac, you place me in a very awkward position. I always get a better spot than that. Sound your A, Professor, I'm coming. *(Crash.)*

My God, things are falling in this town already.

EDGAR: *(Enters right, with his wife, greets MCALLISTER.)* Don't worry, Honey, we've no opposition on the bill. We shall probably be the hit of the show.

MCALLISTER: Hello, Edgar, back with us again?

EDGAR: Seems as if I was in stock here.

MCALLISTER: How are you?

EDGAR: I'm clever, how are you? How's business?

MCALLISTER: Not bad.

EDGAR: That's good.

MCALLISTER: How's your act?

STANLEY: That's bad.

EDGAR: Not good. Not good, great! But you wouldn't know the act, it's all changed. I've got a ukelele in the act.

(Four boys enter, giggling.)

1st BOY *(Crosses to STANLEY—whispers.)*

STANLEY: Right down those steps in the corner.

1st BOY: Thank you so much.

(2nd boy crosses to STANLEY, whispers.)

STANLEY: I've told you, down those steps.

2nd BOY: Thank you, you're so good to me.

(3rd boy crosses to STANLEY.)

STANLEY: I've told you three times, you poor thing, you must be suffering. *(Pushes him down stage left.)*

Down those steps. *(Boy exits—STANLEY crosses center.)*

STEVE: What did he want, Stan?

STANLEY: Wanted to know where the music room was.

STEVE: Where did you come in from, Edgar?

EDGAR: Peoria. And if you think you're funny, play that town. They'll take all the go out of you.

STEVE: Do they feature the vaudeville there?

EDGAR: No, they just say "and vaudeville"; Last week they had—the hell with the blue laws and vaudeville.

(HOOFERS become very noisy and other stage noises annoy PARADISE.)

PARADISE: You—oo—oo, Mac.

(STEVE doesn't hear the first call.)

My God, Mac, you'd think I was on the firing line. I'll be shell-shocked before the second chorus. You'd think they worked the effects for "What Price Glory?"

STANLEY *(To crew):* Lay off the racket. You're throttling the canary. *(To HOOFERS.)* And don't lay your dogs down so heavy.

STEVE *(To PARADISE):* Go ahead with your rehearsal. The boys won't annoy you.

STANLEY: And don't you annoy the boys, Violet.

PARADISE: Lavender, maybe, but violet never.

BRADLEY *(Enters, crossing to PARADISE):* What are the light cues in your act?

PARADISE: It's on the plot . . . but if you have magenta gelatines, please use them instead of the green. Green is so cold—and I must have the warm colour, it's much more artistic.

BRADLEY: We got all them colours.

PARADISE: And I use a colour wheel on the promenade, if you've got one.

BRADLEY: We got that too, is that all?

PARADISE: That's all—thank you.

BRADLEY: That sets you.

(Exits.)

EDGAR *(Downstage to LEADER):* Hello.

LEADER: Do you want to rehearse?

EDGAR: I guess I'd better. Now, the wife and I open the act with a lot of cross-fire talk, and when I kick the wife in the face you play "Together."

LEADER: You don't think we'd play separate?

EDGAR: No, I mean the song, "Together." Has that been sung here?

LEADER: Every week for the past six months.

EDGAR *(STANLEY crosses right):* Oh, I do it different.

(To STANLEY.)

Hey—got a cigarette?

STANLEY: Plenty. *(Exits.)*

EDGAR: I bet he's a great guy. You know, a stage hand hung himself in my dressing room last week. You can imagine how I felt when I came in and found him hanging to the pipes.

LEADER: Did you cut him down?

EDGAR: Well, not right away. He wasn't dead yet. Now, after we sing this song—

STANLEY *(Enters from left):* You go straight to your dressing room.

EDGAR: No, we take a lot of bows.

STANLEY: You take 'em—where do you get 'em from? Say, how did you get on the stage?

EDGAR: I fell out of the balcony.

STANLEY: Well, why don't you get on to yourself and get back to your trade?

EDGAR: I'm at my trade. My father was an actor and my grandfather was an actor.

STANLEY: I suppose if your father and grandfather were bums—you'd be a bum?

EDGAR: No—I'd be a stage hand.

STANLEY: Have a cigar—

(Hands him a cigar.)

I don't want to be near when you light it.

(Exits.)

BRADLEY *(Enters right):* Do you use the spot in your act?

EDGAR: I never put the audience in the dark—I want to get some applause.

BRADLEY: What has a spotlight got to do with applause?

EDGAR: Well, the average fellow that goes to a show takes a girl with him and if you put them in the dark, that guy does everything with his hands but applaud.

BRADLEY: Your act must be worse than last time.

FIRST HOOFER *(To EDGAR):* Have you finished your rehearsal?

SMALL TIMER: Yes, I've finished—oh, hello, Chuck, gee I got some new gags I'll show you. *(Ad lib—Crosses right.)*

FIRST HOOFER: Thanks, why don't you put some in your own show? *(To LEADER):* That guy couldn't show steps to a stoop.

(HOOFERS rehearse steps. As first HOOFER exits.)

Hey, Stan, when do we go on?

STANLEY: You're dancin' it.

HOOFER: "Tanks." *(Exits.)*

BRADLEY *(Offstage):* Hey, youse hoofers use a spotlight in your act?

HOOFER *(Off stage):* Just use de flood.

(Enter TERRILL, followed by JAPANESE VALET with luggage. TERRILL takes position right center and poses.)

TERRILL: Set down the bags, Nikko.

NIKKO: All right.

TERRILL *(Selecting cigarette from case):* A light, Nikko.

NIKKO strikes match and lights TERRILL's cigarette.)

Tell that fellow over there I'd like to speak with him. *(Indicating STEVE.)*

NIKKO *(Crosses to STEVE):* Mister Terrill want talk—talk with you, Honourable Sir.

STEVE: What are you—a wire walker?

NIKKO: Mister Terrill want talk with you, Honourable Sir.

STEVE: There's no wire walker billed this week.

NIKKO *(Points to TERRILL):* Make talk—you—Mister Terrill—make talk. You speak English?

THE PLEASURE MAN 157

STEVE: Do I speak English? Why the hell didn't you say so? *(Crosses to TERRILL.)*

What's the idea of sending that moon-faced kimono over to me? Is he your interpreter?

TERRILL: My valet. Merely my valet. He saves me many extra steps. I suppose I'm dressing in No. 1 as usual. I'm topping the bill here, you know.

STEVE: Yeah—you are. God knows why. How you come to be booked as a headliner is beyond me.

TERRILL: My dear fellow, if I had to worry about the criticisms of stage hands, I wouldn't be a headliner. However, I don't play to stage-hands and, as you know, I pack them in everywhere I appear. The women come in droves to see me. There's the answer—what more could be said?

STEVE: There's a whole lot could be said—about you—but it would take all day for me to tell you. But watch out, Terrill, no nonsense this trip.

TERRILL: It's No. 1. then, isn't it? Nikko, take these bags into No. 1. dressing room.

NIKKO: All right,—I do.

(Exits with bags.)

(BOBBY enters right with bag—sees TERRILL, who crosses to her. She puts bag down.)

TERRILL: Hello, honey. Hello, there. Are you with the dancing act coming in?

BOBBY: Yes, with Dolores and Randall.

TERRILL: Oh, Dolores and Randall? I didn't know they—well, well, that's fine. It must be a great act if you're in it. Oh, my name's Terrill—Rodney Terrill—you've heard of me, of course. Call me Rod. Your name is—?

BOBBY: Bobby.

TERRILL: Now, I thought you'd have a cute name like that. Bobby—so musical, it seems to ripple off the tongue. *(Takes her hand.)*

Weren't you with Gus Edwards?

BOBBY: No, this is the first act I've ever been in. I've never been away from home before. I went to dancing school.

TERRILL: Oh yes—I bet you dance beautifully. You would. You've got grace and poise. I noticed that as soon as you came in. How long have you been with the act, dear?

BOBBY: Only two weeks. This is my first time away from home.

TERRILL *(Looks around):* Ahh, I see. Have you got your Mother with you?

BOBBY: Oh, no.

TERRILL: Well, that's lovely, lovely. Striking out by yourself, eh? Beginning your career all on your own. That's lovely. You'll get along. *(Indicates bag.)* This bothers you. *(Puts bag down.)* You'll be a success if you don't lose your sense of humor. Don't have anything to do with men that aren't sincere. They're apt to tell you anything. How about taking a little dinner with me some night while you're here?

BOBBY: Well, I don't know.

TERRILL: Oh come, Bobby. Actors eat, you know, despite the old crack about starving showfolk. I'll bet you eat prettily, too. I'd love to see those little teeth of yours munching on some—you know they are beautiful teeth—and those lips. Gee, what lips. What beautiful hair you have! Ziegfeld would go wild about you. Say, you'll have dinner with me, tonight, eh?

BOBBY: All right—Rod. *(Starts to go—looks back.)*

TERRILL: That's the spirit.

(Throws kiss to her. As BOBBY exits, FLO enters—They collide.)

FLO: What the hell's the matter with you? Hello, Rod.

TERRILL: Hello, Flo. Lord, I'm glad to see you. I've missed you terribly. I was beginning to think we'd never meet again. The thought nearly drove me mad. *(Takes her hand.)*

FLO: Yeah?

TERRILL: Did you get my letters?

FLO: No. Did you mail 'em in a waste basket?

TERRILL: How can you say a thing like that, dear? I'm surprised. Of course I sent you a letter. Three letters in fact. In one of them, I enclosed a new photograph.

FLO: Who of?

TERRILL: Me, of course. I had it taken especially for you. I'm frightfully sorry you didn't get it. I haven't any more of them.

FLO: Well, that's too bad.

TERRILL: Oh, Flo, I've laid awake nights thinking about you. I've dreamed about you, too—a thousand times. I've gone over in my mind our hours together—do you—remember them, too?

FLO: I couldn't very easily forget them. They made so big an impression on me—then.

TERRILL: Now that we're together again—God, what times we'll have.

FLO: How about tonight—will you take me to dinner?

TERRILL: Tonight? Let me see—tonight. No, Flo, I can't—I've got some very important business to attend to—I'll take you to lunch after rehearsal this morning.

FLO: Are you sure you can't take me to dinner tonight because you've already dated up some other Jane?

TERRILL: Now, Flo, how could you think so hard of me? You know you're the only one for me and—

FLO: Weren't you just talking to Bobby as I came in?

TERRILL: Bobby? Who is Bobby? You mean that girl who went out as you came in? Don't be silly. I just asked her what act she was in and when she told me she was with Dolores and Randall, I was overjoyed because I knew then that you'd be here—*(kisses her hand.)*

Now listen dear, when rehearsals are over, we'll go to some nice little place I know and have lunch. I'm dying to hold you in my arms again, sweetheart.

FLO: I thought we were going just for lunch.

TERRILL: We'll have that, too.

FLO *(Going):* Don't forget, I'm hungry.*(Exits.)*

TERRILL: You'll be fed.

(SCRUBWOMAN enters, crosses right, pauses, looks around, Terrill sees her, turns away, SCRUBWOMAN exits.)

(Enter STANLEY—Crosses right.)

STANLEY: Hey, you missed one.

(Exits.)

STEVE *(Enters—to TERRILL):* Still up to your old tricks? Listen Terrill, I know your kind and I don't have a hell of a lot of use for them either. I want to tell you something. I don't want any visiting in the dressing rooms while you're on the bill this trip, or I'll throw you out of here on your neck.

TERRILL: I told you before, I do not play to stage hands, neither do I take my moral instructions from any stage hands.

STEVE: Now wait a minute. While you're playing this house you're going to obey the rules I make here. Now if you've got anything to rehearse, get it over with. *(Indicates orchestra.)*

You've got the spot position on the bill—fifth place.

(TERRILL goes to LEADER, arranges for rehearsal. STEVE crosses to girls.)

TERRILL: That's as it should be.

STEVE: Are you girls with Dolores and Randall?

GIRLS *(Together):* Yes.

STEVE: Well, you girls are dressing in No. 14.

(GIRLS start picking up their bags, etc. Enter MR. and MRS. RIPLEY HETH-ERINGTON. THEY stand by as STEVE talks to the Girls.)

Now before you girls go to your dressing room, let me tell you something. This goes particularly for this theatre. But if you are the nice girls that I think Mr. Randall would pick for his act, then I'm certain that you won't forget it in any theatre you play.

BOBBY: Mr. McAllister, you don't think—

STEVE: Now young lady, I'm not thinking about it. It is a rule of this house that we do not permit community visiting in the dressing rooms. I don't have much trouble in the theatre because I find the majority of performers on the bills are very decent people and I'm only telling you girls this now, because I saw the little byplay between a couple of you girls and that man—Terrill. I'm quite certain you only wanted to seem smart and chic. Am I right? Now run along and don't forget.

(The GIRLS have mingled expressions of feeling— indignation, embarrassment, guilt. MR. and MRS. HETHERINGTON exchange knowing glances and gestures—whisper to each other.)

MAYBELLE: Thank you very much, Mr. McAllister.

FLO: You can be sure, Mr. McAllister, we won't forget. *(Exit with bags.)*

HETHERINGTON: Mr. McAllister—It is an extreme pleasure for Mrs. Hetherington and myself to be playing once again in your theatre. I sent ahead my property list and scene plot.

STEVE: I'm awfully glad to see you folks back again. I like a good dramatic sketch on my bill. I received the scene and prop plots, but I'm afraid you'll have to use the same old center door fancy. Hey, Al—let down the center door fancy.

(BOYS giggle and chatter.)

Hey, Stan—you take good care of Mr. and Mrs. Hetherington. He'll check up with you on your props.

(BOYS camp—cross center down front.)

(STEVE crosses to BOYS.)

I'll run the whole gang of you off the stage if you don't cut out your clowning. Paradise, send these boys to the dressing room.

PARADISE: All right, Mac—Off you go, boys—to your dressing room.

STANLEY *(To BOYS, as they exit)*: Boys,—save your strength—You have a matinee.

(BOYS exit talking.)

MRS. HETHERINGTON *(To her husband)*: Ugh! Such people. I can't understand them. They're so queer.

HETHERINGTON: Yes, my dear—extraordinarily queer. I think queer is the word. They lack perception, my dear, of the finer qualities which go to make up the true artist of the legitimate drama.

PEACHES: Aren't there peculiar looking people on this bill?

(Looking at MR. and MRS. HETHERINGTON.)

PARADISE: Yes, and some of them are so moth-eaten, they look as though they've been buried and dug up.

STEVE *(Turns to them. DOLORES and RANDALL enter—TERRILL is rehearsing.)*

RANDALL: Dolores, I'll have to straighten this out with the manager. You take care of the rehearsal.

(GIRL comes to DOLORES with music.)

MAYBELLE *(Cross to DOLORES):* Dolores,—do you want your music?

(RANDALL crosses left to STEVE.)

DOLORES *(Right):* In just a moment. There is someone rehearsing now.

RANDALL *(To STEVE):* Are you Mr. McAllister? *(Indicates his electrical apparatus.)*

My electrician tells me he's run into a snag.

STEVE: You'll have to take it up with the stage manager.

(Indicates STANLEY right. RANDALL and BILL cross to him. DOLORES in crossing toward piano meets TERRILL. They greet each other very friendly.)

TERRILL: I knew you were on the bill, Dolores. My God, how I've longed to see you. The three weeks that I haven't seen you have been torture.

(TERRILL screens her from view of RANDALL up stage right.)

DOLORES *(Looking about to see if she is observed by RANDALL):* Oh, Rodney, don't be so careless. Tom's furious. He suspects your interest in me is too intimate. We have had a terrible battle because of you. He's so insanely jealous. Please, for my sake, if you love me as you say you do—do be careful, and I'll see you as often as I can.

PEACHES: Paradise, did you ever have a platonic love affair?

PARADISE *(Left. Looking directly at DOLORES and TERRILL.):* Oh yes, but his wife found it out.

TERRILL: But, Dolores, darling, I'm crazy about you. I love you so that discretion leaves me. When I see your beautiful body with such wondrous poise and grace dance and sway rhythmically about the stage, my blood races through my veins like liquid fire, and consumes all senses except that of my passion for you.

(DOLORES attempts to hush him, but lingers as he draws her close to him by one arm. They whisper balance of conversation. MRS. HETHERINGTON has observed their actions and turns to her husband disgustedly.)

MRS. HETHERINGTON: Ripley, dear, isn't it disgusting? How brazenly and boldly some women in vaudeville conduct themselves before others. *(Indicating DOLORES and RANDALL.)*

HETHERINGTON *(Looking at them):* It is demoralizing! But, my dear, we must see all, hear all and say nothing! You must be famished, my dear,—I insist that you go and have breakfast.*(Exit.)*

(PARADISE has gathered together the BOYS, who are still clowning.)

PARADISE: Mac, where you going to put us to dress?

(To STEVE up stage right.)

STEVE: In Number twelve.

STANLEY: Next to the acrobats—and don't push the chewing gum out of the knot-hole.

PEACHES: You don't think we'd do a thing like that?

PARADISE: Not much! *(As they are trooping off, PARADISE and BUNNY are last to leave. They pass near DOLORES and TERRILL.)*

BUNNY *(To DOLORES):* Listen, sister, you better grab the band and let the drugstore cowboy hit Main Street—the girls will be waiting for him, dearie. *(Exits.)*

TERRILL *(Turns furiously as she walks off):* You keep your remarks to yourself or I'll—

PARADISE: You'll call her husband—

(Cross right.)

to protect the lady's reputation *(Exits).*

(DOLORES takes her music from the GIRLS and confusedly crosses to LEADER—TERRILL restrains himself—PARADISE and BUNNY exit. STANLEY exits on errand down right.)

RANDALL *(To GIRLS in his act):* You will always find on vaudeville bills some certain man who is perfectly willing to be most amusing. Usually these men have only one thought in mind and that is to make you like them—and like them so much that in your little fickle brains you forget the decent things your mother taught you. These men think nothing of visiting you in your dressing room, regardless of how little or how much clothing you may have on. But they usually gauge their time so that you don't have much on—and then under the pretense of a love for you which they never feel— things happen that shouldn't be done—by children.

DOLORES *(To LEADER, who is playing her music):* That's perfect tempo for our dancing—

(Dances a few steps.)

Now the tempo increases until the end of the number which must be very fast.

(Dance for fast finish—RANDALL and STEVE are talking—STEVE points to drops being hung by crew.)

STEVE: Oh, Mr. Randall—

(To RANDALL.)

We're hanging your stuff now—Don't worry about playing the date—I'll see to it that you'll do that in any event—but—

STANLEY *(Who has re-entered—Cross to left center):* See that this bimbo gets a union travellin' card, or get another boy—Only this time don't get one that worked at the Hip.

RANDALL *(To STEVE):* That's mighty decent of you, Mr. McAllister. I'll make it all right with you before we leave.

STEVE *(Indignantly):* No, you won't make it all right with anybody. We don't do things that way here.

STANLEY: It's going to cost you a hundred and fifteen for the man.

RANDALL: How much? Gee, that's steep, isn't it?

STANLEY: That's the union scale and yer kin take it or leave it. You know how it is.

RANDALL: But how about my electrician?

STEVE: Well, he can tell our man what to do.

STANLEY: But he don't dare touch de lights or nothin'.

BILL: Gee, can't I get the stuff out of the crates, even?

STANLEY: Yeah, you can do that—put your spiders and cables and de rest of the stuff over there.

(BILL starts away.)

But don't try ter lay it out, savvy?

EDGAR

(Takes BILL by arm down stage right.)

Are you having trouble with your union card?

BILL: Yeah.

EDGAR: Why didn't you come to me—I'd have taken you over to the Union and fixed the whole thing up for you—

BILL: Who do you know at the Union?

EDGAR: I know the big guy over there—what's his name? Well—anyway—something happened on the bill with me three weeks ago—I took the guy over to the Union and squared up the whole thing up for him. Next time anything like that happens—come to me—I'll fix it up for you.

BILL: If you're such a good fixer—why don't you fix up that lousy act of yours?

RANDALL *(To STEVE):* Thank you ever so much, both of you. Mr. McAllister, I'm doing a little change in the dance numbers and I wonder if there would be any objection to me rehearsing the girls on the stage?

STEVE: None at all, providing you see to it that you are not in the crew's way. *(RANDALL nods his thanks and crosses to DOLORES. STAN-LEY exits.)*

RANDALL: That electrician relative of yours almost got us in a jam in this house. I thought you said he had a travelling card.

DOLORES: Why, darling, what's wrong? We haven't had trouble so far, and besides, I thought he had a card.

RANDALL: Whether he is a relation of yours or not, I just had to make a change. He has managed to bluff his way through this last two weeks, but this time they called his bluff and that bluff is costing the act one hundred and fifteen dollars.

DOLORES: Why worry me about it? If you're letting him out that's all there is to it. We can't afford two electricians though we should have them. You girls run up and get dressed. We must have a rehearsal of the new number.

RANDALL: That is an indifferent attitude, and I don't like it, any more than I like certain other things—

DOLORES *(Flippantly interrupting):* For instance? *(Continues with rehearsal.)*

RANDALL: For instance, young Miss don't-give-a-damn, why were you so anxious to take this particular engagement? I wanted to lay off and build the new numbers. But you insisted on taking this particular engagement. Just what was your object?

DOLORES *(Turning to LEADER, purposely ignoring RANDALL):* That's right, professor, up to the last two bars; but from that point on— adagio with three repeats of those two bars and then with the tempo increasing for the finish.

RANDALL *(Angrily and impatiently seizing her by the arm):* What the hell is the idea of trying to evade and answer? *(Severely.)* Just why were you so anxious to play this engagement? That's what I want to know.

DOLORES *(Flippantly):* Just what am I supposed to say?

RANDALL: You've kept your nose buried pretty close in the routing sheet of the "Billboard" and I want to know what the hell you were looking for in that route list. What kind of a fool do you think I am? I'm way ahead of you, and I give you fair warning: cut it out!

(TED ARNOLD enters and crosses to STANLEY.)

DOLORES: Say, what are you talking about?—Are you trying to pick a fight with me?—Just what are you driving at?

RANDALL: You knew damn well that louse Terrill was on this bill.

(STANLEY crosses to STEVE with ARNOLD—they talk.)

DOLORES: He is?

RANDALL: Yes—he is!

DOLORES: I didn't know that.

RANDALL: Oh, so you didn't know that.

DOLORES *(Turning angrily)*: However, I thought we had that out two weeks ago, and if you keep up this damned jealous imagination of yours, you're going to have a new partner as far as I am concerned—

(Several GIRLS enter and begin practicing.)

RANDALL *(Turns and crosses to McALLISTER.)*: Now you and your electrician explain to Mr. Arnold, our electrician, exactly what you want.

(RANDALL shows ARNOLD what's needed.)

(OTTO BROTHERS enter, talking in German—DOLORES turns her attention to rehearsal with LEADER—STANLEY crosses on stage business and there is a mutual recognition between him and the OTTO BROTHERS.)

HERMANN *(Surprised)*: Ach du lieber Gott! Fritz, choost look who vas diss!

STANLEY: Ah, the Otto brothers!

(They hug each other in genuine affection.)

HERMANN: Ach, how long iss it since I seen you, aindt it?

STANLEY: The Flying Dutchmen, Hermann, Fritz and Carl. I haven't seen you since my Robinson Circus days.

FRITZ: Yah, yah, yah—das iss recht—dass iss ein, zwei, drei—ach, das iss seven years! Are you playin' on der bill, Stanley?

STANLEY: I should say not. I own the theatre. I'm the property man of this theatre. No more fallin' around and breaking my neck.

HERMANN: Pye Golly, Fritz, didn't I always told you Stanley was alvays too smart for a dumb act?

STANLEY: Where's the rest of the troupe? Ain't Carl witcha no more?

HERMANN: Sure—Carl—he's vidt us, only he aindt vid us—dot's der trouble—vy ve can't play diss date.

STANLEY: What do you mean yer can't play this date? He's witcha only he ain't? Gee, yer billed here—yer gotta play it. Whatsa matter wit' Carl?

FRITZ: Oh, he hast gefallen und busted by der collar-button—der wertabress.

STANLEY: What's he mean?

HERMANN: No choost dots it. I vired by der house manatcher, und den I didn't send dot vire. Ve came ofer tinkin' maype ve could vork a routine by Fritz und me—Ach, Gott, maype Stanley—No I guess not.

STANLEY (Anticipating HERMANN's thought): Gee, I was tinkin' de same thing.

FRITZ: Vot's dot?

STANLEY: Are you still as sure of your holds as you used to be?

HERMANN: Yah, yah, I'm sure of my holds—almost—only shlip vunce in a vile. Vy choost look, Carl hass peen vorkin' top on comedy shlip hold—You know vat he does Stan, you know you used to do dot. Und only two times I drop him in all dese years.

ARNOLD (To RANDALL): You really need three electricians to handle an act like this. Who handles the moon while I handle the olivettes?

RANDALL: You won't have to worry about that. The house man handles the switch. You're working in unison off two spider-boxes and the moon has a mechanical riser.

(He demonstrates what he means.)

(STEVE crosses to STANLEY and OTTO BROTHERS and addresses himself to HERMANN.)

STEVE: Are you the acrobats?

HERMANN: Yah, yah, Herr direktor—but vun partner iss—er—iss—er.

STEVE: Well, you close the bill.

STANLEY: Hey Steve. Wait a minute—let him explain.

FRITZ: Herr, direktor, choost vat Hermann mean, iss choost like diss—

HERMANN: Dot's not der vay it vas. Dot's not der vay it vas.

STANLEY: Let Hermann tell it. He knows more than the two of you.

HERMANN: You see it was choost like diss. Carl he vass up dere, und it was shloppy und shlippery, und it vas so varm—und—er—und—er.

STANLEY (Interrupts): He's trying to tell yer Steve dat yer got no tumblin' act. Unless they can get a routine put together for two people.

But if they do that, they got no comedy in the act. I know because I used to do the stuff that Carl was doin', back in the old circus days with the Robinson show.

STEVE: Stan, we can hardly get an act here to take their place now. *(To HERMANN.)*

Why didn't you let me know this?

HERMANN: Vy, vy—I made for you a telegram vire.

STEVE: I didn't get your wire.

HERMANN: I know dot. I didn't send dot vire. I come myself—choost because maype Fritz und me—somehow might be able to vork der date und—und—

STANLEY: Say, listen—have you any money? Hey, Steve, I'd like to help the boys out. I know all the stuff and with an hour's practice I can be up in it. I got everything set on stage and so rather than get a new act in time for tonight, I can help them out—and if you like it, all right—if you don't—it's up to you—What d'ya say?

HERMANN: Ach Gott, Stanley, you do dot for me? Choost like oldt time. You know dot, Stan. You vas better den Carl anyvay!

STEVE: If you think you can do it, Stan, and the props of all the other acts are taken care of, it'll be all right with me, but I hope you don't break your foolish neck.

STANLEY: There's nothin' to it, Steve, it's an easy pipe for this baby—

HERMANN: Yah, yah, dot vas chust like off der log fallin' for Schtan.

FRITZ: He's good.

STEVE: I hope his falling will be no harder than that. *(Turns away then back to STANLEY.)*

Say, Stan, who is this fellow Arnold, the electrician on the dancing act? He acts strange. Do you know him?

STANLEY: Sure I know him—he's a pal of mine. He's a crossword puzzle to most of the bunch at the Union. You see, he don't say much. Seems to have something on his mind all the time. He comes from Boulder Creek—worked at nearly all the theatres in these parts, but won't take a steady job in any of them. He went to college and is an electrical engineer. He knows his stuff, Steve, and minds his own business. This is the first time we pulled him off the list—The Orpheum gets him every couple of weeks.

(ARNOLD getting cables and lamps in position for light rehearsals. DOLORES and the GIRLS dressed for rehearsal enter. RANDALL crosses to LEADER. Gives instruction on music tempo. OTTO BROTHERS and STANLEY talk in dumb show. RANDALL turns to girls.)

RANDALL: Ready Dolores—Ready girls—come on snap into it— Position—Right from the beginning.

(Signals LEADER. Dance starts, continues with occasional directions from RANDALL.)

CURTAIN

ACT TWO

SCENE ONE

(Double-deck dressing rooms and corridor leading to the stage.

At rise of curtain, TERRILL discovered in his dressing room partly made up and rehearsing a song number before a mirror. To his entire satisfaction, he has a dauber in his one hand retouching his makeup during rehearsal. The other dressing rooms are unoccupied and dark.

Applause and music heard off stage.

Enter through corridor from stage, four BOYS, in female attire. They are sent to their dressing rooms, an ad lib running conversation being carried on as they go up steps.)

BUNNY: Peaches dear, did you see that glorious Adonis directing traffic at Broad and Main Street?

PEACHES: Do you mean the one on the horse, dearie? You know that's the statue of some General.

BUNNY: Oh, perhaps it's General Coxey. They would direct anything around here dearie.

(Enter from dressing room, CHUCK and JOE.)

JOE: What a mess you made of that step, you dumbbell. Here's the way it goes.

(THEY rehearse the dance step.)

CHUCK: That fool step is too intrik-kate—

JOE *(Abruptly stopping):* You tumbled all over it dis show—Boy, what a time I'm having making your feet and your brain work together.

CHUCK: I don't wanta use me brain when I use me feet. Besides dat, I'm tired.

(Stops abruptly in his dancing.)

Dis step tires me too much.

JOE: If you would cut out runnin' around with the janes on the bill, a little dance step wouldn't make you tired.

CHUCK: Why, yer told me that before and I'm gettin' tired of you tellin' me who I can go wit'.

(As JOE exits to his dressing room, CHUCK pauses at bottom of steps.)

(STANLEY enters from upstairs, comes down steps.)

STANLEY: Hello, Chuck.

CHUCK: Did yer ketch the show, Stan? What did yer think of it?

STANLEY: All right. Great.

(Continues walking back stage.)

CHUCK *(Calls him)*: Say, Stan, have you noticed dis partner of mine?

STANLEY: Yeah—what about him?

CHUCK: That's just it—I don't get him—can't figger him out.

STANLEY: What's strange about him?

CHUCK: Dat's what I been tryin' to find out. Yer see, I only teamed up wit' him two weeks ago. My old partner was bumped off in a auto wreck. So I gets this bird. Well, he's been actin' funny from the start. He don't seem reg'lar to me. I'm beginnin' to be suspicious.

STANLEY: Well, if you're suspicious of him, he must do something odd.

CHUCK: He does. The first week he was wit' me every thing was ok, but the second week in his spare time, I found out he makes lampshades. Now that ain't right. I wouldn't mind if he got drunk or shot crap in his spare time—but makin' lampshades—phooey—that's all wet. Here he is now,—look him over—

(Enter JOE.)

STANLEY *(Looking him up and down)*: I guess you're right. Whoops!

(JOE turns quickly around.)

I knew that'd get him.

JOE: Did you call me?

STANLEY: Yeah—I understand you make lovely lampshades?

JOE: Yes—want to buy one?

STANLEY: I'm quite interested.

JOE: I've got a dozen of them finished—in all the latest colors.

STANLEY: I'll get one for my boudoir.

JOE: Lovely—I'll bring some down tomorrow, and you can take your choice. Mr. Stanley's your name, isn't it? *(Exits.)*

STANLEY *(To CHUCK):* He's all right—nearly. There's no harm in lampshades. He's just an aesthetic type.

CHUCK: Oh, yeah?—well maybe I was wrong about him. If he's as you say, just an elastic type, why I guess I'll have to overlook his funny actions.—But even so, I'm gonna keep my eye on him.

STANLEY: Yeah, you better watch him.

(During the last speech DOLORES and RANDALL enter their dressing room, switching on lights as they enter.)

RANDALL: Well, I'm sorry, but that's the way I feel about it, nevertheless.

DOLORES: If you don't stop picking on me because I talked to Terrill last show, you and I are going to have a battle. I'm tired of being bullied all the time.

RANDALL: Well, I'm not going to allow my wife to be so damn loose that she becomes the subject of questionable ridicule among stage hands and the other actors on the bill.

DOLORES: Your insane jealousy runs away with you. I'm only trying to be courteous and congenial with other people on the bill. And since you're picking on me about this monologue artist, I'm going to tell you this. I'm getting tired of the manner in which you maul Flo— and the numerous rehearsals you think you must have with her to perfect her dancing. Do you think that I'm such a fool I can't see it's only for the purpose of having her body close to yours in all its blonde nakedness? And the tenderness with which you caress her and pull her about . . .

RANDALL *(Interrupts her angrily):* Now stop that right where you are! Don't try to cover up a guilty conscience with some pretended show of jealousy on your part. Let me tell you something, if you don't want the beauty of this male milliner, Terrill, mussed up, don't let me catch you talking to him again.

(During above conversation DOLORES and RANDALL are beginning their disrobing and laying out their make-up. TERRILL has crossed and been lis-

tening at the door. The HOOFERS have been dancing and stopping intermittently to correct some dance steps. At the conclusion of RANDALL's speech, there is a knock at the door. He opens it and discovers ARNOLD, the electrician.)

ARNOLD: Mr. Randall, will you come out and give me the change in lighting instructions? Your man hasn't shown up.

(RANDALL exits with ARNOLD. TERRILL listens as he hears the door close, gets note from dressing table, hurries to door and slips the note under it. DOLORES jumps up, goes to door, gets note and reads it. During this business:)

BUNNY *(Speaks on raps):* Peaches, sweetheart, I think you're cheating on me.

PEACHES: Oh, don't be such a moll. How could I cheat on you?

BUNNY: Who burned the cigarette hole in your costume?

PEACHES *(While PEACHES speaks, DOLORES' and RANDALL's GIRLS enter. CHUCK stops FLO):* Oh, damn it—after I pricked my fingers a thousand times in making the beautiful thing. Men are such uncouth things. It must have been that hoofer.

BUNNY: What were you doing with a hoofer? I thought you promised no mixing on the bill. You're going to get in a hell of a jam some day.

CHUCK: Say kid, will you go to dinner with me?

FLO: You better save it. You'll need it tomorrow.

(Goes up stairs with BOBBY.)

CHUCK: Gee, you're a thoughtful kid. You look good to me—you look like a million dollars.

FLO *(Stops on balcony, looks over):* Yes—and just as hard to make.

PEACHES: O, I must tell you about it!

(Simultaneous with this conversation the GIRLS in DOLORES' and RANDALL's act come in three and then two— the hoofers try to flirt with the first three as they start upstairs to dressing room. The other two tarry a while with the hoofers, chat and giggle and then proceed up stairs and enter dressing room. DOLORES has finished reading her note for the third time, while she has disrobed and put on her makeup kimono. She kisses note and hides it

among her effects. TERRILL goes to door and taps signal and DOLORES answers with two taps. Following the two taps, TERRILL and DOLORES throw kiss to each other through the door. TERRILL continues throwing kisses until OTTO and STANLEY enter room—THEY pause inside, look at TERRILL.)

STANLEY: A blockhead throwin' kisses to a wood-pile.

OTTO *(Grunts and says):* Verrückt!

(Starts taking things off at dressing table.)

TERRILL *(Turns haughtily upon two intruders):* Of course you wouldn't understand, being so subnormally developed. I was just taking my last bow and throwing my salutations to my audience—a thing which must be very carefully rehearsed. I am an artist, and every move I make must be gauged for its psychological effect . . . That's the reason I'm topping the bill here . . .

STANLEY

(Gives him razzberry with mouth noise—as he starts to disrobe.)

(TERRILL has turned admiringly to his looking-glass as he finishes his speech. He turns suddenly on STANLEY.)

TERRILL: A person of your mentality would do a thing like that. That's one of the reasons you're a dumb act.

OTTO: I'll tank you nod to insinuation—Mr. Ter-er-Ter-er . . .

STANLEY: Mr. Terrible . . .

TERRILL *(Reaching into pocket—produces card, hands it to OTTO):* My card.

OTTO *(OTTO looks at card):* Ach! Bad luck. Diss iss ace of spades. Himmel, somebody die maype, no?

(As TERRILL exchanges card for one of his name cards.)

STANLEY: Yes, he's a lady-killer—

TERRILL: My real card—the jack of hearts.

(During conversation TERRILL turns to and from his mirror putting on finishing touches. The GIRLS are making up. One is stretching with her leg on make-up table. FLO persistently whistles snatches of song while making up, to the annoyance of the other GIRLS— The BOYS have been laughing and

talking in dumb-show while donning their male attire and putting on street make-up. The HOOFERS have been in and out of their dressing room—Backstage across the corridor, stagehands have been passing to and fro.)

BOBBY *(Complains of whistling. Stops in stretching exercise—to FLO):* Say, listen, Flo, cut that whistling. I've got all the hard luck I want.

FLO: The hardest luck you ever had is—you lost Rodney—and I got the dinner.

JEWEL: You'll both have harder luck if this act closes.

FLO: Well, what's the matter with the act?

BOBBY: Let it close. I found a sugar-daddy in town.

JANE: Yeah—but sugar-daddies turn sour if you're out of work.

JEWEL: You know, kid, you're only an attraction as long as you're behind the footlights, and they think they got something the other guy can't have. But then they throw you over—

JANE: And believe me, kid, they always do—the sudden stop makes you write home to mother.

(During scene with GIRLS in dressing-room, TERRILL sees FRITZ in underwear and gives look of disgust.)

STANLEY: This is going to be a tought week on you.

(Just before this line, FRITZ shakes out his trousers violently.)

FLO: Tell us what's the matter with the act.

JEWEL: Oh, the act's all right, but some day there's goin' to be a split between Dolores and Randall and that split ain't far off.

FLO: Just what d'you mean by that crack?

BOBBY: Ha, ha! You might've got the dinner, but the demi-tasse is gonna be damn bitter, kid.

FLO: You're talkin' like a pair of nuts. I can't see anything wrong.

(NIKKO sprays room with atomizer.)

STANLEY: What the hell is this?—Do you think we are insects?

JANE: You're playin' one of the hoofers against Rodney—and you're too busy playin' love-checkers to see what's happen' in the act.

JEWEL: If you weren't so dumb you'd see that Terrill's making a play for Dolores and she's falling for it like a sap—

JANE: Not only that, but Randall's getting wise to it, too—

JEWEL: —so get ready for the blow-up. When a jane falls for a ham like that, anything can happen.

FLO: Well, let it happen. I been understudying her dance for a long time.

(GIRLS all laugh at her remark and kid her. Enter PARADISE. EDGAR to him at bottom of steps.)

EDGAR: Paradise, will you settle an argument for me? My wife says your gown was made by so and so—and I says it was made by what's his name.

PARADISE *(Pretends to ignore the remark.)*

TERRILL *(Turning from mirror as he finishes making up):* Look and behold why girls leave home—

FRITZ: What again?

STANLEY: Mr. Terrill—will you do me a favor?

TERRILL: Anything within reason—

STANLEY: How, how do you get these women? What's the attraction, that's what I want to know!

TERRILL: It is charm, poise, personality, Capital IT—it.

FRITZ: What is it—this it?

TERRILL: Well, it isn't a handspring, so probably you wouldn't understand it. It's a gift—it can't be acquired. It is my magnetic attraction—all the women fall for me, I can't keep them away. It is embarrassing at times.

STANLEY: Don't you ever get tired out?

TERRILL: Occasionally, I do get a bit fatigued.

STANLEY: Did you ever try Lydia Pinkham?

TERRILL: I never played the town she lives in.

STANLEY: You remind me of one of her pills.

TERRILL: Meaning not hard to take.

STANLEY: But take two of them and see what happens—

(PARADISE talking at EDGAR's door. STANLEY noting this. DOLORES has written her note and hides it as RANDALL enters.)

RANDALL: Just look at this light plot. I can't make it out myself. No wonder that Arnold can't understand it. I'm going to keep him and let that four-flushing relative of yours go. And I'm tired of having jams with the Union.

DOLORES: If he won't do, just let him go—it can't be helped. But don't let it excite you and upset you because it will interfere with your performance.

RANDALL *(Crossing to her):* Oh, I'm awfully glad you take it that way, sweetheart. I like Bill, but he's been doing an awful lot of fumbling with our lights. And this week above all, we can't muff any part of it. Because Thompson, the Orpheum's West Coast Manager, wired he'd catch the act this week. We might get forty weeks out of it.

DOLORES: You dear, big boy—always fretting and worrying. Put Arnold on and between us, we'll see that the girls do their best.

RANDALL *(Taking her in his arms):* You wonderful pal—Oh, Dolores, if anything should come between us, I don't know what would happen to me.

DOLORES: Then please don't be so jealous. You don't trust me—do you?

RANDALL: It isn't that—it's that I know—

(ARNOLD knocks at door, enters.)

ARNOLD: I've got to run down-town and get some gelatins.

(Exits, after getting money from Randall. LESTER QUEEN and TOTO enter from left. ARNOLD exits to street.)

RANDALL *(Crossing down to DOLORES):* I must rearrange everything for the next show—so I will get made up first.

(STANLEY enters singing—LESTER QUEEN stops him.)

LESTER *(Handing card to STANLEY):* Would you mind giving this card to the Bird of Paradise. Why, Stan, you remember me? Lester Queen?

STANLEY: Oh, yes, what are you doing in town?

LESTER: Laying off as usual—but it won't be for long.

STANLEY: I'll say, "Queenie is calling."

LESTER: Yes,—Don't forget, from London, Paris and New York.

(Walks to dressing room door. One of the OTTO BROTHERS puts his head out door.)

Oh, my God!

(Walks away.)

STANLEY: Paradise—your lost Queen's here—

(Enter PARADISE.)

LESTER: Hello, Paradise, you're looking wonderful—your act's marvelous.

PARADISE: And I feel lousy.

LESTER *(Does back kick):* Well, the real reason I came here—Toto is throwing a grand costume party tonight—and I want the crowd to come over. Say, where's that heavy lover on the bill? That big boudoir man—

PARADISE: Oh, you mean Terrill? You're going to invite that cluck?

LESTER: Why not? I think he has an ear for music!

PARADISE: Well, he's off key to me.

(LESTER QUEEN stands with PARADISE and TOTO PARADISE tells LESTER that TERRILL is in dressing room One with OTTO BROTHERS.)

LESTER: The acrobats? I just love—acrobatics.

(Enters TERRILL's dressing room and greets him.)

What a terribly gorgeous robe you have.

TERRILL: Yes, it's just a little thing I picked up in Paris.

LESTER: With what else?

TERRILL: No, I wasn't thinking of women that day.

LESTER: Oh, by the way, would you mind coming to a very smart party tonight given by a very brilliant person in town—by Toto? You remember, Toto use to do a dog act.

TERRILL: Yes, I remember—a canine act.

LESTER: Can we count on you?

TERRILL: Well, I always have a lot of engagements after the show. Tonight a very prominent society woman in town is giving a very exclusive party for me, so I'm afraid—

LESTER: But we will be very disappointed. Almost everyone on the bill is coming—the Bird of Paradise, the boys, Mr. and Mrs. Randall,

(Turns towards STANLEY) Stanley, the acrobats . . . *(To STANLEY):* You're coming over, aren't you?

STANLEY: Try to keep us away.

LESTER *(To TERRILL)*: Oh, you will come, won't you?

TERRILL: Well, I'll tell you, old boy, I don't think the party I'm going to will keep me very late. Perhaps I'll run over.

LESTER: Then, I can count on you, and you, and you—

(As he strokes the OTTO BROTHERS' heads.)

Lovely—

(Leaves dressing room and crosses to PARADISE.)

We'll have the cars over here at 11 o'clock.

(Exit, LESTER, TOTO and PARADISE, ad libbing. TED ARNOLD enters, carrying gelatins, crosses to TERRILL's dressing room, knocks and enters. TERRILL has just finished retelling an exploit to STANLEY and the OTTO BROTHERS. He has set out on his dressing table a number of photographs of women. ARNOLD addresses STANLEY.)

STANLEY: Come on in. Hello, Ted.

TERRILL: Whose dressing room is this, Stan? Ours?

ARNOLD: Say, Stan, do you know if there is anything up in the prop room that would look well in that new number Randall is trying out tonight?

STANLEY *(Scratches head):* I'll take a look after I get made up and let you know.

TERRILL: The only thing that's needed to make Randall's new number a success, is me. But of course, I have no idea of helping him out.

ARNOLD *(Looking up sharply at TERRILL, and then permitting his gaze to travel around the room, spies the photographs):* You've got quite a collection of beautiful girls, Mr. Terrill.

(Moves over to take a better look at them.)

TERRILL: Yes—some of them are pretty good—in fact more of them are bad. I pride myself on my good taste in women.

ARNOLD *(Picks up a photo and glances quickly at TERRILL):* Do you mind?—Here's a pretty girl. Who is she? Is she an actress?

(Keeps his eyes fastened on TERRILL's face. TERRILL takes the photo, looks at it.)

TERRILL: Let me see? I just don't recall . . . Oh, yes—now I have it. She's a jane that lives in this town. She fell for me like a shot bird. A fair number.

ARNOLD: Is that so?

TERRILL: Sure—But they're all easy for me. You see, it's all in the method.

ARNOLD: Don't you ever fall in love?

TERRILL: Of course I do, but only for a week or so at a time. Otherwise I would never be able to cover all the available territory—you know what I mean.

STANLEY: He's just a pleasure man.

TERRILL: Yes, I give them pleasure on and off.

ARNOLD: Oh, I see!

STANLEY: It's all in fun with him.

ARNOLD: I see.

(Turns to STANLEY.)

Stan, will you do that for me?

STANLEY: You bet.

(ARNOLD with a backward glance at TERRILL, exits into corridor where STEVE greets him and asks him about an electrical effect for the DOLORES and RANDALL act.)

ARNOLD *(As he exits):* You won't forget?

STANLEY: I won't forget.

(STEVE comes on from stage to end of corridor with TED ARNOLD.)

STEVE: I'm trying to dope out something to improve the setting of that dancing act. They need original lighting in that woodland nymph number. What can you suggest? We should have something around here to give color to that setting. I think we have some stuff in number four that you could rig up into a new effect. Look it over and see what you can do.

ARNOLD: All right. I've got an idea. I'll see how it'll work out.

(ARNOLD hurries up steps, turns right, at top. As he does so, STEVE calls.)

STEVE: Hey, Brad!

(GRIP comes on.)

Get that straightened out there.

(Indicates pile of material in corridor.)

Somebody'll break their neck on it.

RANDALL: Dolores, I want to speak to Mr. McAllister. I will be back in a moment. *(Exits.)*

STEVE: I wish you fellows would be a little careful around here.

(STANLEY who is making up, hears STEVE's voice.)

STANLEY: Anything wrong, Steve?

STEVE: No. Just getting this stuff off here, Stan.

(STANLEY spreading make-up on his face, crosses to him.)

Well, feel a little nervous getting back into harness again?

STANLEY: Oh, I'll be all right.

STEVE: Good luck—knock them cold.

STANLEY: That's what I'd like to do to everybody in the theatre.

(Exits to dressing room. Enter MARY ANN from left.)

MARY ANN *(To Steve):* Would it be possible to see Mr. Terrill?

(CALL BOY enters.)

CALL BOY: Mr. Randall would like to see you on the stage, Mr. McAllister.

STEVE: Tell Mr. Terrill, a young lady to see him.

(Exit.)

CALL BOY *(Knocks on TERRILL's door and opens it):* First call Mr. Terrill— Mr. Terrill, there is a young lady to see you. *(Closes door.)*

(To MARY ANN): He will see you in just a minute.

TERRILL: The line forms at the left. *(Exits.)*

STANLEY: Just a pleasure man.

(STANLEY goes to get shoes as DOLORES slips her note to TERRILL under door. STANLEY picks it up. Ad lib business.)

TERRILL: Hello, dearie.

MARY ANN: I knew you were here and I just had to come.

TERRILL: Why yes, I remember you—Mary Ann—Glad to see you. Why how have you been? Did you get my letters?

MARY ANN: No. No. You mean you sent me a letter—O—O—

TERRILL: Yes, what's the matter?

MARY ANN: Then you didn't forget! You meant what you told me! You do care?

TERRILL: Of course, I care—dearie. Of course I care. *(He kisses her on the cheek.)* Why, you're nervous, you're trembling.

MARY ANN: I haven't slept for days, weeks, months, thinking about you—wishing, hoping, praying, that you'd come back. And today I learned you were here. O God! How can I tell you? It's just too terrible!

TERRILL: What is this? What's it all about?

MARY ANN: Are you going to keep your promise?

TERRILL: Promise? What promise?

MARY ANN: Don't you remember? You promised to marry me!

TERRILL: Marry you?

MARY ANN: You don't understand. You've got to now!

TERRILL: What are you trying to do—pull a fast one on me? Listen little lady, I'm too smart a guy to fall for anything like this. . . . And another thing, from now on you keep your trap shut about this.

MARY ANN: But Rod, you've got to—you've got to!

TERRILL: Marry you. Why, you're crazy!

(TERRILL thrusts her roughly from him. She strikes the railing of stairway, screams and falls in faint. PARADISE has entered during scene and screams.

He rushes to her as TERRILL hurriedly exits to stage. Enter from dressing room, OTTO BROTHERS and STANLEY. HOOFERS enter from dressing room left. ARNOLD appears at head of stairs, carrying some electrical apparatus. He pauses, sees confusion, and hurries downstairs, not knowing who the unconscious form is.)

PARADISE *(On knees, raising MARY ANN's head):* You poor kid, you had an awful fall.

(Looking up.) Does anybody know this girl?

ARNOLD *(Leaning over PARADISE's shoulder):* Good God! It's Mary Ann! What happened? Let's get her a place to lie down.

(To STANLEY.) Get some aromatic and a glass of water and bring it to number seven.

(They pick her up and carry her off stage. HOOFERS look at each other. PARADISE and OTTO BROTHERS follow ARNOLD down corridor toward stage.)

FLO *(Opens door into corridor, looks out, and turns back puzzled):* Gee, I thought I heard a woman scream. Did you girls hear it?

JEWEL: No, you heard them queens next door, campin'.

(At this point GRIP enters DOLORES' dressing room unceremoniously places MARY ANN on lounge. STANLEY enters right behind with water and aromatic and mixes her a dose. DOLORES places pillow under her head.)

DOLORES: Why, what happened to the poor kid?

PARADISE: She had an awful fall.—Like happens to all us poor girls.

(DOLORES gives PARADISE a scornful look.)

Oh, it's coming to you, dearie.

BLACKOUT

ACT TWO

SCENE TWO

*(Same as Scene One. At rise of curtain, we discover the PERFORMERS collect-
ed in the corridor and on the steps, leading to second tier dressing rooms.
While GROUP is discussing in dumb show, excitedly, OTTO comes from left
corridor, enters his dressing room, closes door, sits down and makes up.
DOLORES is rather hysterical and daubing her eyes. PARADISE is the center
of an interrogating group in the corridor through which STANLEY and
STEVE push their way downstage.)*

STANLEY: I tell yer Steve, I don't know anything about it, except I
heard a scream, and I found the girl flopped on the floor with this
queen hangin' over her. The hoofers they . . .

PARADISE: Say, just what do you mean by insinuating, that I . . . ?

STEVE: Now just wait a minute. Here, you girls, get back in your dressing rooms and if you fellers—

are going out, go; if not, get back in your dressing room.

(To the HOOFERS.): And the same goes fer you.

*(Excepting STANLEY and PARADISE, the others return reluctantly to dress-
ing rooms.)*

(To PARADISE): Did you see what happened to this young lady?

PARADISE: Well, it certainly was anything but what he says.

STEVE: That's not what I asked you. Did you see what happened?

PARADISE: Well, I didn't see everything that happened, but when I
came off stage after finishing my act, I nearly collided with Mr.
Terrill who was coming out of his dressing room, and proceeded on
about my business. I had to walk around the young lady who was
standing at the bottom of the steps as though undecided what she
was going to do. I went on up the steps. When I got half way up I
heard a terrible scream, which naturally frightened me. . . . And
looking down, I saw the poor girl in a faint on the floor. Oh, it was
horrible! She fell just as if somebody had hit her. I rushes down, seeing a sister in distress and almost ruined my gown stooping down
and raising the poor dear's head. Of course at that point, this bimbo
and those hoofers came running out of their dressing rooms.
Naturally they saw me bending over her. I'm not heartless, you
know. I have feelings.

STEVE *(Advances to HOOFERS' door and knocks. HOOFERS come to door and he calls them outside—during preceding dialogue, the GIRLS have been listening at the doors of their respective dressing rooms, sneaking down corridor and looking over edge of balcony and ducking back again, and otherwise indicating their curiosity by their gestures.)*

BUNNY: Oh, Peaches, don't be so curious.

(STEVE knocks at door.)

Come in and sit down. When Paradise comes up you know very well she'll tell us all she knows, because she's not able to keep anything to herself. She's such an awful gab.

STEVE *(To HOOFERS):* Did you hear any noise in the corridor here, before the scream?

HOOFERS *(Together):* No.

STEVE: Well, if anybody fell down those steps, you'd be able to hear it in your dressing room, wouldn't you?

JOE: Gee, I'll say we would. We hear everything that goes up and down them.

STANLEY: Hey, Steve, I got to get in and get made-up. That's all you want of me, ain't it?

STEVE: That's all, Stan.

(STANLEY advances to dressing room as CALL BOY comes to STEVE.)

CALL BOY: Ted wants you on the phone, Mr. McAllister.

(As STEVE abruptly turns and hurries offstage, hoofers shrug their shoulders and start into dressing room. TERRILL strolls nonchalantly on from stage. PARADISE confronts him. THEY glare at each other. RANDALL who has been consoling and petting Dolores, after having finished his make-up, answers the door as ARNOLD knocks and is seen standing outside door with gelatins in his hand.)

BRADLEY: Mr. Randall, some gelatins have just come for you.

RANDALL: I'll be right with you.

(Turns to DOLORES.)

Sweetheart, lie down and take a little rest. We have three-quarters of an hour, yet. And I'll be busy with Arnold that long. Bill hasn't shown up at all. *(He embraces her affectionately and exits.)*

PARADISE: Say you—*(Crosses to Terrill.)*

At last I've got you just where I want you. I always knew you were a rotter.

TERRILL: I suppose you told everything you think you know. *(Contemptuous smile.)*

You don't think they'd believe you in preference to me.

PARADISE: Oh, they'll believe me all right, in preference to you. I've taken care of that.

TERRILL: What are you trying to do? Blackmail me?

PARADISE: Now don't call names and don't try to scare me, for I don't care—What I know, I know, and that's that.

TERRILL: Well, let me tell you this—If I hear you have told anything I'll beat your head off!

PARADISE: No, you won't beat my head off because I've got it on you and if I open my mouth—why you haven't got guts enough to hit anything but a poor, little, weak woman. Only a dirty louse would do the vile thing I know you've done and if you're going to do any punching of my head, you better begin right now, but I know you're nothing but a false alarm. And if you're a man, thank God, I'm a female impersonator. Why, you yellow pup—you couldn't even lick a lollypop!

TERRILL: Just a little bitch.

(PARADISE continues to dressing room. TERRILL pulls himself together and hurriedly enters dressing room. In a braggadoccio manner he poses before OTTO and STANLEY.)

TERRILL: Boys, I tell you, it's a gift—I had that audience in the palm of my hand—they laughed and cried right with me.

STANLEY: You mean right at you.

TERRILL: You see, they don't get acts like mine in this house, often—with my ability and art, my style, my magnetism, my appearance. Why, you'd have thought those young flappers were going to jump up on the stage and kiss me.

OTTO: Yah, yah! Kiss you goot-pye!

TERRILL *(Taking a handful of mash notes from his pocket)*: And as for mash notes—Listen to this one. And this is only one of thousands I get. Why look, a handful—a handful—just given to me as I came off stage.

STANLEY: Yes—a handful of bologny!

TERRILL *(Reading letter as though he hadn't been interrupted):* Listen and learn, "Adorable Man . . . I have been entranced and thrilled by the grandeur of your personality, poise and magnetism. For such a man the greatest sacrifice would be too small a price. You seem to be the affinity of my soul—my dream man"—The balance is too personal . . . I'll read this one . . .

STANLEY: I don't want to hear any of 'em. I know 'em by heart. I found one on de floor and stuck it in your mirror.

(TERRILL goes to his mirror and reads note.)

PARADISE *(Who has been relating in dumb show the details of business downstairs):* Yes, and I just laid him out stinkin', the shopworn mess. I can't see what a girl can see in a pushover like that. I felt like smacking his face. It takes me a long time to get started, but when I do, I fly higher than Lindbergh ever dared to, and I haven't got a plane either. If I'd have stayed one minute longer, it would have taken him at least two weeks to dig the heels of my slippers out of his anatomy. The only thing he hasn't made is one of the lions in front of the public library.

BUNNY: Oh, Paradise, sweetheart, don't be so upset, you won't be worth a thing for Toto's party.

MAYBELLE: I wish those Molls next door would cut out that bragging. I don't know how you girls feel, but I feel all upset with that woman screaming and the excitement around here.

JANE: Oh, do you feel that way too? Gee, it makes me think of home. There was always somebody screamin' in our house.

JEWEL: Just 'tend to your knittin' kids, and be thankful it wasn't some one in our act doin' the screamin'.

FLO: Oh, Jewel, you make me tired, they ought to call you Calamity Jane, you're always carryin' a wet blanket around with you.

(TERRILL, after reading over his note a couple of times, turns to STANLEY.)

TERRILL: What do you mean by reading my note?

STANLEY: I didn't know it was your note. I only guessed that. It had no name on it. And when I read it, it was addressed to my beloved Adanoids—an' I knew it wasn't for me 'cause I had mine cut out.

TERRILL: You're with the right thing—a dumb act. It's addressed to my "beloved Adonis"—Adonis was a Greek god . . .

STANLEY: Gee, I thought it was for you, 'cause you remind me of a grease-ball. And when I got down to the second line and it says: "the glorious thrill you gave me, in our long, lingering kiss" . . . Den I knew it wasn't fer me. . . . So I just stuck it on your mirror. I didn't know which one of your flames it come from.

TERRILL: Did you say you found it . . . or some one give it to you. How did you get it?

(HOOFERS join MAYBELLE and JANE on Balcony. Dance steps.)

STANLEY: Oh, it was slid in under that door. Somebody was behind it pushin' it. Maybe it was the old man Randall, I don't know.

TERRILL: Oh, don't be ridiculous. I know who it is. It's Flo. I have so many of them. All the girls in that act are crazy about me. Flo must have been with Dolores and sneaked this in under the door.

OTTO *(To TERRILL)*: Ach, you talk girls—piffle, piffle, piffle!

(To STANLEY.)

You want ve should rehoise dat last part again? Perfect makes practice. No?

(Opens door, looks out in corridor.)

Dere iss room oudt here—plendy!

(STANLEY and OTTO exit into corridor. As they do, TERRILL closes door, goes to door between rooms and listens, taps signal. DOLORES who switches off her light and stretches herself out for a rest on her couch. TERRILL leaves his room, watches rehearsal of OTTO and STANLEY for a moment or two and then exits into corridor leading to stage.)

PARADISE: I tell you, boys, I don't know anymore than I've already told you, but I have a sneaking suspicion that Terrill has had something to do with some sort of a past that poor girl had suffered.

BUNNY: But, Paradise, weren't you able to find out who the girl is?

PARADISE: No, and down here it may be God's country, but I'm taking no chances on getting my hips in a sling by asking questions. I'll get the dirt from Toto, but what I hear I'll keep to myself, because I'm not going to get mixed up in any scandal.

(TERRILL enters DOLORES' dressing room quickly, gives quick sign of caution to DOLORES—a furtive glance out the door up and down corridor—closes door, comes to DOLORES, embraces her, passionate kiss.)

TERRILL: Your note thrilled me so, sweetheart, I just had to come.

DOLORES: But he may come back any minute.

TERRILL: No. He's busy with the new electrician, he won't come back. You're secondary to him, you know that. His act comes first and then you. But you're everything to me—first, last and always. Ever since the first time I laid eyes on you, I've been mad about you. All I could do was eat, drink, sleep, think nothing but you.

DOLORES: Oh, you're wonderful, marvelous—

TERRILL: I love you, I need you, I want you.

DOLORES: But not here, not now—I'll try and see you tonight after the show.

(RANDALL enters, unseen by DOLORES and TERRILL.)

But please go—now.

TERRILL: I can't, I can't—To hold you in my arms, to kiss you, love you, to have you—oh, my marvelous, glorious—

(Wrapped in each other's arms.)

DOLORES: You must go, you have gone crazy, and think nothing of my safety or of your own. Tom would kill you if he found you here. Go, I tell you. Go, for God's sake go.

(As they struggle during her pleading with him to go, RANDALL petrified by what he looks upon. DOLORES sees him, screams and swoons. TERRILL looks quickly as RANDALL advances.)

RANDALL: You dirty, sneaking skunk—

(RANDALL plants a blow on TERRILL's jaw. THEY fight. RANDALL beats TERRILL and knocks him through the door between the dressing rooms. They fight until they are separated by STANLEY. OTTO and STEVE rush on and drag the two of them out into the corridor, where the GIRLS and PARADISE are looking on from the stairs and the balcony. RANDALL tries to tear himself loose, shouting.)

You rotten, lousy bastard—I'll kill you as soon as I lay my hands on you—You goddamn son of a bitch!

QUICK CURTAIN

ACT THREE

SCENE ONE

(The drawing room of TOTO's apartment. At rise of curtain, all the guests are dancing to a jazz orchestra. At the conclusion of the first number several new arrivals are announced by the master of affairs. As each enters, a few bars of music are played.)

FIRST BOY: I hear you're working in a millinery shop.

SECOND BOY: Yes, I trim rough sailors.

THIRD BOY: My, what a low-cut gown you've got!

FOURTH BOY: Why, Beulah, a woman with a back like mine can be as low as she wants to be.

FIRST BOY: I hear you're studying to be an opera singer.

THIRD BOY: Oh, Yes, and I knows so many songs.

FIRST BOY: You must have a large repertoire.

THIRD BOY: Must I have that, too?

FOURTH BOY: Oh, look, I can almost do the split.

SECOND BOY: Be careful, dearie, you'll wear out your welcome.

FIRST BOY: I've had so many operations since I last saw you, I've been cut up, so, I look like a slot machine.

FOURTH BOY: That's nothing, I have a gash from here to here. *(Illustrates.)*

STANLEY *(Looking about):* Hello fellers! Hello boys! Say, what a party this is—band and everything—some party!

CHUCK *(Looking the place over. To STANLEY):* Oh boy! What a swell dump this is!

STANLEY *(Crossing to CHUCK):* Don't be calling this joint a dump!

(All guests laugh and ad lib.)

BILL *(Crossing from LESTER to STANLEY):* Dey oughten't ter have unions in this town. Dis is a capitalist joint. *(Smelling the air.)*

I smell whiskey.

(Howls from guests.)

STANLEY: Yeah, you've got a great nose for whiskey. It took more than just smelling it to put that shade of henna on your beezer. *(Laughter.)*

TOTO *(Coming toward the three of them):* I'm so glad you came—I'm so glad you came.

BILL *(Turning to TOTO):* Say, what kind of a party is dis? Where's the giggle water?

TOTO *(Assuringly):* Just rest your hips a moment. You'll get yours.

(LESTER takes the arm of CHUCK and BILL and leads them toward the table with punch bowl. The noise of the guests increases as they mill about. TOTO and STANLEY chat. Enter TERRILL and DOLORES, laughing as though at some very funny story. They pause just inside of the door, still laughing. STANLEY seeing them, shouts in a kidding manner.)

STANLEY: Oh, the Pleasure Man is here—

(DOLORES turns toward him. TERRILL looks him over smilingly.)

DOLORES: Good evening, Stan.

STANLEY: Oh, hello, Miss Dolores. Where is your husband?

TERRILL *(Condescendingly, crossing to STANLEY):* Well, how is the Beau Brummell tonight?

STANLEY *(Imitating TERRILL's manner):* Oh, everything's very Algonquin, very Algonquin. In fact it is quite the bologny. You are here ahead of me. I'd have got here sooner, but I stopped to see Ted Arnold. He's the new man on the lights of the dancing act—his sister is pretty sick—poor kid—nice kid too. I tried to bring Ted with me, but he wouldn't leave his sister alone.

TERRILL *(Taking cigarette from case, looking at STANLEY searchingly as he lights):* Awfully sorry about his sister. I've heard she's a nice little thing.

(Abruptly turning to DOLORES): Will you have a highball, Dolores?

(Crosses to her and takes her arm.)

DOLORES *(Upset at STANLEY's remark):* No, I don't think—

TERRILL *(Coaxingly):* Oh, come on, join the spirit of the festivities, Dolores.

DOLORES (*Smiling half-heartedly, as TERRILL leads her toward punch bowl*): Perhaps I will. I feel that I need something. I really don't feel well at all.

TERRILL (*As they cross*): Oh, come on, Dolores. You just imagine it.

STANLEY (*Turning toward them*): Imagine it? Say, can't a lady feel sick if she wants to?

CHUCK (*Taking from pocket a bottle of gin*): Where shall I put this gin? (*Guests all laugh and ad lib.*)

BILL (*Leaving crowd at table—half lit—Crosses to STANLEY unsteadily*): A few more o' dem mint tulips an' I won't care for no unions.

(*Taking STANLEY by the elbow.*)

C'mon, lemme squirt you a glassful.

(*They cross to table. Ad lib from guests.*)

STANLEY (*Looking about room for OTTO BROTHERS*): Where's the Otto Brothers? Ain't they here yet? I guess they stopped off at Moe's to get their pants pressed.

LESTER (*Crossing to center downstage*): Why didn't they tell me? I would have pressed their pants gorgeously—and gladly—(*Laughter and ad lib.*)

(*Looking off as OTTO BROTHERS are heard off stage arguing in German.*)

The Otto Brothers have arrived.

(*Enter OTTO BROTHERS to the strains of music from the jazz band. OTTO BROTHERS come down, arguing in German about the address. STANLEY crosses to them and greets them heartily. TOTO crosses and greets them. FRITZ gesticulating, hits him in face. TOTO screams. Guests ad lib.*)

STANLEY: Hey, where have you been? We thought the tailor burned up your pants.

HERMANN: No—No—Ve vent by de wrong place—Fritz said dar number vas 102 und it was 201—

FRITZ: Dots not right—der number vas 201—you know dot—

HERMANN (*Pushing FRITZ*): Dat's not right—you vas wrong—dot's right.

FRITZ: I vas not wrong—dat's right—you vas wrong.

(Laughter from guests.)

STANLEY: Don't it say on the card?

HERMANN: On de card ve don't got.

FRITZ: Sure, it says on dat card.

STANLEY: Well?

HERMANN: But ve didn't got dat card mit us.

FRITZ: Ve left it in der mirror-glass by der dressing room.

STANLEY: Take your hats off—this ain't no coffee pot.

(Ad lib and laughter. TOTO comes to them again.)

FRITZ: Have you got any good beer?

TOTO: Oceans of it—Go right over there and give your tonsils a treat.

(FRITZ lifts hat with both hands and whoops. They cross with STANLEY to table. Band strikes up a number.)

LESTER: Who is feeling gay enough to start the show?

(Ad lib from all.)

(Music supplemented by ad lib remarks and general noise made by the guests.)

(Bell is heard ringing—Several of the guests run to door— They come back excited.)

PEACHES: It's Randall—He's drunk and he's looking for his wife— What shall I tell him? *(TERRILL and DOLORES exit.)*

PARADISE: Tell him she's not here—Do you want him to come in and make an arena out of this place?

LESTER: Oh, let him in. There'll be a grand fight—and all the gorgeous cops in town will be here.

PARADISE: Yes, you'd love that. The last time the wagon backed up you almost broke your legs slipping down the fire-escape.

(As Waltz strain dies, RANDALL enters slowly, obviously drunk and in savage mood. Dancing couples are gradually aware of his presence as he moves in to center and they fall away to each side and music stops.)

RANDALL: Where is she?

(No one answers.)

Where is she?

BUNNY: Your wife isn't here, Mr. Randall. *(Goes to him.)*

RANDALL: Don't tell me she isn't here—I know she is and I want her.

(Pushes BUNNY away.)

THE COBRA *(GUEST in drag)*: My God, isn't he rough!

RANDALL: My wife and Terrill left the theatre together and I have damn good reasons to believe they're here.

PARADISE: Why act like that, Mr. Randall? You may be mistaken about your wife—why not give her a chance? None of us are perfect . . . We all make mistakes, you know.

STANLEY *(Crossing to RANDALL, putting his arm around him while HER-MANN does likewise at his right):* That's right, Mr. Randall, you're all wrong—your wife isn't here.

RANDALL: Is that right, Stan?

STANLEY: Of course.

TOTO: Why, Mr. Randall, you ought to be ashamed of yourself break-ing into our party and frightening us all in this manner. It will take me three hours to relax—my heart is beating like a tom-tom.

STANLEY: Come on, Mr. Randall, we'll put you into a taxi—Maybe your wife is back at the hotel waiting for you now.

RANDALL: I'm sorry I interrupted your party—I apologize—I'll go but I'll get that rat—I'll get him—if it's the last thing I ever do.

(STANLEY, RANDALL and HERMANN exit, with RANDALL building up an "I'll get him" exit.)

CURTAIN

SCENE TWO

(The same. At rise of curtain, STANLEY, TOTO, DOLORES and RANDALL. PARADISE, STEVE, CHIEF of POLICE with two ASSISTANT OFFICERS in plain clothes all onstage.)

CHIEF: Mr. McAllister, the murdered man was a performer at your theatre, was he not?

STEVE: Yes—he was a headliner on the bill and frequently played this town.

CHIEF: Was Rodney Terrill a man who had enemies in this town?

STEVE: Sir, he had enemies in every town he every played in. I don't believe he had one true friend in this world.

CHIEF: I see. Now was there to your knowledge, any performer on your bill who was particularly hostile to Terrill?

STEVE: He was disliked by all of them, Chief, with the probably exception of some of the girls. He had a great deal of charm for the ladies, Chief.

CHIEF: Hmm. Was there any one person that you know of, who might have been glad to see him out of the way?

STEVE *(Hesitating):* Well—he attempted to assault a woman in her dressing room, and was discovered by her husband, who gave him a sound thrashing.

CHIEF: Ah—who was that woman?

(Looks around at those present, DOLORES shrinks back at her husband's side.)

STEVE: The lady present, Chief.

TOTO *(Cutting in):* Not me, Chief.

PARADISE: Nor I.

CHIEF *(Looking at them with scorn):* Now, Mr. McAllister, tell me—I've known of such cases before—Did the husband make any threats? They usually do.

STEVE *(Looking certainly at RANDALL who nods his head wearily):* Well, Mr. Randall, the lady's husband, in his rage, threatened to kill Terrill. But Chief, I've known Mr. Randall a long time—I—I'd personally stake my reputation on his innocence of any murderous act.

CHIEF: The hand of murder fits anyone, Mr. McAllister. We're all potential murderers—given a motive, the opportunity and the provocation of fear. *(Then to TOTO.)*

Say—you!

TOTO *(Jumps):* God—don't be so rough!

CHIEF: What was your idea in throwing this party?

TOTO: Well, Chief, I'll tell you—You see, I know most of the performers that play at Mr. McAllister's theatre. I used to be a performer myself. And a good one, too. Some say I still am. Now, I inherited quite a lot of money. So I like to spend it on my old friends in the profession when they come to town. Last night I invited the whole bill over for a gay time. I'm so lonesome here.

CHIEF: I know all that. But what about this man, Terrill? Did you invite him, when he was so disliked?

TOTO: Oh, he just floated over all night. He was in and out of this room. In fact everyone was in and out of every room in the house. The place is a mess. I didn't even see Terrill go upstairs. God knows I don't follow my guests around, although I know of some persons that do. I remember now that Terrill was around with Miss Dolores most of the time.

CHIEF: Oh, then she came here with Terrill?

TOTO: Really, I couldn't say. I didn't see them come in. I only know they were here.

CHIEF *(To DOLORES):* You came here with Terrill, didn't you?

DOLORES: Yes.

CHIEF: Where was your husband?

DOLORES: I left him at the theatre. He—well, we weren't on speaking terms.

CHIEF: So you came here with the man who tried to attack you? And after your husband had beaten him for it?

DOLORES: Mr. Terrill apologized to me. And he seemed so sincere that when he said he would like to be just a good friend—why I believed him. So I came here with him—Tom wouldn't forgive me—wouldn't talk to me. Oh, I didn't know what I was doing. I love Tom, but

Rodney—Mr. Terrill, was fascinating. He told me he loved me—and I—I foolishly, I know now, was thrilled at the thought of having made so charming a man care for me.

CHIEF: Your husband then was not at the party at all?

DOLORES: I didn't see him, but I was told he had come here looking for me. They were afraid he would start a fight if he knew I was here with Mr. Terrill, so they told him I was not at the party.

CHIEF: Did any of you here see and speak to Mr. Randall when he came in?

PARADISE: Oh, we all saw him. He was intoxicated, and he insisted that his wife was here. Finally we got him to go without searching the place.

CHIEF: What did Mr. Randall have to say?

PARADISE: Oh, he called Terrill a rat. And said that he'd get him. Of course he was drunk and didn't know what he was saying.

CHIEF: A jury will have to be the judge of that. Mr. Randall, where were you at the time of the murder, which was approximately 2:30 a.m.

RANDALL: I—I can't tell you.

CHIEF: You mean you won't?

RANDALL: No—I mean I don't know—I don't remember—I was terribly drunk. I just remember coming here to look for my wife. After I left here, I don't know where I went.

CHIEF: What were you doing in the garden, where my man discovered you?

RANDALL: I—I don't know. I can't think how I got there. As I just told you, after I left here I don't remember what happened to me. I must have wandered around—finally coming back here to look for my wife again, convinced that she was here. The next thing I knew, one of your men had seized me and brought me in. I must have just come to.

STANLEY: If Mr. Randall killed Terrill, it was no more than the rat deserved. Chief—Terrill was just a Pleasure Man—he used to brag that he was a Pleasure Man. At first I thought he was great—I wanted to be like him—making the dames fall for me. I even imitated him. I wanted to be a Pleasure Man too. But now, I see what a snake he was . . . Why didn't he leave good women alone. . . . There are Pleasure Women too. . . . Why didn't he pick out his own kind? Oh, Lord, from now on, I'm just going to be myself.

CHIEF: I don't suppose you ever studied surgery, Mr. Randall?

RANDALL *(Surprised):* Why no.

CHIEF: Mr. Randall, I place you under arrest on suspicion of murder of Rodney Terrill.

STEVE: But Chief—you have no proof—

CHIEF: Circumstantial evidence warrants the arrest.

DOLORES *(Throwing her arms around RANDALL):* Oh, Tom—you didn't—you couldn't—you couldn't—tell them you didn't!

RANDALL *(Wearily shaking his head):* I don't know . . . I don't know . . .

PARADISE *(Meaningfully):* I thought it wouldn't be long before that brute Terrill got his . . . striking down a woman like he did Ted Arnold's sister. I understand the poor girl is dying from the effects of it.

CHIEF: What's this? Who is Ted Arnold?

STANLEY: He's the electrician we called in to help out on Dolores' and Randall's act. I know the boy well. He's a fine fellow. I left him at his home looking after his sister, just before I came to the party.

CHIEF: Oh.

(Takes up some papers—calls one of his assistants.)

Here, take my report to the district attorney's office. *(Reads.)*

"Rodney Terrill, actor, was the victim of some person as yet unestablished. Death was due to an operation performed by someone who had a knowledge of surgery and who used instruments which were found, with some degree of surgical skill. Thomas Randall, actor, has been placed under arrest on suspicion, based on circumstantial evidence.

(The OFFICER takes the report from the CHIEF. STEVE and STANLEY exchange glances— DOLORES sobs quietly. OFFICER enters with TED ARNOLD.)

CHIEF: What's this?

OFFICER: Chief, —I think we've got our man. He surrendered himself. I brought him here for further information—

STEVE: Good God, Stan.

CHIEF: What's your name?

ARNOLD: Ted Arnold.

CHIEF: Tell us what you know.

ARNOLD *(As he is handcuffed):* I'm willing to tell everything . . . God! It'll help me to tell. To-night—what I did—that's only part of it. For the past two months this thing has been torturing me. Ever since I knew that my sister was used for some man's dirty sport. I didn't know who he was—until today. But this morning—from the moment I saw him—I knew. Then I saw my sister's picture in his dressing-room. And he spoke of her as if she were just one figure in the dirty parade that his life was. Then I found out that it was he who hurt her this afternoon—hurt her so that she may not live. And right from that—as tho' it were nothing—I knew that he was starting his filth with Randall's wife—It drove me mad—I was insane—but I didn't think he would die—I didn't want him to die. I did—what I did—because I wanted him to live—in pain—and in shame—and to know that he could never again use people for his rotten pleasure.

STEVE: But, my God, boy—You're not only a murderer! What you did was obscene!

ARNOLD: Obscene—obscene—Mr. McAllister—when I was in college—in the laboratory—we experimented with rats—with vermin—with poisonous things—we worked on them—so that they could never propagate their own kind—the life I took from that man Terrill—was no higher or better than that of a poisonous beast. Men can fight dirt with dirt, Mr. McAllister—and still fight for what's clean—I was crazed—or I couldn't have done it—but now I'm not insane—and I know what I did was right—and I'm glad—glad. . . . Take me away now, officer. I'm ready to go.

CURTAIN

MAE WEST SHOW RAIDED

(NEWS photo)

NEW RAID STOPS THEM! — Makeup, skirts and all, a couple of female impersonators flounce into patrol wagon at Biltmore theatre after yesterday's crowded matinee. Mae West's "Pleasure Man" was cut short by second police raid and the entire cast was taken for a ride to the police station. —*Story on page 3.*

The police raid on *The Pleasure Man* was even more sensational than the last act.

The Daily News

THE CASE
AGAINST MAE WEST

The Case for the Prosecution

Legal Documents Relating to *Sex* and *The Pleasure Man*

In 1873 the U.S. Post Office named Anthony Comstock a special agent. Over the course of his long career, Comstock claimed to have destroyed "sixteen tons of vampire literature," and convicted of obscenity "enough persons to fill a passenger train of sixty-one coaches." The English prosecuted Zola, Flaubert, de Maupassant. Anthony Comstock kept Americans safely ignorant of Balzac and Tolstoy.

Surprisingly, challenges to the laws concerning "decency" began to come from a small band of young American women. Margaret Anderson started *The Little Review* in Chicago and published Emma Goldman's essays on anarchism and "free love." She moved the review to Greenwich Village, and with Jane Heap, began to publish Joyce's *Ulysses*, episode by episode, from the first installment through the middle of the book when they were arrested. In 1920 they were tried, convicted and fined one hundred doolars for publishing literature considered obscene. From Paris, Sylvia Beach followed events closely. With a loan of $3000 from her mother in New Jersey, Beach had opened Shakespeare and Company in 1919, and with considerable daring, published *Ulysses* in 1922. The first printing sold out, and the great game of smuggling *Ulysses* from Paris into the U.S. and England began.

In the United States, the war against books was heating up. Theodore Dreiser's *American Tragedy,* published in December, 1925, was almost immediately banned in Boston. Donald Friede, Horace Liveright's partner, went to Boston to make a test case and got himself arrested for selling a copy. Clarence Darrow defended the author, but the jury brought in a guilty verdict and the defense lost its appeal to the State Supreme Court, which dismissed

Mae West at the trial for *The Pleasure Man* in 1928.   UPI/Corbis-Bettman
Charges against the play were dropped.

out of hand the "novel" argument that banning *American Tragedy* violated freedom of the press." "That contention . . . requires no discussion."*

If the suffragettes could go to jail for demanding the vote, if Margaret Anderson and Jane Heap could stand trial for defending their right to publish what they chose, Mae West could certainly join that small army of "obstreperous women" and defend her own plays.

The legal papers in this section come from the Municipal Archives of the City of New York. They are incomplete records of criminal prosecutions of *Sex* and *The Pleasure Man* in 1928 and 1930. The documents bear witness to the city's determination to end West's theatrical career, and her determination to defend herself in court. These papers have been lightly edited for consistency and clarity.

Sex opened at Daly's 63rd Street Theatre on April 26, 1926, and was raided on February 21, 1927, after 385 performances. The District Attorney argued that Sex *was obscene and endangered the morals of youth. A jury found West and the other principals guilty. West was fined $500 and sentenced to ten days on Welfare Island. She had herself driven to jail in an open car carrying armloads of white roses, she claimed the warden let her keep her silk underwear, and she gave $1000 to the Mae West Memorial Library in the Women's House of Detention. "Considering what* Sex *got me," she said, "a few days in the pen 'n' a $500 fine ain't too bad a deal."*

---

*from Edward de Grazia, *Girls Lean Back Everywhere: The Law of Obscenity and the Assault on Genius,* Random House, Vintage Books, 1993, pp. 5, 7, 20, 138–39.

1. CASE #168495, GRAND JURY INDICTMENT OF MAE WEST, WILLIAM MORGANSTERN, JAMES TIMONY, JOHN CORT, THE MORAL PRODUCING COMPANY AND THE CAST OF ACTORS.

List of Witnesses:
Patrick D. Kenneally, 3rd Division
Frank Keeney
John J. Byrnes
Adeline Leidzbach
Harry Cohen
Irving M. Feurelicht
Edward F. Cullebon
Ralph Pape

Filed, 2nd day of March, 1927. Pleads not guilty.

THE PEOPLE
vs.

Clarence William Morganstern
John Cort
James A. Timony
Mae West
Barry O'Neill
Eeda Von Beulow
Lyons Wickland
Pacie Ripple
Gordon Burby
David Hughes
Daniel J. Hamilton
Constance Morganstern
Ann Reader
   Defendants

Warren Sterling
Thomas V. Morrison
Alfred L. Rigali
John Coleman
Mary Morrisey
Ida Mantell
Conde Brewer
Ivan Jordan
Florence Doherty
Pete Segreto
Edward Elsner
63rd St. Theatres Limited Inc.
and Moral Productions Corporation

Joan H. Banton District Attorney
COURT OF GENERAL SESSIONS OF THE
COUNTY OF NEW YORK.

THE GRAND JURY OF THE COUNTY OF NEW YORK, by this indictment, accuse THE SAID DEFENDANTS of the Crime of UNLAWFULLY PREPARING, ADVERTISING, GIVING, PRESENTING AND PARTICIPATING IN AN OBSCENE, INDECENT, IMMORAL AND IMPURE DRAMA, PLAY, EXHIBITION, SHOW AND ENTERTAINMENT, committed as follows:

The said defendants, on the fifth day of February, nineteen hundred twenty-seven, and for a long time prior thereto, and thence continuously to the date of the finding of this indictment, at a certain building and theatre in said county situate and known as Daly's Theatre, unlawfully did prepare, advertise, give, present and participate in an obscene, indecent, immoral and impure drama, play, exhibition, show and entertainment then and there called "SEX," a more particular description of which said drama, play, exhibition, show and entertainment would be offensive to this Court and improper to be spread upon the records thereof, wherefore such description is not here given, which said drama, play, exhibition, show and entertainment at all times herein mentioned would and did tend to the corruption of the morals of youth and others, and in such act and acts unlawfully [alone and with] each other the said defendants did then aid and abet; against the form of the statute in such case made and provided, and against the peace of the People of the State of New York and their dignity.

SECOND COUNT.

AND THE GRAND JURY AFORESAID, by this indictment, further accuse THE SAID DEFENDANTS of the Crime of MAINTAINING A PUBLIC NUISANCE, committed as follows:

The said defendants, at the time aforesaid, in the county aforesaid, contriving and wickedly intending, so far as in them lay, to debauch and corrupt the morals of youth and of other persons and to raise and create in their minds inordinate and lustful desires, unlawfully, wickedly and scandalously did keep and maintain a certain theatre and play house there commonly known as Daly's Theatre, for the purpose of exhibiting and exposing to the sight of any persons willing to see and desirous of seeing the same and of paying for admission into the said theatre, a certain wicked, lewd, scandalous, bawdy, obscene, indecent, infamous, immoral and impure exhibition, show and entertainment, being the same exhibition, show and entertainment described in the first count of this indictment, to which reference is hereby made, and in the said theatre, at the time aforesaid, did unlawfully, wickedly and scandalously, for lucre and gain, produce, present, exhibit and display the said exhibition, show and entertainment to the sight and view of divers and many people, all to the great offense of public decency, against the order and economy of the state and to the common nuisance of all the people; against the form of the statue in such case made and provided, and against the peace of the People of the State of New York and their dignity.

THIRD COUNT.

AND THE GRAND JURY AFORESAID, by this indictment, further accuse THE SAID DEFENDANTS of the Crime of UNLAWFULLY PERMITTING A PLACE TO BE USED FOR AN IMMORAL PLAY, committed as follows:

The said defendant, 63rd St. Theatres Ltd., Inc., at the time aforesaid, in the county aforesaid, was a corporation and the owner and manager of the building, place and theatre commonly known as Daly's Theatre, mentioned and described in the first count of this indictment, to which reference is hereby made; and then and there unlawfully, as such owner and manager, the said defendant corporation unlawfully and knowingly did lease, let, permit and assent to the said building, place and theatre unlawfully to be used for the purpose of the said wicked, lewd, scandalous, bawdy, obscene, indecent, infamous, immoral and impure exhibition, show and entertainment called *Sex*, being the same exhibition, show and entertainment mentioned and described in the first count of this indictment;

And all the other said defendants were then and there unlawfully concerned in the commission of the said unlawfully permitting a place to be used for an immoral play, and crime by the said defendant, 63rd St. Theatres Ltd., Inc., in the manner and form aforesaid, and did then and there unlawfully aid and abet the said defendant, 63rd St. Theatres Ltd., Inc., in the commission of the same in the manner and form aforesaid, and did then and there unlawfully counsel, command, induce and procure the said defendant, 63rd St. Theatres Ltd., Inc., the said unlawfully permitting a place to be used for an immoral play, and crime, in the manner and form aforesaid then and there to do and commit; against the form of the statute in such case made and provided, and against the peace of the People of the State of New York and their dignity.

JOAB H. BANTON,
District Attorney.

[Norman Schloss, Mae West's attorney, attempted to have the charges dismissed and then to have the case moved. Both efforts failed, and then he filed to have the case heard by a jury rather than by a three judge panel. The court agreed and the case was heard by a special jury in general sessions. With a flair for theatricality and comedy equal to Mae West's, Schloss defended *Sex* as a work of art comparable to *A Tale of Two Cities*, *Hamlet* and the *Bible*. —L.S.]

2. DISTRICT ATTORNEY'S MEMORANDUM IN OPPOSITION TO DEFENSE MOTION FOR TRANSFER OF THE TRIAL TO ANOTHER COURT'S JURISDICTION.

SUPREME COURT: NEW YORK COUNTY
THE PEOPLE OF THE STATE OF NEW YORK

-against-

CLARENCE WILLIAM MORGANSTERN, MAE WEST, BARRIE O'NEAL, EEDA VON BEULOW, LYONS WICKLAND, PACIE RIPPLE, GORDON BURBY, DAVID HUGHES, DANIEL J. HAMILTON, CONSTANCE MORGANSTERN, ANN READER, WARREN STERLING, THOMAS V. MORRISON, ALFRED L. RIGALI, JOHN COLEMAN, MARY MORRISEY, IDA MANTELL, CONDE BREWER, IVAN JORDAN, FLORENCE DOHERTY, PETER SEGRETO, EDWARD ELSNER

JOAB H. BANTON   JAMES GARRETT WALLACE
District Attorney   Assistant District Attorney
New York County.   Of Counsel.

February, 1927

The defendants herein are charged, by an information by the District Attorney in the Court of Special Sessions of the City of New York, with the misdemeanor of unlawfully giving and presenting an indecent, immoral, and impure play, in violation of Section 1140A of the Penal Law, and of unlawfully doing an act which offends public decency in violation of Section 1530 of the Penal Law.

They now move for a certificate that it is reasonable that the charge against them be prosecuted by indictment, pursuant to the provisions of Section 31, Subdivision 1 of the Inferior Criminal Courts Act (L. 1910, Chap. 659, as amended by L. 1911, Chap. 576). That section provides that the Court of Special Sessions shall have, in the first instance, exclusive jurisdiction to hear and determine all charges of misdemeanor committed within the City of New York, except charges of libel; but that it shall be divested of jurisdiction to proceed with the hearing and determination of any charges of misdemeanor in the following case:

"(c) If, before the commencement of any such trial, a Justice of the Supreme Court in the Judicial Department where the trial would be had; or, if the charge be triable in the County of New York, a Judge authorized to hold a Court of General Sessions of the Peace in and for the County of New York; or, if the charge be triable in another county, a county judge thereof, shall certify that it is reasonable that such charge be prosecuted by indictment."

Applications of this character are addressed to the discretion of the Court. They are not granted as a matter of course. The Court must be satisfied that it is reasonable that the charge be prosecuted by indictment. Reasonable, in this connection, has been defined to mean just, proper, fair, and equitable. The burden of showing the reasonableness of the application is upon the defendant. He must show something more than a mere preference for a jury trial, to which he is not entitled as a matter of right. If the motion is made merely for the purpose of delaying the trial, it should not be granted.

Peo. V. Levy, 24 Misc. 469
Peo. V. Wade, 26 Misc. 585
Peo. V. Rosenberg, 59 Misc. 342
Peo. V. Willis, 59 Misc. 371
Peo. V. Porter, 108 Misc. 100
Peo. V. Byrne, 163 N. Y. Supp. 680
Peo. V. Butts 121 App. Div. 226
Peo. V. Title G. & T. Co., 180 App. Div. 64

It is claimed: (1) That the question involved here is preeminently one for trial by jury; and (2) that the consequences of a conviction are such that it is reasonable that the issue should be tried by a jury. It is thus sought to bring the case herein within the grounds enumerated in the case of People vs. Rosenberg (supra). We submit that the defendants have not brought themselves within these grounds.

(1) The defendant Morganstern is the manager and producer of the play "Sex" which is the alleged indecent show or play in question, and the other defendants are actors therein who participated in the presentation of this play. They have been held for trial in the Court of Special Sessions on an information charging violation of Sections 1140A and 1530, Penal Law. The test of criminality, as set forth in Section 1140 of the Penal Law, is whether a play is obscene, indecent, etc., and would tend to the corruption of the morals of youth or others (Penal Law, Sec. 1140A). Section 1530 of the Penal Law makes it a misdemeanor known as a "public nuisance" to unlawfully do an act which offends public decency. The question as to whether the play is indecent within the meaning of the statutes is one of fact (Peo. v. Muller, 96 N. Y. 408;

Peo. v. Doris, 14 App. Div. 117). This is conceded by the defendants. Where only a question of fact is involved the defendant must show, to justify the issuance of a certificate, that the question is an intricate or complicated one, which may be far-reaching in its effects as a precedent. No such situation is here involved. The sole effect of trial of this case, no matter what the decision is, will be the effect it has upon the persons directly involved, inasmuch as cases of this kind have heretofore been tried both in Special and in General Sessions, and no precedents of any far-reaching importance can be decided by the failure to transfer in this particular instance. One of the leading cases involving the trial of an immoral show is People v. Doris (supra). That was tried in Special Sessions, and the Judges found that the play was immoral and tended to corrupt, and the Appellate Division upheld that conviction.

(2) There is no property right involved in the case at bar. Such a right, within the meaning of the cases, is involved only in cases where the conviction would not only subject the defendant to fine, imprisonment, or both, but would also, ipso facto, work a forfeiture of a property right—as, e.g., a license possessed by a defendant to carry on a legitimate occupation (People v. Rosenberg, supra; People v. Porter, supra). In this case no license would be forfeited as the result of the conviction of these defendants if convicted. The sole property rights involved in this are the good will and box office attractiveness of the play itself, if any, and such rights should not be considered by the Court as of any importance in a case where a play is one of such character as is the play herein.

On a similar application heard this day, February 23, 1927, in Part I of the Court of General Sessions, County of New York, Judge Allen, in denying a motion to transfer a play, said:

"I see no need for delaying this decision even for the period necessary for the purpose of submitting briefs. I have long been of the opinion that the Justices of the Court of Special Sessions are well qualified to pass upon any question that may come before them for decision. They are able men, learned in the law, men of sound judgment and of broad experience, irrespective of whether property rights or any other rights are involved, I do not think for a moment that any party to a proceeding before those three Judges would be prejudiced in any respect. To my mind they are far better equipped by reason of their experience upon the bench to pass upon the question involved here than would be a jury of twelve laymen in a trial presided over by one of the judges of this Court. Counsel, you will have your day in court, and whatever verdict is rendered will be a sound and honest one. This court has a heavy calendar to contend with, and we are doing our very best here to reduce it and clean out the Tombs prison. A trial of this kind is bound to take considerable time, and we have red tape to go through in presenting the case before the Grand Jury, and then there are various other delays before we get to trial. Now, this is a matter of public interest. The trial should be expedited. Let it be expedited in the Court where it belongs, in the Court of Special Sessions. Motion denied."

Judge Allen well sums up the delays necessary incident to a trial where a misdemeanor is transferred from the Court of Special Sessions to the Court of General Sessions. The Court of Special Sessions, composed of three Judges, is the Court in which in the natural and usual course of events all misdemeanors should come to trial. In a case of this kind in which there is no extraordinary situation present to the Court, the Supreme Court, even though it has the power, should not interfere to divest the Court of Special Sessions of its jurisdiction. The Court of General Sessions is, as Judge Allen says, more than fully occupied with the trial of important felony cases. The question as to whether or not the actors and managers in this play have presented an indecent show or exhibition, or committed an act which offends public decency, is a matter of importance to them but is not a matter of extraordinary public importance so as to justify the transfer of this case to a higher court, nor will any precedent be established by the denial of this application that will bind the Supreme Court or any other Court in the future on any other application. The questions of fact and the questions of law involved in this case may as well be tried in the Court of Special Sessions as in the court where felonies are customarily tried.

THE APPLICATION SHOULD BE DENIED.

Respectfully submitted,

JOAB H. BANTON
DISTRICT ATTORNEY
NEW YORK COUNTY

JAMES GARRETT WALLACE
Of Counsel

February, 1927.

3. DISTRICT ATTORNEY'S MEMORANDUM ON LEGAL PRECEDENTS FOR ARGUMENT IN THE PEOPLE OF THE STATE OF NEW YORK VS. CLARENCE WILLIAM MORGANSTERN, ET. AL.

COURT OF GENERAL SESSIONS OF THE COUNTY OF NEW YORK.

THE PEOPLE OF THE STATE OF NEW YORK

-against-

CLARENCE WILLIAM MORGANSTERN, ET AL.

There are just two questions involved in this case:

I. The connection or participation of the various defendants in the acts charged in the indictment, namely, the presentation of the play "Sex" on the 15th of February, 1927, at Daly's Theater.

II. The question as to whether or not the play is obscene, indecent, immoral or impure, and would tend to the corruption of the morals of youth, or others, within the meaning of Section 1140A of the Penal Law.

The following authorities are respectfully called to the attention of the Court:

Peo. vs. Muller, 96 N. Y. 408
Queen vs. Hecklin, 3 Eng. L.R.Q.B. 369
Peo. vs. Doris, 14 App. Div. 117
U. S. vs. Bennett, 16 Blatch. Rep. 366
U. S. vs. Means, 42 Fed. Rep. 605
U. S. vs. Hahn, 45 Fed. Rep. 44

CRIMINAL INTENT OR KNOWLEDGE

Where a picture is sold or shown, a play advertised or given, or a book published, under this or analogous statutes, the intent with which it is advertised, given, sold or portrayed is immaterial. Criminal intent is knowledge. The term is defined by Penal Law Section, Subdivision 4, as follows:

"The term *knowingly* imparts a knowledge that the facts exist, which constitute the act or omission of crime, and does not require knowledge of the unlawfulness of the act or omission."

In People vs. Muller, Supra, the Court held:

"The defendant's counsel, at the conclusion of the evidence made several requests to charge, which were denied by the trial judge. The leading purpose of those requests was to induce the Court to lay down the rule that the intent of a defendant in selling a picture claimed to be indecent and obscene is an important element in determining his guilt. The statute makes the selling of an obscene and indecent picture a misdemeanor. There is no exception by reason of any special intent in making the sale. The object of the statute was to suppress the traffic in obscene publications and to protect the community against the contamination and pollution arising from their exhibition and distribution."

In Regina vs. Hecklin, Supra, Cockburne, C. J., said:

"I take it where a man publishes a work manifestly obscene, he must be taken to account for the intention which is implied from that act, and that as soon as you have an illegal act thus established, quoad [with respect to] the intention, and quoad [with respect to] the act; it does not lie in the mouth of the man who does it to say, 'Well I was breaking the law, but I was breaking it for some wholesome and salutary purpose." The law does not allow that; you must abide by the law, and if you would accomplish that object you must do it in a legal manner or let it alone. You must not do it in a manner that is illegal."

In Steele vs. Brannon, 7 L.R.C.L. Series, p. 267:

"The probable effect of the publication of this book being prejudiced to public morality and decency, the appellant must be taken to have intended the natural consequences of such publication, even though the book was published with the objects referred to by his counsel."

In U. S. vs. Harmon, 45 F. R., 421:

"These laws, as in the case of polygamy, are based upon public policy, and the law is arbitrary and holds the party responsible for the consequences of his acts when the means of knowledge are within his reach. It is a part of the common law of the land that indecent exposures, the uttering of obscene words in public, and the like, are indictable offenses. It rests upon the universal consensus that such things are impure, indecent and hurtful to the public morals and the common welfare; and as every man is supposed to know this fact, when he knowingly violates the statute, and gives publicity to such matters, he stands without an excuse in law."

Further quoting from the same case Judge Phillip said in answer to a defense interposed by the defendant that what he had done was an necessity in order to correct existing evils:

"* * * Reduced to its essence, the ultimate position of defendant is this: that although the language employed in the given article may be obscene, as heretofore defined, yet as it was a necessary vehicle to convey to the popular mind the aggravations of the abuses in sexual commerce inveighed against, and the object of the publisher being to correct the evil and thereby alleviate human condition, the author should be deemed a public benefactor, rather than a malefactor. In short, the proposition is that a man can do no public wrong who believes that what he does is for the ultimate public good. The underlying vice of all this character of argument is that it leaves out of view the existence of the social compact and the idea of government by law. If the end sought justifies the means, and there was no arbiter but the individual conscience of the actor to determine the fact whether the means are justifiable, homicide, infanticide, pillage and incontinence might run riot; and it is not extravagant to predict that the success of such philosophy would remit us to that barbaric condition where

'No common weal the human tribe allied,
Bound by no law, by no fixed morals tied,
Each snatched the booty which his fortune brought,
And wise in instinct, each his welfare sought.'

It is the very incarnation of the spirit of anarchy for a citizen to proclaim that like the heathen he is a law unto himself * * *"

Judge Philips continuing and alluding to the language in this publication, said:

"* * * When the defendant and his co-adjutors say that such language and subject-matter are only impure to the overprudish it but illustrates how familiarity with obscenity blunts the sensibilities, depraves good taste, and perverts the judgment. To the pure all things are pure, is too poetical for the actualities of practical life. There is in the popular conception and heart such a thing as modesty * * *"

In Grimm vs. U.S., 15 Sup. Ct. Rep. 471, the Court said:

"It is unnecessary that unlawful intent as to any particular picture be charged or proved. It is enough that in a certain place there could be obtained pictures of that character, either already made and for sale or distribution, or from some one willing to make them, and that the defendant, aware of this, used the mails to convey to others the like knowledge."

4. THE PEOPLE VS. WILLIAM MORGANSTERN, MAE WEST, ET. AL., #168495, CITY MAGISTRATE'S COURT, 10TH DISTRICT, 2/15/27. DESCRIPTIONS OF THE SCENES, ACTIONS AND DIALOGUE OF THE PLAY PROVIDED THE BASIS FOR ITS PROSECUTION.

The People vs. Wm. Morgenstern
CITY MAGISTRATE'S COURT
BOROUGH OF MANHATTAN
THE PEOPLE OF THE STATE OF NEW YORK
on complaint of James S. Bolan,
against-
C. WILLIAM MORGANSTERN, EDWARD ELSNER, MAE WEST, BARRY O'NEILL, EEDA VON BEULOW, LYONS WICKLAND, PACIE RIPPLE, GORDON BURBY, DAVID HUGHES, D.J. HAMILTON, CONSTANCE MORGANSTERN, ANN READER, WARREN STERLING, THOMAS V. MORRISON, ALFRED L. RIGALI, FRANK R. WOOD, MARYE MORRISEY, IDA MANTWELL, CONDE BREWER, FRED LE QUORNE, FLORENCE DOHERTY, AND PETE SEGRETO. DEFENDANTS

STATE OF NEW YORK
CITY AND COUNTY OF
NEW YORK
JAMES S. BOLAN, being duly sworn, deposes and says, I am a Deputy Inspector of the Police Department of the City of New York, On Saturday, February 5th, 1927, in the City and County of New York, and for a long time prior thereto, the defendants above unlawfully advertised, gave, presented and participated in, an obscene, indecent, immoral and impure drama, play, exhibition, show and entertainment which then and there tend to the corruption of the morals of youth and others, and committed unlawfully an act which then and there offended against public decency in that on the said date at a certain theatre and playhouse known as Daly's Theatre, situated there 24 West 63rd Street, the above named defendants unlawfully advertised, gave, presented and participated in a play then and there known as "Sex"; that said play then and there consisted of three certain "acts" and six "episodes", two "episodes" taking place in each act. "Episode" 1, as appears from the annexed programme, called Exhibit A, which deponent received at the time of his visit to said theatre, takes place in the living room of Margie LaMont in Montreal. The "episode" takes place in a room that purports to be for the encouragement of lewdness, fornication and unlawful sexual intercourses, and the defendant, Mae West, who appears in the character of Margie LaMont throughout said scene, portrays the character of a prostitute

engaged in plying her trade at that place. In such scene or "episode" the defendant, Warren Sterling, who portrays the character of Rocky Waldron, takes the part of a pimp and procurer engaged in collecting moneys from such prostitutes who appear in the "episode", and the defendant, Gordon Burby, portrays character of one Dawson who, as a corrupt policeman, seeks to obtain "protection" money from the said pimp and prostitute. In the said "episode" the defendant Ann Reader portrays the character of Agnes Scott, another prostitute engaged in plying her trade in these premises thus exhibited. In the same "episode" the defendant D. J. Hamilton portraying the character of Ensign Jones, and Barry O'Neill portraying the character of Lieutenant Gregg, appear as patrons of this disorderly resort and the prostitutes aforesaid and endeavor to enter into arrangements with the said Mae West, in the character of Margie LaMont, to commit an act of prostitution with them.

The second "episode" takes place four hours later in the same disorderly resort. In it appears the same prostitute, Margie LaMont, portrayed by the defendant Mae West, the same Lieutenant Gregg, portrayed by defendant Barry O'Neill, the same Dawson, portrayed by defendant Gordon Burby, the same pimp, portrayed by Warren Sterling, and a new character who has not heretofore appeared, known as Clara Smith by the defendant Eeda Von Beulow. Clara Smith proves to be the wife of a wealthy man in Connecticut who is traveling without her husband and who informs the pimp, Rocky Waldron, in this "episode" that she is in Montreal looking for a thrill, and he solicits her to take him home with her. This married woman away from her husband then becomes friendly with the pimp, Rocky Waldron, and kisses him. He drugs and robs her; and it is at this point that the drunken prostitute, Margie LaMont, comes into the room with the drunken Lieutenant Gregg who, in "episode" 1 some four hours ago, had solicited her to have sexual intercourse with him. They had a conversation in which she invites him to stay for the evening, and he turns over to her a roll of money in bill form. She kisses him and sits on his lap. He then describes to her a trip that the fleet to which he is attached is to make to Trinidad and solicits this prostitute to accompany him on that trip. She thereupon dances before him in a way that causes him to grab her and say "You'd make a savage out of any man". Their attention is attracted to the character Clara Smith. The character Dawson enters and enquires as to the identity of the said Clara Smith, and upon the said Clara Smith informing the character, Dawson, that she was there as a result of what Margie LaMont had done, Margie LaMont threatens to get even with said Clara Smith and the act thereupon terminates.

Act II "episode" 1 takes place in the cafe in Hotel Port au Prince, Trinidad, to which place the prostitute, Margie LaMont, following out the request of

Lieutenant Gregg, in "episode" 2, has come with Lieutenant Gregg. In this "episode" the prostitute dances before the sailors of the fleet and the officers in a way that causes Ensign Jones, the same character in which "episode" 1 had solicited Margie LaMont to commit an act of prostitution with him, to say "You'd make a bulldog break its chain", the said dance having been performed by the defendant Mae West by moving her buttocks and other parts of her body in such a way as to suggest an act of sexual intercourse. In this scene defendant Lyons Wickland, portraying the character of Jimmy Stanton, makes his appearance, He is introduced to the prostitute with whom he falls in love. The second "episode" in the same act takes place after an interval of one week and is at the same scene as "episode" 1 of that act. In these scene the same prostitute, Agnes Scott, portrayed by defendant Ann Reader, again appears and announces to the prostitute Margie LaMont that she had heard that Margie LaMont was following the fleet and doing well, and for that reason she had come along. Jimmy Stanton asked the prostitute Margie LaMont to marry him and it is arranged that Jimmy Stanton and Margie LaMont shall leave for the United States the following morning.

The first "episode" of Act III takes place in Robert Stanton's home in Westchester, Robert Stanton being the father of Jimmy Stanton. It is then discovered that the character, Clara Smith, who in "episode" 2 of Act I was the married woman away from her husband, brought into the disorderly house in Montreal by the pimp, Rocky Waldron, is the mother of Jimmy Stanton who is in love with the prostitute Margie LaMont. Mutual recriminations take place between the prostitute and the character of Clara Stanton, alias Clara Smith, in which after Clara Smith has called the prostitute a woman of the street, the prostitute, after announcing that hers was a profession followed to earn a living, tells the mother of the man whom she expects to marry that such mother was a prostitute except that the mother gave her virtue away without pay. At another point all the characters have left the scene except Jimmy Stanton and the prostitute Margie LaMont. Jimmy embraces Margie LaMont and goes through with her the business of making love to her by lying on top of her on a couch, each embracing the other. When this is terminated and Jimmy Stanton offers to call a maid to show the prostitute to her room, Margie LaMont answers "Can't you show me to my room?" The character Jimmy Stanton takes her to her room. On the threshold, after kissing and embracing, they step into that room and the scene ends.

Prior to the termination of the act, and at the same time of the talk referred to between the character Clara Stanton and Margie LaMont, Margie LaMont tells Clara Stanton that inasmuch as Clara Stanton had used the home of Margie LaMont in Montreal, she, Margie LaMont, intended to use Clara Stanton's home to have sexual intercourse with Jimmy Stanton and test out whether or not he really was in love with her. The language they used does not contain the words "sexual intercourse" but the purport and tenor of the business and language is to that effect.

"Episode" 2 of Act III takes place the following morning in the same scene and is opened by Jimmy Stanton stealing out of the prostitute's room into which he had gone as indicated at the end of the last act, after kissing and embracing her. In this last "episode" the pimp, Rocky Waldron, again appears, but the forgiving prostitute, Margie LaMont, upon his threatening to kill her, does not turn him over to the police but gives him another chance, so the pimp escapes justice. Margie LaMont confesses to Jimmy Stanton that she is a prostitute but indicates that she has reformed and is going to marry Lieutenant Gregg, the navy lieutenant who, in "episode" 1 and 2, solicited her to commit an act of prostitution with him.

The foregoing is a public performance at which the general public was admitted upon the payment of a price for tickets. At the time of my observing the said play, several hundred other persons were present of both sexes as part of the public audience watching the play. I was accompanied by Sergeant Patrick D. Keneally and Patrolman James T. Powers, both attached to the Third Division of the Municipal Police Department of the City of New York.

There is annexed hereto and made a part of this affidavit as Exhibit B a more detailed summary of what occurred during the play at the time of my visit and observation of the same with verbatim excerpts from and reports of dialogues that occurred in the course of the exhibition and play. The audience was not only of both sexes but was chiefly made up of young persons whose ages appeared to me to be between 17 and 20 years.

As appears from the said exhibit and hereto annexed, and from Exhibit C hereto annexed, the defendant C. William Morganstern advertises and presents, and the defendant Edward Elsner directs and at all times herein mentioned did advertise, present and direct the said play, exhibition and show. Exhibit C was at the time purchased in the lobby of the said theatre from persons who purported to be employees of the said theatre, by Sergeant Patrick D. Keneally, and Exhibit A was received from one of the ushers in the theatre as the programme of the play, after the tickets of admission had been presented to the person in charge of the gate and entrance obtained as a result thereof.

The corroborative affidavit of Sergeant Patrick D. Keneally and Patrolman James T. Powers, both of whom accompanied me at the time, are hereto annexed and made a part of this affidavit.

As to the other persons named as defendants and for whom warrants are sought, they each aided and abetted in that they played parts in the presentation of said play, exhibition and show, as appears from the exhibit marked "People's Exhibit A".

WHEREFORE deponent asks that warrants be issued for the arrest of the above named persons and that they may be dealt with according to law.

James S. Bolan
Subscribed and sworn to
before me this 9th
day of February 1927
William McAdoo
Chief City Magistrate

[*The Pleasure Man* had its tryout in Bridgeport, Connecticut. The play was moved to the Bronx Opera House for the week of September 17, 1928, and moved again for the week of September 24 to the Boulevard Theatre, in Jackson Heights, Queens. But when it opened in Manhattan on October 1 at the Biltmore Theatre on Broadway, the police raided the play. Nathan Burkan, Mae West's attorney, obtained a temporary injunction, but Equity warned the actors not to appear again. When they showed up for the Wednesday matinee, the police broke into the theatre in the second act and herded the cast, in full costume, into a paddy wagon. Audiences who knew the police raid was in store paid $70 and $100 a ticket for the second performance, but West made no money on *The Pleasure Man*. On the contrary, it cost her $60,000 to bail out the cast of fifty-eight actors and for the legal defense that ended in a dismissal of the indictment. —L.S.]

5. COVER SHEET AND INDICTMENT AGAINST MAE WEST AND 58 OTHERS, CASE #174820., CALENDAR NO. 53001, SUPERSEDED BY CASE #174820 1/2, CALENDAR NO. 53002. OCTOBER 4 AND 5TH, 1928.

COURT OF GENERAL SESSIONS OF THE
COUNTY OF NEW YORK

THE PEOPLE OF THE STATE OF NEW YORK
-against-
MAE WEST, CARL REED, CHARLES EDWARD
DAVENPORT, STAN STANLEY, ALAN BROOKS,
JAY HOLLY, WILLIAM AUGUSTIN, CAMILIA
CAMPBELL, EDGAR BARRIER, ELAINE IVANS,
LEO HOWE, LESTER SHEEHAN, MARTHA VAUGHN,
EDWARD HEARN, WILLIAM SELIG, HERMAN
LENZEN, JULIE CHILDREY, MARGARET BRAGAW,
ANNA KELLER, JANE RICH, FRANK LESLIE,
WILLIAM CAVANAGH, CHARLES ORDWAY,
CHUCK CONNORS the Second, FRED DICKENS,
HARRY ARMAND, SYLVAN REPETTI, GENE DREW alias Gene Grew,
ALBERT DORANDO, LEW LORRAINE, JO HUDDLES-
TON, WALTER MacDONALD, GENE PEARSON,
HOWARD CHANDLER, JAMES AYERS, AUGUSTA
BOYLSTON, MARGUERITE LEO, KATE JULIANNE,
MAY DAVIS, EDWARD ROSEMAN, JOEJ DELANEY,
ROBERT COOKSEY, ROBERT DeMARCHE, JAMES
CLARK, CHARLES ZLATOFF, GEORGE CARTIER,

PHILIP KIRSCHEN, PHILIP GROSSMAN, RICHARD
READ, FRED CARLTON, JACK DENTON, HARRY
BONER, RUDOLPH CORMILLO, TOMMY DENTON,
FRANK RINDHAGE, FRANK SPENSER, KUNI HARA,
WALLY JAMES, TOD LEWIS,
DEFENDANTS.

THE GRAND JURY OF THE COUNTY OF NEW YORK, by this indictment, accuse THE SAID DEFENDANTS of the Crime of UNLAWFULLY PREPARING, ADVERTISING, GIVING, DIRECTING, PRESENTING AND PARTICIPATING IN AN OBSCENE, INDECENT, IMMORAL AND IMPURE DRAMA, PLAY EXHIBITION, SHOW AND ENTERTAINMENT, committed as follows:

The said defendants, on the first day of October, nineteen hundred twenty-eight, and for some time thereafter, at a certain building and theatre in said county situate and known as the Biltmore Theatre, unlawfully did prepare, advertise, give, present and participate in an obscene, indecent, immoral and impure drama, play, exhibition, show and entertainment, and obscene, indecent, immoral, impure scenes, tableaux, incidents, parts and portions of said obscene, indecent, immoral and impure drama, play and exhibition, which said obscene, indecent, immoral and impure drama, play, exhibition, show and entertainment was then and there called "PLEASURE MAN," a more particular description of which said obscene, indecent, immoral and impure drama, play, exhibition, show and entertainment and said scenes, tableaux, incidents, parts and portions thereof would be offensive to this Court and improper to be spread upon the records thereof, wherefore such description is not here given, which said drama, play, exhibition, show and entertainment and said scenes, tableaux, incidents, parts and portions thereof tend and at all times herein mentioned tended and would tend to the corruption of the morals of youth and others, and in such acts unlawfully each of the said defendants did aid and abet; against the form of the statute in such case made and provided, and against the peace of the People of the State of New York and their dignity.

SECOND COUNT.

AND THE GRAND JURY AFORESAID, by this indictment, further accuse THE SAID DEFENDANTS of the Crime of UNLAWFULLY ADVERTISING, GIVING, PRESENTING AND PARTICIPATING IN AN IMMORAL PLAY AND EXHIBITION, committed as follows:

The said defendants, on the day and in the year aforesaid, in the county aforesaid, unlawfully did prepare, advertise, give, direct, present and participate in a certain exhibition, show and entertainment, being the same exhibition, show and entertainment described in the first count of this indictment, to which reference is hereby made, and certain scenes and tableaux in said exhibition, show and entertainment, all then and there depicting and dealing with the subject of sex degeneracy and sex perversion; against the form of the statute in such case made and provided, and against the peace of the People of the State of New York and their dignity.

THIRD COUNT.

AND THE GRAND JURY AFORESAID, by this indictment, further accuse THE SAID DEFENDANTS of the Crime of MAINTAINING A PUBLIC NUISANCE, committed as follows:

The said defendants, on the day and in the year aforesaid, in the county aforesaid, contriving and wickedly intending so far as in them lay, to debauch and corrupt the morals of youth and of other persons and to raise and create in their minds inordinate and lustful desires, unlawfully, wickedly and scandalously did keep and maintain a certain theatre and playhouse there commonly known as the Biltmore Theatre for the purpose of exhibiting and exposing to the sight of any persons willing to see and desirous of seeing the same and of paying for admission into the said theatre, a certain wicked, lewd, scandalous, bawdy, obscene, indecent, infamous, immoral and impure exhibition, show and entertainment, being the same exhibition, show and entertainment described in the first count of this indictment, to which reference is hereby made, and in the said theatre, at the time aforesaid, did unlawfully, wickedly and scandalously, for lucre and gain, produce, present, exhibit and display the said exhibition, show and entertainment to the sight and view of diverse and many people, all to the great offense of public decency, against the order and economy of the state and to the common nuisance of all the people, and against the form of the statute in such case made and provided, and against the peace of the People of the State of New York and their dignity.

JOAB H. BANTON,
District Attorney.

6. MAE WEST'S REPLY AFFIDAVIT FILED IN ANSWER TO CHARGES AGAINST PLEASURE MAN. IN PAPERS DRAWN UP BY HER ATTORNEY, NATHAN BURKAN, MAE WEST OFFERED A READING OF HER PLAY THAT DENIED ALL ALLEGATIONS OF INDECENCY.

SUPREME COURT: NEW YORK COUNTY.
CARL REED, MAE WEST

Plaintiffs,

-against-

CHARLES WARREN, both individually, and in his official capacity as Commissioner of Police of the City of New York, JAMES S. BOLAN, Deputy Chief Inspector of the Police Department of the City of New York, JAMES J. WALKER, both individually and in his official capacity as Mayor of the City of New York, WILLIAM F. QUIGLEY, both individually and in his official capacity as License Commissioner of the City of New York, JOAB H. BANTON, both individually and in his official capacity as District Attorney of the County of New York, and the officers under the command of any of the said defendants and their agents, et al.
Defendants

STATE OF NEW YORK
COUNTY OF NEW YORK

MAE WEST, being duly sworn, deposes and says:
I am an actress and playwright, and have had many years experience on the stage. In the Spring of 1928, I commenced to write an original play around the adventures of a troupe of vaudeville actors. I had been on the vaudeville stage myself for many years, and was familiar with this phase of life. I wrote the play within a period of about 2 or 3 months.
The story of the play, in synopsis form, is briefly as follows:

SYNOPSIS OF "THE PLEASURE MAN"

The locale of the play is a small town in the middle-west.
The play opens with a scene in a vaudeville theatre of the town, showing the bare stage with scrubwomen who have just cleaned the dressing rooms. Stage hands are shown moving trunks and scenery. The manager of the theatre comes on, ready to look over the new acts that were billed for the current week. The house musicians are shown ready to rehearse the music for the new acts.

Various acts come on for rehearsal. The first act is a man and wife act—Edgar "It" Morton and wife. The second act is the Bird of Paradise, a female impersonator with his four manikins, also female impersonators. Another act—Dolores and Randall, who are husband and wife, with four girls; this is a dancing act. Another act, Hethingwater [stet] and wife. The headline is Rodney Terrill. He takes the star part in the play and is designated as "The Pleasure Man." There is also an acrobatic team.

"The Pleasure Man" is shown as a pronounced voluptuary; he seeks many adventures with the fair sex and seems to have a craze for women, his complex being to have them fall desperately in love with him. He has charm and personality and exercises them constantly, seeking an intrigue with almost every woman he meets. Not only does he seek the women of his own profession, but those in the towns in which he plays as well.

The first act of the play shows Terrill carrying on various flirtations with the feminine members on the vaudeville bill.

He is particularly interested in Dolores of the team of Dolores and Randall. Randall, her husband, senses the incipient affair and admonishes his wife not to have anything to do with "The Pleasure Man."

The manager of the theatre, who also knows Terrill's reputation (Terrill having played in this theatre on a prior occasion) warns the various girls on the bill to beware of the blandishments of this modern Don Juan.

The stage manager, Stan Stanley, who was at one time an acrobat, fills in a gap in the acrobatic act and helps out and various comic lines are interpolated in that way. Having had no conquests of his own, Stanley secretly admires "The Pleasure Man" for his ability to charm the fair sex, and makes strenuous efforts to imitate him.

The end of the first act closes with the curtain coming down on the stage, showing the vaudeville bill about to commence.

The second act is set back-stage, four dressing rooms being shown.

The star dressing room is being shared by Terrill, the headliner, and the acrobats, including Stanley.

In the next dressing room are Dolores and Randall.

The dressing room above Terrill's is occupied by the Bird of Paradise and the four manikins; all female impersonators.

In the next room are the girls of the Dolores and Randall act, four dancing girls.

The actors are seen in the various dressing rooms, making up for the performance.

The girls in the upper dressing room are discussing the affair that is going on between Dolores and Terrill.

The female impersonators are seen disrobing.

Music is heard off-stage, as the different actors close their acts and the applause of the audience is heard.

The actors are seen coming back from the stage and other actors are shown going on to their acts.

A knock is heard at Terrill's door, and he is told that a lady wishes to see him. He goes out and meets one Mary Ann, a young woman who lives in the town. She tells him that he has gotten her into trouble and asks him to keep his promise to her to marry her. Terrill spurns her, she pleads with him. Just then, the signal is given for him to go on with his act, and he throws the girl against the wall and she falls to the floor and faints. He leaves her there and goes on to the stage.

The other artists, hearing the commotion, rush out of their dressing rooms and find the girl on the floor.

It seems that an electrician, Ted Arnold, who is working in the theatre, is the brother of Mary Ann, and that he has recognized his sister's picture on Terrill's dressing table.

The brother has also heard the commotion and rushes in to find his sister lying on the floor. He picks her up and carries her into the rest room.

Terrill returns from his act.

A vaudevillian, named Lester Queen, enters. He knows almost all of the actors personally and invites them all to a party that night to be given by one Toto, who is a wealthy resident of the town and was a former vaudevillian who presented a canine act. Most of the artists agree to be at the party that night. Lester tells them that as the cars will be waiting for them after the show, they need not bother taking off their make-up, as the party will be a costume party.

The Bird of Paradise, the female impersonator, who had seen Terrill throw the girl to the floor, threatens to expose him.

Randall has gone out. His wife, Dolores, is alone in her dressing room; Terrill enters her room and a tender love scene ensues between Terrill and Dolores. Randall re-enters the room and finds his wife in Terrill's arms. There is a fight between the two men. The struggle is carried on from the dressing room to the corridor. Stage hands and others intervene and separate the men, and Randall screams at Terrill, "I'll get you, yet, you dirty rat. God damn you." Whereupon the curtain falls.

The curtain for the third act rises upon Toto's home, where the party is in full swing. The female impersonators, in costume, are present. Various invited guests, residents of the town, are present, wearing evening clothes. Terrill, Dolores, the acrobats, Stanley, the stage manager, and other members of the bill, mingle with the guests. There is music and dancing. The various acts do their specialties for the entertainment of the other guests; the entertainment consisting of songs and dances such as are usually seen in high class vaudeville shows.

During the height of the merriment, Randall enters, very much intoxicated, looking for his wife, Dolores. He had learned that she had gone to the party with Terrill. Terrill and Dolores, having heard Randall come in, dance off into an ante-room, and the various artists, in order to avoid a scene, try to persuade Randall that his wife is not at the party. He exits, threatening that he will kill Terrill when he finds him.

The party immediately breaks up.

After the guests leave, Terrill and Dolores return from the ante-room. Terrill has now become intoxicated and reckless. He tries to persuade Dolores to spend the night with him at this house, telling her that everything has been arranged; that he has a room upstairs. She refuses and runs away from him, but as she leaves him, he says: "I'll expect you back!"

Terrill takes a few more drinks and finally staggers to a room upstairs.

Toto comes in and tells his butler to turn the lights out and retire. The butler turns out the lights and is about to retire. As he does so, a slam is heard upstairs, as if someone had gone out of Terrill's room. The butler exits. The stage is dark. Dolores is seen returning. She ascends the stairs to Terrill's room.

A second or two later, a terrific scream is heard from Dolores, who comes down the stairs greatly agitated. The scene also brings Toto downstairs. Toto rushes over to Dolores and asks her what has happened. She points up to the stairs and cries "Terrill". Toto runs upstairs.

Dolores staggers over to the couch, thoroughly exhausted. Toto comes running back to her and she says: "Toto, for God's sake, do something, quick!" Toto rushes to the telephone, clicking the receiver madly. He asks for the police station. Dolores tries to prevent his calling the police, but Toto gets the police station on the wire and shouts "Come at once; something terrible has happened". The curtain falls slowly on this scene, while Toto says, "I can't explain over the telephone."

The curtain is lowered for a minute, indicating a lapse of two hours.

The curtain rises on the same scene. The Chief of Police is sitting at the table, questioning Toto, the various members of the household, as well as the members of the vaudeville show who had been at the party, including Stanley, the stage manager, Randall, Dolores, the manager of the theatre and the Bird of Paradise.

In the course of questioning, it is brought out that Terrill had been killed, his death having been caused by means of an operation.

Suspicion is fastened upon Randall, because he had been heard to threaten Terrill. Randall is placed under arrest and is about to be taken away, when a detective walks in with Ted Arnold, the electrician and brother of Mary Ann. Ted confesses that he killed Terrill. He says: "I didn't mean to kill him. I only wanted to maim him so he would never be attractive to any other man's sister; so he wouldn't use any other woman for his filthy sport."

The last lines of the play are spoken by Stanley, who comes forward in horror and tells the chief of police that Terrill got what he richly deserved; that he was merely a "Pleasure Man" and a menace to women; that Terrill's fate would be a lesson to him for the rest of his life.

After the play was finished, I arranged for the production thereof with Mr. Carl Reed, and Mr. Reed engaged a cast of players, had scenery made for the show, purchased equipment and commenced rehearsals.

The play opened on September 17th, 1928, at the Bronx Opera House. It was successful from the start, and the public acclaimed it as an interesting dramatic production.

Most of the play is built around bits of comedy, particularly as it develops in backstage life.

During the performances the audience at each performance seemed very pleased, and applauded the actors generously.

The play received favorable comment from the press. I attach hereto and make part of this affidavit copies of the review of several of the leading newspapers, particularly, the review that appeared in "The New York Evening Post" and in the "Brooklyn Daily Eagle". The said reviews show that there was nothing in this play that was objectionable, indecent or immoral.

The play, indeed, tells a moral story, and teaches a lesson not to be forgotten. The play teaches succinctly that punishment will follow a wrongdoer. The lines of the play are wholesome and not objectionable, and I will hand up, on the argument of this motion, a copy of the manuscript of the play or acting version of the play.

This play, "THE PLEASURE MAN", was performed in the Bronx Opera House, Bronx County, City of New York, from September 17, 1928 to September 22, 1928, a period of one week.

I was informed by the manager of the theatre that Mr. McGeeghan, District Attorney of Bronx County, had seen the play, and that he had suggested the elimination of one song. This was agreed to by Mr. Reed and Mr. McGeeghan, as I am informed and believe, expressed himself as satisfied with the play and made no attempt to interfere with its production.

The following week, commencing Sept. 24, 1928, the play was presented at the Boulevard Theatre, Jackson Heights, Queens, New York City. No attempt was made to interfere with the play by the authorities of that County, although I was informed and believe that they saw the play on the opening night, and the play ran a full week at that theatre.

Mr. Reed, as he will more specifically show in his affidavit, made a booking contract with the Chenins for the production of the play at the Biltmore Theatre, located on West 47th Street, Borough of Manhattan, City of New York.

The play was produced at that theatre on the evening of October 1, 1928.

On that evening, I am informed and believe, without warning or notice, the defendants sent various police officers to the Biltmore Theatre and arrested each and every member of the cast of the play, consisting of about fifty-four members. The police officers also arrested me at performance in which I was playing in a play entitled "DIAMOND LIL", at the Royale Theatre on West 45th Street, New York City, and I and the artists so arrested were arraigned a little before midnight at the Night Court before a Police Magistrate sitting therein, charged with giving an immoral exhibition under Section 1140a of the Penal Code of the State of New York.

I was arrested about five minutes of eleven, when I closed my performance in "Diamond Lil". At that time the play "THE PLEASURE MAN" had not yet been finished, so that clearly the defendants herein had premeditated the arrest regardless of the nature of the play.

We were again arraigned today in the Magistrate's Court on West 54th Street, and the matter was adjourned until Thursday, October 4, 1928.

In the meantime the actors and actresses playing in the production have become very much worried over their arrest, and the arrest has had a demoralizing effect upon the morale of the cast.

The defendants have threatened to arrest the members of the cast and to arrest me again if any further performances of the play are given.

I deny that the said play "THE PLEASURE MAN" is indecent or immoral. I deny that it is in any sense objectionable. It is good, clean, wholesome dramatic entertainment.

The acts of the defendants are arbitrary and tyrannical. The threats to arrest the members of the cast and to arrest me again and again are made for the purpose of demoralizing the cast, so that no further performances of the play will be given.

If the production of the play should be interrupted, it will mean that we will lose the booking of the theatre, and that the investment of the producer will be swept away.

Moreover, it will mean great loss and damage to me, because I have a contract with the producer under which I receive royalties during each and every week that the play is presented, and if the play should be closed down I will lose royalties for an indefinite time and the amount of my loss cannot be estimated or calculated, and my damage will be irreparable.

If the defendants are permitted to continue their plan of arresting the members of the cast and me for each performance of the play, the play will have to shut down, and irreparable damage will be caused.

Therefore I pray that an injunction be granted, restraining the defendants from making any further arrests or doing anything to demoralize or intimidate the members of the cast of this play.

For all of which no previous application has been made.

That the reason an order to show cause is asked for is that it is of the utmost urgency that a speedy adjudication of this motion be made as the injury complained of is causing the plaintiffs great damage.

Sworn to before me this
2nd day of October, 1928 .(signed) MAE WEST

Marion L. Ekin
Notary Public, New York Co.
Clerk's No. 133, Register's No. 9139.
Commission expires March 30, 1929.

[Carl Reed described the development of the project and affirmed the characters were all "normal men and women." The play was "clean, wholesome, and interesting." Moreover, the first night audience included "distinguished and prominent people." He concluded by pointing out the financial loss he [and by implication other Broadway producers] would suffer if he were found guilty and fined. —L.S.]

7. CARL REED'S REPLY AFFIDAVIT IN ANSWER TO CHARGES AGAINST PLEASURE MAN.

SUPREME COURT: NEW YORK COUNTY
CARL REED, MAE WEST,

Plaintiffs,

—against—

CHARLES WARREN both individually and in his official capacity as Commission of Police of the City of New York, JAMES S. BOLAN, Deputy Chief Inspector of the Police Department of the City of New York, JAMES J. WALKER, both individually and in his official capacity as Mayor of the City of New York, WILLIAM F. QUIGLEY, both individually and in his official capacity as License Commissioner of the City of New York, JOAB H. BANTON, both individually and in his official capacity as District Attorney of the County of New York, and the officers under the command of any of the said defendants and their agents, et al.

Defendants

STATE OF NEW YORK
COUNTY OF NEW YORK

CARL REED, being duly sworn, deposes and says:
I am a theatrical producer, and have been such for a great many years. I produced many successful plays, among them being "Aloma of the South Seas", "Stronger Than Love" at the Belasco Theatre, "So this is Politics" at the Henry Miller Theatre, "The Creaking Chair" at the Lyceum Theatre, and "Sport of Kings" at the Lyceum Theatre.
Early in August, 1928, Miss May {sic} West submitted to me a synopsis of a story. I read the same with interest, and Miss West told me that she would have a completed play on that story in time to go to rehearsal, if I was interested and desired to make a production thereof.
I told her that I liked the story. She thereafter brought a manuscript of the

play to me. It was then entitled "Back Stage". We found that the title "Back Stage" had been used in a motion picture, and rather than have any law suits we decided to change the title, and we hit upon the title "THE PLEASURE MAN".

I thereupon arranged for a production of the same. I entered into 54 contracts with actors and actresses, including a jazz band, and obligated myself to pay salaries to the star actors and actresses for the run of the play, and to the minor artists for the usual period of a run with a two weeks notice clause.

I purchased some of the scenery, and had other parts of the scenery made to order at an expense involving about $25,000. I spent $3,000 to $4,000. in advertising the play. The production cost of $25,000. including not only the scenery but the wardrobe and lighting and scenic effects, and other accessories of the play.

I also entered into a contract with Miss West under which I agreed to pay her royalties for each and every week that the play was produced. The play was rehearsed and produced at the Bronx Opera House, Borough of Bronx, City of New York, on September 17, 1928.

The production was successful from the start, and the public and critics were unanimous in their approval. The play was clean, wholesome and good, and in fact it was a play with a moral, and intended to preach a sermon to the audience.

I received many letters and telegrams from people in the profession and from other walks of life, all of them commendatory and all of them unanimous in their praise of the play. Many great artists of the stage saw the play and praised it.

I did not receive a single communication from any person complaining of the show or criticizing it in any shape form or manner. No one came to the box office and made any complaint about the play. The public apparently approved of the play and of the subject and the manner in which it was presented. Mr. McGeehan, the defendant, informed the house manager of the theatre that he thought one of the songs should be eliminated, and I, without hesitation, acceded to his wishes and eliminated the song.

No other suggestion was made to me by any man in public life or by anyone in authority to change any of the lines or take out any songs or to make any other changes in the play.

During that week in the Bronx, with a popular scale of prices from 50¢ to $1.50, we took in approximately $5,800. at the box office, which is a substantial sum in that theatre for a try-out show, performances being in the nature of try-out performances as is customary with new plays before bringing them to New York City.

After the week in the Bronx, I presented the play for the week commencing September 24th, 1928, at the Boulevard Theatre, Jackson Heights, Queens.

The box office receipts that week with the same scale of prices were about $8,500., again a very good substantial sum, and an indication that the play would be a tremendous success.

I was informed by the house manager of the fact that many people in the audience came more than once to see the play. The play appealed strongly because of its theatrical flavor showing life back of the stage, and showing the comedy and tragedy of that life. It appealed particularly because of its moral flavor showing the punishment that is meted out to a willful and persistent transgressor.

The characters of the play are all normal men and women. There are no abnormalities, no sex perversions and no filth in this play. It is clean and wholesome, and I deny that there is anything indecent or immoral in the presentation of this play.

I entered into a contract with the Chanin Theatre Corporation for the production of the play at the Biltmore Theatre on or about the 29th day of August, 1928. Before this contract was made I had many other offers from managers and lessees of theatres in the City of New York who asked me to give them the booking for this play. I attach hereto and make part of this affidavit a copy of the contract between the Chanin Theatres Corporation and myself.

I am informed and believe that the Chanin Theatres Corporation, which booked this play for the theatre, has a contract with the Chambrook Realty Co., Inc., and that the Chambrook Realty Co., Inc. is the lessee of said Biltmore Theatre and operates the same.

Both the Chambrook Realty Co. Inc. and the Chanin Theatres Corporation are interested in the production to the extent that one is to receive a booking fee for its services, and the other is to receive a rental for the use of its theatre, and they also will be damaged irreparably by the acts of the defendants hereinafter complained of.

The opening performance in New York City was given on October 1st, 1928, at the Biltmore Theatre. The public manifested great approval. I was present at the performance and mingled with the audience and nowhere did I hear a word of disapproval, nowhere a word of complaint, but on the contrary everyone thought that the play was clean, wholesome, interesting and particularly dramatic and effective.

In the audience I noted many of the most prominent people in the City of New York whom I recognized. Indeed the audience was a most distinguished and representative audience. I received many letters and telegrams of congratulations, and not one communication criticized the play in any aspect.

The performance commenced about 8:40 P. M. At the commencement of the second act police officials walked back stage, and I was informed that these officials representing and acting as agents of the defendants herein, had left word that no member of the cast was to leave the theatre but that they would be placed under arrest and taken to court immediately at the conclusion of the performance. When the performance was over, a little after 11 o'clock, the members of the cast were arrested by the police officials and arraigned in the night court.

Bail was given in the night court, and the defendants were released and the matter was set down for City Magistrate Edward Weil in the 54th Street Police Court for October 2nd, 1928. On that day the defendants were again arraigned upon an information dated and filed the 2nd day of October, 1928, a copy of which information is hereto annexed and made part of this affidavit. On that day the matter was adjourned to Thursday, October 4th, 1928.

The defendants herein have embarked upon a course of intimidation. They are determined to suppress this play and to prevent me from continuing the production thereof; to destroy my investment; to compel me to breach many contracts with others without giving me a hearing on the merits of the play.

I have been informed and believe that it is the intention of the Defendant Charles Warren, Police Commissioner, at the instigation and at the request of the other defendants herein to arrest and re-arrest each and everyone of the members of the cast and Miss West at each and every performance of the play on the same charge to the end that I will be unable to continue the further production of this play.

The arrest which was made on the evening of October 1st, 1928 has had a demoralizing effect upon the morale of the cast. The acts of the defendants, if permitted to go unrestrained, will disturb this morale entirely and make it impossible for me to give any further performances of the play in which event I will suffer irreparable damage, which cannot be computed.

I will lose my enormous investments; I will lose an opportunity to acquire profits from the further presentation of the play in the City of New York for a season or perhaps more, and I will lost the right to put on road shows or to sell stock or repertoire rights in the play, and I will lose an opportunity to acquire moneys for the motion picture rights in the play, all of which are very valuable and run into large sums of money, and I will suffer injury to such an extent that no adequate remedy at law is available to me in this matter.

Moreover, the other plaintiffs herein will likewise suffer irreparable damage and injury if the defendants succeed in their course of intimidation and demoralization.

The acts of the police officials and the acts of the defendants herein are illegal, arbitrary and tyrannical.

This play has a valuable property right. The advance sale of seats indicates that this play will take in from $20,000 to $25,000 per week.

In addition to the rights above enumerated and to the moneys which will accrue from the continued presentation of the play, I have been offered substantial sums for the foreign rights and also for a second company of the play for a run in Chicago, Illinois.

All this property and valuable good will, will be destroyed by these defendants if they succeed in harassing the plaintiffs in the manner hereinabove described, by continued arrests, and if they are unrestrained in interfering with and hampering me in the production of this play. The acts of the defendants are high-handed because they constitute an illegal intimidation against which I have no remedy, and against which the other plaintiffs are without any remedy, except however, the restraining arm of a court of equity.

This action is not at issue but a summons has been issued herein and served simultaneously with the order to show cause and affidavits. That the earliest term, so I have been informed and verily believe, at which this action can be noticed for trial is November, 1928.

For the above reasons, plaintiffs seek a temporary injunction restraining the defendants from making any further arrests of any of the members of the cast of the play "THE PLEASURE MAN" or of Miss West or of anyone else connected with the production of this play, and from interfering with this play "THE PLEASURE MAN", and from doing anything calculated to harass, annoy or intimidate the members of the cast of this or from taking any steps to close the plaintiff's play, directly or indirectly, and from any act or acts tending to harrass, impede or prevent me from the production of the said play at the Biltmore Theatre in the City of New York or elsewhere.

That the reason that an order to show cause is asked for is that it is of the utmost urgency that a speedy adjudication of this motion be made as the injury complained of is causing the plaintiffs great injury.

That no previous application for this order has been made.

Sworn to before me this
2nd day of October, 1928. (Signed) CARL REED.

(Marion L. Elkin
Notary Public N. Y. Co.
Clerk's No. 133 Register's No. 9130)
Commission expires March 30, 1929.

[The prosecution provided scene by scene description of action that take place on the stage, with specific allusions to jokes about homosexuality, to the "large number of male degenerates," to "sex degeneracy and sex perversion," to a "fairies convention" and the use of the word "queers." In March, 1927, the New York State Legislature passed legislation banning all depictions of homosexuality on the stage. —L.S.]

8. NOTES FOR PROSECUTION ARGUMENTS IN PEOPLE VS. MAE WEST ET AL. #174820 1/2

Prosecutor's Notes

Jury sole judges of facts.

Must consider interest of witnesses.

Defendant most interested.

People's witnesses, police officers. Who else can you get to be around for two years, make notes and keep refreshed, etc.

Police told the truth.

No motive to concoct story.

[officer James] Powers a stenographer.

His notes, in all probability, more accurate than present memory of any other witness.

Police properly made full memorandum shortly after performance, when facts were fresh in their mind.

We would have been glad to produce book or script of play if we could have found one.

Could not get prompt book or actors' parts.

No witness called by defense ever saw manuscript (prompt book) according to their testimony.

If there is in existence a manuscript of this play, it is within the control of the defense, and they have not produced it.

Infer that they did not dare submit the real manuscript.

What kind of a play with no prompt book on hand in case an actor "gives up" in his lines.

The best of them do it sometimes, particularly when play is new.

Who is on trial.

Not the People's witnesses for being policemen and obeying orders.

Not the D.A. for attempting to enforce the law.

Defense would like to try anything but case against defendants.

Defendants on trial for violating law.

Only question is, what did they do on October 1st, 1928?

Did they present and participate in an obscene, etc., play?

Did they prior to that date prepare and advertise that play?

If you find that the defendants or any of them prepared this play, wrote it, rehearsed it, directed it, produced it so as to make it ready for stage presentation on October 1st, 1928, and that the play is one condemned under this section of the statute, then any of these defendants who prepared or advertised or produced this play should be found guilty under the law.

This Court, I believe, will charge you that a person can aid and abet in the commission of an offense without being actually present at the time when the offense is committed.

Question for the jury is what took place on stage on October 1st, 1928.

Was the play obscene, etc. and tended to corrupt, in whole or in part enacted?

OR

Was the play produced in whole or in part, depicted or dealt with sex degeneracy or sex perversion?

This 2nd section doesn't mean sodomy. The People of this state, thru their legislature, have said in so many words to theatrical producers, authors, managers and actors, "You must not depict or deal with sex degeneracy or sex perversion on the stage. If you do you commit a crime."

It does not say, "You may not depict or deal with sex degeneracy in a serious drama, but you may do so in a comedy." It doesn't say, "You may do so if you make a joke of it."

It says that subject is bound for stage purposes. Deal with it at your peril.

Legislature had a right to make that law, and the people of the stage must obey it.

Law not intended to apply to acts of sodomy. You can hardly expect these to be enacted on stage in public.

What was play? On what did it depend for its box office appeal? In the age old simple story of its main theme, a girl ruined and a boy _____ by a faithless lover? No change.

On the lines and situations as put forth here by the defense?

NOT AT ALL.

It was a deliberate attempt to capitalize by depicting on the stage, the portrayal of the action, speeches, manners and obscene jokes of a large number of male degenerates to depict and deal with these types on the stage in such a manner that a sensation would be created that would draw to the theatre the prurient mind, and the curious, to the end that the pockets of the author and producer would be FILLED.

Let us analyze the testimony and see if this is not so.

FIRST SCENE:

Scrubwomen: I've had it—Yes, more than once. I've had my time—Yes, with the whole fire department.

As told by People.

As told by defense—"I don't remember."

SHE DIDN'T WANT TO COMMIT DELIBERATE PERJURY.

Opening note of play. What is the meaning?

Blame on author and manager, rather than on actors.

SCENE: BIRD OF PARADISE:

PEOPLE:

"I get down on my knees (pause)"

I'm a female impersonator."

"I sing mammy songs" (not in [James] Powers' notes).

DEFENSE: "What kind of an act do you do?"

Howe—"I sing mammy songs.

No attempt at joke; no comedy; no situation. A mere walk. As People describe it, a play for a laugh on an obscene allusion to degenerate practices.

You can see the effect if a male in men's attire, acting like a fairy, in view of Harvey's definition of what "goes down on knees" means.

Depict by manner, walk and speech with double meaning sex degeneracy and sex perversion.

It means that or nothing. Which is it credible to believe happened?

Shortly after this, Stanley has a line, "It looks like a convention.

The only point, the only _____ in that was the appearance soon after [Leo] Howe, of two males who were acting and talking _____ FAIRY.

Stanley didn't mean a Democratic Convention. He meant a fairie's convention.

He follows it up later, when three more of a similar type appear, as described by People's witnesses, "I told you it was a convention. Here are some more delegates."

The object of these lines, in addition to whatever comedy effect they had, was to call attention to these persons who were depicting male degenerates. They were not doing any female impersonation. If, as People's witnesses say, they were acting in an effeminate manner, walking like and talking like women, they were depicting fairies or degenerates.

Connors says this didn't happen at all.

Connors put on to tell the whole story of the play, an actor with few lines and appearances, according to his own testimony, has apparently spent a large part of his time since the date of arrest, preparing for his appearance in court.

If defense admitted fact like this, they would admit whole case against them.

Mrs. H:
"They're so queer.
"I'll say they're *queer.*"
People's witness.
Defense—the learned Chuck.
They're so odd—Yes; my dear."

I think odd is the word. They lack the true perception that goes to make up the artist of the legitimate stage.

These characters being talked about apparently only walked on conversing among themselves. No one claims they had any dialogue with the Hetheringtons that would call for a speech on their artistic perceptions. But if they were acting like fairies, H's speech wold mean something, if QUEER is understood.

"DID YOU EVER HAVE A chronic/platonic LOVE AFFAIR?
"YES, BUT HIS WIFE FOUND IT OUT."
Connors—it never happened.

Significance of this scene between two males—in men's dress.
The broom incident.

People's witness: S touched him. He whooped.
STANLEY: "I whacked him and knocked him off stage."

The acrobats.
The stunt as described in a play full of men depicting and portraying male degenerates, has a peculiar significance, which it otherwise might not have.

As done by them it is _____.

It consists largely of falling down.

Head is not in trousers long enough for any comedy effect, decent or indecent. Pants brought to court so arranged that it was difficult for small man to get into them at all.

A PALPABLE FAKE.

Designed to appeal to the sort of people that might be attracted to the theatre by a show of this character.

No one called by defense saw men with women's underclothing for bodies, and brassieres, kimonos, sewing—all point fact to audience that these men were not mere female impersonators, but degenerates, who, even offstage, when not performing, adopted the mannerisms of women.

Same effect from scene between Connors and his dancing partner. (We didn't see Dickens [who played Joe].)

Stanley: Dickens was just a big lamp shade manufacturer.
Connors said no lamp shade was produced. Stanley said yes.
Connors lost his memory as to some things while traveling with "Diamond Lil."
"Not a dry seat in house" line cut, and says [Officer] James Powers got it, [Lieutenant James] Coy got it—they only saw show in Biltmore; had no script.

Stanley _____ Sheehan to draw attention of audience to type and get a laugh.
No point or joke otherwise.
Scene when Stanley opens door of dressing room. He says nobody screams.
No comedy in scene unless something happens, or if man acted like a man.
Even make an improper suggestion out of scene when Par[adise] tries to help girl.
If you're a man, thank God I'm something else.
MEANING OF THAT SPEECH.

THIRD ACT
No excuse for gathering of men in women's clothes at this party. They were not portraying female impersonators, but depicting degenerates or fairies at a fairies' party, given by a man who depicts a fairy type.

THE SONGS. ANALYZE THEM.
ANALYZE CONNORS' WORDS.

[Chuck Connors, the self-styled "Mayor of Chinatown," was a Bowery character of the 1890's. An acrobat who styled himself Chuck Connors, II, played one of the "hoofers" in PLEASURE MAN, and when that play closed, Mae West kept him in the touring company of DIAMOND LIL. The cross-examination was obviously tied to proving to the jury that in PLEASURE MAN, the cast was not acting the parts of gay men but were themselves practicing homosexuals. —L.S.]

9. MEMORANDUM ON CROSS-EXAMINATION OF [CHUCK] CONNORS.

Has a good memory and can he remember who was on the stage on October 1st, 1928 and who participated in every scene?

What character did [Lester] Sheehan portray in the play?

When Sheehan came on, was he supposed to be a man living in the town, inviting them to a party of another man living in the town?

Sheehan was not one of the female impersonators in the 2nd act.

Sheehan appeared in woman's dress in 3rd act.

Is Chuck Connors his true name?

Ever convicted of a crime?

What have you been doing since "THE PLEASURE MAN" closed?

Have you been in the employ of Mae West since that time?

Did you appear in the cast of "DIAMOND LIL" after "THE PLEASURE MAN" closed?

Have you received any money from Mae West since the play closed?

With whom have you talked about this case since the arrest?

Who engaged Mr. Burkan as your counsel?

Did you engage him or was he hired by Miss West as your attorney?

How many times have you gone over the story you told on the witness stand?

You were a comparatively unimportant person on the stage, in very few scenes, and have very few lines. Isn't that a fact?

(See affidavit)

You say you live at Langwell Hotel, 44th St. and Broadway. How long have you lived there?

Are you married or single?

Whom do you live with?

When did you last see Ed Hearn, your former partner?

Where did he live when you last saw him?

Did you state in your affidavit that you were one of the authors of this play and put in scenes and lines of your own?

How many times have you been in Burkan's office since the arrest?

How many times have you seen Mae West since the arrest?

In the first act ,did you see a scene between Stanley and Augustin [William

Augustin played the part of Steve McAllister] in which they had a conversation about shoes?

In the first act, what you were representing to the audience was a stage of a small town theatre in the morning when the acts were coming on in rehearsal, but when there was no show supposed to be coming on in this small town theatre.

And in the second act you are depicting and portraying a scene on the backstage of this theatre at a time when the show that was being given in the small town theatre was supposed to be going on somewhere off stage where the audience in the Biltmore Theatre could not see it.

When the actors came on in the second act, they were supposed to have left the stage where they had given their performance or they were on their way to the stage of the small town theatre.

Do you know who gave Sheehan the name of Lester Queen in the show?

Were you on the stage when Stanley was kicking Hetherington?

Did you see Stanley run upstairs after kicking Hetherington.

Did he pull open door of dressing room where there was an individual in a kimono?

Did that individual scream like a frightened woman and draw the kimono around him as though he were concealing his person?

Did you see Stanley go into a dressing room where Dolores was?

Did you see four men in women's attire who were depicting female impersonators in the 2nd act, come on the stage and go to their dressing room?

Who were those four men?

3rd act.

[This memorandum is unsigned. —L.S.]

[The trial itself did not begin until 1930, and by court time, thirty-four indictments were dismissed, and proceedings commenced against twenty-four defendants. Although the prosecution mounted a spirited attack, the sensational aspects of the case had diminished. The jury declared itself deadlocked, and the District Attorney declined to retry the case. *VARIETY* announced MAE WEST BEAT IT. —L.S.]

10. [RECOMMENDATION]
THE COURT OF GENERAL SESSIONS
OF THE COUNTY OF NEW YORK.
Cal. No. 53 002
Ind. No. 174, 820 1/2
THE PEOPLE OF THE STATE OF NEW YORK

—against—

MAE WEST, CARL REED, CHARLES EDWARD
DAVENPORT, STAN STANLEY, ALAN BROOKS,
EDGAR BARRIER, LEO HOWE, LESTER
SHEEHAN, EDWARD HEARN, WILLIAM SELIG,
HERMAN LENSEN, CHUCK CONNORS 2nd,
FRED DICKENS, HARRY ARMAND, SYLVAN
REPETTI, GENE DREW, ALBERT DORANDO,
JO HUDDLETON, WALTER MacDONALD, GENE
PEARSON, HOWARD CHANDLER, MAY DAVIS,
WALLY JONES, CHARLES ORDWAY and TED
LEWIS,
Defendants.

RECOMMENDATION

The defendants were indicted on the 5th day of October, 1928, charged with a violation of Section 1140-a of the Penal Law, and with the crime of Maintaining a Public Nuisance. They were tried before Judge Bertini and a jury in Part IX of the Court of General Sessions on the 17th day of March, 1930. During the course of the trial, on motion of the District Attorney, the case against certain of the defendants was taken from the consideration of the jury and they were acquitted by direction of the Court. The case against the other defendants resulted in a disagreement of the jury on April 3, 1930.

I do not believe that public justice requires a retrial of this action. The first trial was protracted, and I do not believe that a better result would be obtained upon retrial of the case. I, therefore, recommend that the bail of all of these defendants be discharged.

Dated, New York, N. Y., November 3, 1930.

Respectfully submitted, James G. Wallace,
ASSISTANT DISTRICT ATTORNEY

[Joab Banton]

A GLOSSARY OF TECHNICAL STAGE TERMS

from *The Drag*

spot: an actor's place in the order of the acts billed in vaudeville.

light plots: line or sight cues are recorded for light changes and the plot is assembled in play sequence, an electrician's cue sheet, indicating location of props.

scene plots: a list or diagram showing the scenery to be used in each scene of the production.

spider box: a multiple pin connection, a pin connection or "spider" box, an electrical plug to connect outlets and plugs, a receptacle suitable to stage use because it is flat and rectangular.

olivette: a black metal housing for lights, painted white or silver inside, grooved to hold gelatines, swivel connection to floor stand.

baby spots: a small spotlight to use 100-250-400 watt lamps.

douser: a cutoff device in an arc light.

door fancy: (draperies?).

riser: a stage platform, the step position of a spotlight.

moon box: an artificial effect machine used to simulate the moon; a container holding a lamp is moved on lines behind a transparent drop.

call boy: a person employed to call actors, at the stage manager's signal, to be ready to come on stage.

gelatine slide: a color wheel with each color having its own number.

grip: a stagehand who helps the chief carpenter on or below the stage level, especially in scene shifting.

gaffer: a lighting technician.

bunch lights: a row of lamps in an open metal box with a reflector, used as floodlights, mounted on a standard in the wings; a light stand.

CPSIA information can be obtained at www.ICGtesting.com
Printed in the USA
BVOW11s0755190814

363317BV00008B/20/P